SWINBURNE'S HELL AND HICK'S UNIVERSALISM

This book seeks to establish whether a Christian position must entail a belief in hell or whether Christians can hold a coherent theory of universal salvation. Richard Swinburne's defence of hell depends on the argument that hell is necessary if humans are to be genuinely free. It becomes clear that the contemporary discussion of hell and universalism cannot be separated from the issues of human freedom and God's knowledge, and so Hall centres the discussion round the question 'Are we Free to Reject God?' John Hick argues that although we are free to reject God there will eventually be an universalist outcome. Having examined the contrasting arguments of Hick and Swinburne, Hall builds on Hick's position to develop an argument for Christian universal salvation which holds in balance our freedom in relation to God and the assurance that all will finally be saved.

ASHGATE NEW CRITICAL THINKING IN RELIGION, THEOLOGY & BIBLICAL STUDIES

The Ashgate New Critical Thinking in Religion, Theology and Biblical Studies series brings high quality research monograph publishing back into focus for authors, international libraries, and student, academic and research readers. Headed by an international editorial advisory board of acclaimed scholars spanning the breadth of religious studies, theology and biblical studies, this open-ended monograph series presents cutting-edge research from both established and new authors in the field. With specialist focus yet clear contextual presentation of contemporary research, books in the series take research into important new directions and open the field to new critical debate within the discipline, in areas of related study, and in key areas for contemporary society.

Other Titles in the Series:

Swinburne's Hell and Hick's Universalism

Are We Free To Reject God?

LINDSEY HALL

ASHGATE

Published by
Ashgate Publishing Limited
Gower House
Croft Road
Aldershot
Hampshire GU11 3HR
England

Ashgate Publishing Company
Suite 420
101 Cherry Street
Burlington, VT 05401-4405
USA

Ashgate website: http//www.ashgate.com

British Library Cataloguing in Publication Data
Hall, Lindsey
    Swinburne's hell and Hick's universalism : are we free to
    reject God?. - (Ashgate new critical thinking in religion,
    theology and biblical studies)
    1.Hick, John, 1922- - Views on hell 2.Swinburne, Richard -
    Views on hell 3.Hell
    I.Title
    236.2'5

Library of Congress Cataloging-in-Publication Data
Hall, Lindsey, 1976-
    Swinburne's hell and Hick's universalism : are we free to reject God? / Lindsey Hall.
        p. cm.-- (Ashgate new critical thinking in religion, theology, and biblical studies)
    Includes bibliographical references and index.
    ISBN 0-7546-3400-0 (alk. paper)
    1. Future punishment--Christianity. 2. Hell--Christianity. 3. Swinburne, Richard. 4.
Universalism. 5. Hick, John. I. Title. II. Series.

BT837 .H23 2003
236'.2--dc21
                                                        2002027698

ISBN 0 7546 3400 0

Printed in Great Britain by Antony Rowe Ltd, Chippenham, Wiltshire

For my parents with love and thanks

Contents

Preface

Many people have commented that it must be depressing reading and thinking so much about hell. Others are doubtful that one can retain any interest whilst studying the same subject for so long. I have found neither to be the case. Our beliefs about heaven and hell affect how we perceive and relate to people of different faiths or none, and sometimes even those of our own faith. It is my belief that the doctrine of hell has led Christians to view others in a very negative way and that this has distracted us from the real business of Christianity. Belief in hell has meant that we have been so concerned with securing our own final salvation that we have neglected the salvation of others and made judgements that we are not entitled to make.

I first became interested in this topic when required to write an essay on hell during my undergraduate degree. Despite a background of Church attendance and commitment to the Christian faith, I had never given the topic any serious consideration. I conducted a straw poll of friends and was amazed to learn that many of them did indeed believe in the existence of hell and in some cases were committed to Christianity precisely because of a fear of eternal damnation. I was intrigued by this belief in what I had assumed to be an outdated idea, the main purpose of which had been to brow beat the masses into Church attendance and Christian adherence. The idea of any sort of hell seemed very remote from my understanding of God but I clearly needed to give it serious consideration. The essay question I eventually chose was a defence of universalism, the bibliography for which consisted solely of one author, John Hick. I was unsure whether this was primarily representative of my approach to essay writing as an undergraduate or whether it did in fact reflect a paucity of writing in this area.

I was fortunate enough to be able to spend four years exploring what had become for me a burning question and this book is a version of my Ph.D. thesis accepted by the University of Bristol at the end of 2001. I set out to prove to myself (and of course to the satisfaction of examiners) that it was possible to assert a final universalist outcome and to retain a broadly Christian framework. And indeed I find myself more convinced than ever that Christian faith does not require belief in an eternal hell. Having studied the topic in considerably more depth, I have found a surprisingly small amount of writing which ultimately proclaims a universal salvation. Despite a resurgence in the number of works defending the existence of hell, there is still a shortage of work by those on the other side of the fence. It seems to me that there is still room for more to be written on this subject in order for it to be presented as a serious option for the Christian.

During my time at the University of Bristol I was privileged to have supervision from Gavin D'Costa. I am greatly indebted to him for the benefit of his wisdom and for all of the help and encouragement he has given. I am also grateful to John Hick and Richard Swinburne who assisted with bibliographical and biographical information, and of course to everyone at Ashgate, particularly Sarah Lloyd, and their readers. I am very grateful to many friends and family who were supportive during the (seemingly endless) period of research and who have been excited about the book. Bristol friends particularly have probably heard more about the project than they care to know! Many thanks to all those who helped with getting hold of articles and reading drafts of chapters or assisted in other practical ways. My biggest thanks, as ever, must go to my family who are always so generous in their support. I have dedicated this book to my parents who believed unfailingly in the importance of this project and my ability to see it through.

Lindsey Hall
Spring 2003

Chapter 1

The Debate About Hell

Introduction

The debate about hell has occupied Christian thought throughout the centuries. The doctrine of hell has never been unequivocally defined and thus there have been many suggestions of what constitutes hell and who will be sent there. These suggestions have ranged from discussing the temperature and offensive smell of hell to the ideas of suffering the pain of separation from God or passing out of existence, which are popular today. The idea of some sort of eternal torment for the wicked after death has been prevalent since the beginning of Christianity, but it has always been controversial. Arguments have ensued not only over the nature of hell, but also many have challenged the existence of hell in favour of belief in the salvation of all people. Thus the debate about hell has always been a heated one. However during the twentieth century, the debate cooled and hell seemed to be largely removed from the theological agenda. Although many churches and indeed many theologians have been silent on the subject of hell there is one growing group amongst whom discussion of hell has been prominent. The Evangelical Churches in Britain and America have been more concerned to preach about hell than many of the mainstream churches, but although it still featured heavily in evangelical belief systems, published articles on hell had significantly decreased. The recognition of this situation may well account for the large proportion of evangelical literature concerning the doctrine of hell to have been produced in the last twenty or so years.[1] Many of the books and articles that have been published during this time bemoan the fact that this topic has been sorely neglected both by academics and in the preaching of the Christian Church.

This influx of material was no doubt also prompted by the fear that universalism was becoming generally accepted in the mainstream churches. A further reason for this renewed interest in the question of hell may be the massive current interest in the relationship between Christianity and other Religions. Although this issue has existed in Christianity from the beginning it has never been so prevalent as in today's world. Despite Christianity's conflict from the earliest days with those adhering to other belief systems many Christian doctrines have been established and grown in something of a vacuum. John Hick writes:

---

[1] See bibliography for evangelical writings on hell.

> Christian theology ... was developed, not indeed in ignorance, but
> nevertheless in essential unawareness, of the other religions of the
> world. I do not think it is an exaggeration to say that traditional
> Christian theology simply ignored the greater part of the human
> race![2]

Thus today's world with its enhanced awareness of other faiths challenges the Christian position that all outside of Christianity are sentenced to an eternity in hell.

In this book I will look at defences and denials of the doctrine of hell in order to establish whether there is an overwhelming defence of hell which will cause us to think that it was necessary for God to have created it. The most prominent and forceful modern defence of hell is the Free Will Defence. This states that in order to honour our human freedom, it was necessary for God to create hell so that we could, if we so desired, ultimately choose to reject God. Many who support this defence of hell reject other defences. For example, Jerry L. Walls defends the existence of hell in *Hell: The Logic of Damnation* but writes that his argument: 'involves a strong commitment to the value of libertarian freedom. This value judgement is surely one of the main pillars of the orthodox Christian doctrine of hell and indeed, I think the doctrine would topple without it'.[3] Thus the necessity of hell will be established by asking the question: 'Are we free to reject God?'. Whilst this will be the main focus of the book, it will in places be appropriate to look at other defences of hell and discuss the way in which they respond to the problem of hell.

My aim in this book is to establish whether one can hold a theologically and philosophically defensible position which rejects the existence of hell. There could of course be the option that there is no afterlife at all. However the concept of afterlife has been an integral part of Christian thought since its beginnings and for the purposes of this book I will assume that it is coherent to talk of an afterlife. Gerald Bray writes: 'Any consideration of the subject of hell ought naturally to begin with the Biblical evidence'.[4] Although the evidence and testimony of scripture is, of course, essential in establishing a Christian position, the aim of this book is primarily to explore the topic of hell in relation to concepts of philosophy of religion. There will be some discussion of the Biblical material throughout this work, but it will not make up the main focus of this book. I will look at both Swinburne and Hick's use of Biblical material and finally in chapter 6 I will examine universalist approaches to Scripture in order to establish whether the Bible can support a universalist position.

In this book I aim to examine not only whether the existence of an eternal hell is compatible with a loving God but further whether there is any good reason

---

[2] John Hick, 'The Reconstruction of Christian Belief for Today and Tomorrow: 2' *Theology* vol. 73 (1970) p.399.

[3] Walls, 1992 p.136.

[4] Gerald Bray, 'Hell: Eternal Punishment or Total Annihilation?' *Evangel* summer (1992) p.19.

for God to have created hell at all. Hans Urs Von Balthasar maintains that hell is not created by God. Sachs summarizes his argument: 'One should not say that God has created hell. If anything, hell is the creation, or better, the 'anticreation' of the sinner, who obstinately refuses God's divine will and eternal purpose in creating'.[5] However, even if a person creates his/her own hell by rejecting God, all states if not directly created by God are allowed and kept in existence by God. Thus God must allow a person to retreat into and stay in the hell which he/she has created for him/herself. This is not to assert that if God sees fit to create a place of everlasting torment, God should also provide a justification of it in order to satisfy philosophers of religion. However if the doctrine of hell is to be defended on the grounds of its philosophical and theological coherence it must also be open to challenge on these grounds. The writers of the ACUTE report assert: 'The Christian doctrine of hell is ultimately a construct of systematic theology'.[6] As noted above, examination of the Biblical material pertaining to the problem of hell will not constitute the core of this book. Rather I will seek to demonstrate that philosophically the creation of an eternal hell by a loving God is unnecessary. The relationship between theology and matters of faith and belief is a difficult one and thus it might be possible that an individual could accept the conclusions of this book as an academic investigation, and yet reject them on the grounds of Biblical revelation. Although my approach to this subject will primarily be to consider it as a question of philosophy of religion, I do not intend for it to be removed from issues of faith. However, I recognise that those who believe in the absolute authority of the Bible as the only source of revelation are likely to find this approach unacceptable and consequently reject the conclusions reached. For those who believe that religious faith is more about seeking truth through a combination of Biblical revelation, reason and experience this book may be of greater relevance. I hope to show not only that rejecting the doctrine of hell is philosophically defensible, but also a position which can be maintained within a broadly Christian framework.

In order to do this I will look at two particular responses to the problem of hell. A topic as wide as this one invariably requires that some parameters be placed around the study. Thus I will focus on the question through the work of Richard Swinburne and John Hick. My aim in concentrating in turn on Swinburne and Hick is to look at their very different understandings of the problem of hell in order to consider the question: 'Are we free to reject God?'. Both Hick and Swinburne claim that we are free to do so, and for Swinburne that is the key to his argument. Hick also claims that we are free to reject God; however he believes that ultimately no one will. Whether Hick can actually respond affirmatively to this question is a matter of some debate. There is no debate over whether Swinburne endorses our freedom to reject God, however there is much to be debated over the price he pays

---

[5] John Sachs, 'Current Eschatology: Universal Salvation and the Problem of Hell' *Theological Studies* vol.52 (1991) p.235. He is referring to Hans Urs Von Balthasar, *Dare We Hope 'That All Men Be Saved'?* (1988) San Francisco: Ignatius pp.53 - 55.
[6] ACUTE, 2000 p.36.

to ensure this freedom. Although very different in their beliefs, Hick and Swinburne have similarities in the aspects of philosophy of religion which have interested them and their initial approach to philosophy. They are both rationalists, and at one time were both theists. Thus their contrasting theories provide an interesting and useful framework in which to ask the question: 'Are we free to reject God?'.

In this chapter I will introduce the issues which will be of the greatest importance to this work. I will establish the 'problem of hell' and discuss the 'moment of decision', that is the point when one decides for or against hell. I will then define the different understandings of hell and universalism before looking at the different types of human freedom and God's knowledge. This will then allow us to proceed with examining the work of Hick and Swinburne on this subject in subsequent chapters.

The Problem of Hell

In order to define the problem of hell, it will be helpful to look first, at the more familiar problem of evil. The problem of evil has occupied philosophers and theologians for centuries. Kenneth Surin in *Theology and the Problem of Evil* explains:

> The so-called 'problem of evil' is deemed by its proponents to have a venerable ancestry, and was apparently first formulated by Epicurus (341 - 270 BC) in the form of a dilemma which perhaps receives its most succinct formulation in the words of David Hume (1711 - 76): 'Is he willing to prevent evil, but not able? then he is impotent. Is he able, but not willing? then he is malevolent. Is he both able and willing? whence then is evil?'.[7]

The problem of evil today is more commonly formulated in this three point statement:

1) God is omnipotent.
2) God is benevolent.
3) Evil exists.

This is the logical form of the problem of evil, which can also be discussed in its evidential form. Indeed it is the evidence of evil in the world that causes many to deny the existence of a good and all-powerful God.

The existence of hell cannot be formulated in the same evidential way, as we do not have first hand experience of hell as we do of evil. However, in its

---

[7] Kenneth Surin, *Theology and the Problem of Evil* (1986) Oxford: Blackwell. He is quoting from David Hume, *Dialogues Concerning Natural Religion* (ed.) H.D. Aiken (1948) New York: Harper p.66.

logical form the problem of evil and the problem of hell can be formulated in a similar way. Thus the statement of the problem of hell would be:
1) God is all powerful.
2) God is benevolent.
3) Hell exists.

This statement poses a similar problem to Christian belief as the problem of evil, although according to Hick it is even worse. He writes: 'the sufferings of the damned in hell, since they are interminable, can never lead to any constructive end beyond themselves and are thus the very type of ultimately wasted and pointless anguish'.[8] Thus the existence of an eternal hell cannot have an eschatological purpose. As Jonathan Kvanvig in *The Problem of Hell* writes:

> The evil of hell leads nowhere; at no point in the future will something of value make up for the evil of hell or will some reward be granted to those who endure the suffering of hell. Hell is apparently paradigmatic as an example of truly pointless, gratuitous evil. Thus arises the problem of hell.[9]

The problem of hell, unlike the problem of evil, cannot point to future purpose for its solution.

The options then, as they are with the problem of evil, are to deny the truth of (1), (2) or (3) of the statement or offer some explanation of how they are actually compatible. In the problem of evil, few have attempted to deny the truth of (3). Evil exists. However, with the problem of hell, the denial of (3) Hell exists, is not only a familiar response but is a straightforward one given that the existence of hell cannot be proved. To some however the statement that hell exists is not dispensable. Kvanvig supposes that we have good reason to believe in hell. In what Kvanvig calls McTaggart's Dilemma, John McTaggart, writes that there must be some good reason to believe in hell, or we need not even contemplate its existence.

> Either there is good reason to believe in hell or there is not. If there is no good reason for belief in hell, no one should believe in it. After all, without some good reason to believe in hell, the option of believing in hell is no better than any other merely possible catastrophe ... So, for the doctrine of hell to be respectable, there must be good reason to believe in it. The difficulty for this option, however, is that the only possible kinds of reasons are self-defeating. The only evidence there might be for hell is based on revelation from the one who can consign us to hell, and yet no one who claims that hell exists and outlines conditions for avoiding it can be trusted. So,

---

[8] Hick, 1966 p.342.
[9] Kvanvig, 1993 p.3.

on either horn of the dilemma, the conclusion to be drawn, according
to McTaggart is that belief in hell is not intellectually respectable.[10]

The weight of Christian tradition does not allow us to approach the problem of hell
assuming that it does not exist and therefore placing the burden of proof entirely on
those who do believe in its existence. Kvanvig claims that: 'The doctrine of hell is
no mere addendum to the primary claims of the Christian faith. Instead, the sacred
scriptures of the Christian faith found the doctrine in the eschatological nature of
Christianity'.[11] The predominant view throughout the history of Christianity has
clearly been in some sort of separation of fates in the afterlife. However neither on
these grounds, will we assume that hell must exist. Rather I will look at arguments
both for and against and see which can best respond to the problem of hell. Whilst
many have accepted the doctrine of hell in some form, many who are Christians
have rejected the idea of hell. As Kvanvig writes: 'To many - even to many who
would declare their allegiance to the revelation of God in Christ, hell is the
paradigm of truly pointless, gratuitous suffering'.[12]

As well as the difference between the ultimate purpose of evil and the lack
of teleological purpose of hell, Kvanvig observes that there are further differences
between the problem of hell and the problem of evil. He claims that:

> The problem of hell differs from the general problem of evil in the
> following way. On the majority of important evils, most theological
> traditions are silent; they do not say why the evils occur or how such
> evils fit into the divine scheme. Theologies rarely say why natural
> disasters occur or what purpose they serve, for example. Such is not
> the case, however with the doctrine of hell. The point of hell is fully
> explicit in the theological traditions in question, and the explicitness
> of this point gives rise to the problem of hell.[13]

The problem of evil requires a theodicy to explain how God can allow evil to exist.
However the problem of hell in its strongest form is that it is inflicted by God in
response to our behaviour in this life. Thus the sort of response which is required
for the problem of evil is not available for the problem of hell. Kvanvig observes
that there is a further difference between the problem of hell and the problem of
evil. He explains that:

> Protesting that God is not as mighty as some have thought and hence
> cannot do anything about hell will not do, for in any of the religious

---

[10] Kvanvig, 1993 p.10. He is quoting John McTaggart, *Some Dogma's of Religion* (1906)
London: Arnold pp.213-215
[11] Kvanvig, 1993 p.11
[12] Kvanvig, 1993 p.12
[13] Kvanvig, 1993 p.9

outlooks that give rise to the problem of hell, the fundamental afterlife options are present as a result of God's direct activity.[14]

Hell can only exist if it was created and is maintained in existence by God. Henri Blocher notes that some may argue that if God allows evil now it is consistent to claim that God would also allow evil in the afterlife. He writes:

> Some orthodox writers would carry further the last considerations and argue from God's permission of evil in history to the propriety of the same in eternity: if it is compatible with divine love and holiness now, it must be forever also.[15]

However Kvanvig has observed that this does not follow because of the significant differences between the problem of hell and the problem of evil. Thus the different theodicies which respond to the problem of evil cannot simply be applied to the problem of hell. Rather specific theodicies must be developed in response to the problem of hell.

The point at which one's eternal fate is sealed will be significant in this book and is integral to some doctrines of hell and universalism.

The Moment of Decision

A significant issue in the recent discussion about hell has concerned the moment of decision. That is the time when one must choose decisively for or against God and consequently for heaven or hell.[16] Traditional Christian theology has generally maintained that after death one's final state is eternally fixed. However many theologians considering this subject have suggested that after death there may be further opportunities in which to decide one's end. The most established of these is, of course, the Roman Catholic idea of purgatory. Traditional Roman Catholic thought claims that purgatory is an in-between stage for many people between this life and heaven. It allows those who did not fully prepare themselves for the Beatific Vision in this life to be purged of sin and thus prepared for the company of heaven.

There is the further option that all people make their decision in the moment of death, or after death when they will have an encounter with Christ. The idea of an encounter with Christ in the moment of death, which John Sanders calls

---

[14] Kvanvig, 1993 p.164.

[15] Blocher, 1994 pp.293-294.

[16] The moment of decision will only apply to some understandings of hell. For example on the strong view of hell, one does not decide for or against God but is sent to hell as a result of God's judgement thus any decision on the part of the individual is precluded.

the 'final option theory' is, he observes 'primarily Roman Catholic'.[17] One leading advocate of this position is Ladislaus Boros who claims that this theory allows all people including those who die in infancy to be able to make an informed decision for or against God. He writes: 'In death the infant enters into the full possession of its spirituality, i.e. into a state of adulthood … The result of this is that no one dies as an infant, though he may leave us in infancy'.[18] Sander's offers this summary of the final option theory: 'All human beings come, at the moment of death, to a point of development whereby they are enabled to make either an act of faith for salvation or an act of sin for damnation'.[19] Thus the final option theory means that one's ultimate fate is actually fixed at death, but is not determined until the moment of death when all people are in a developed state and able to make an informed decision. The final option theory means that the Gospel is revealed to all people, but does not necessitate universal salvation as not all people will make their decision for God.

This is similar to the idea of post-mortem evangelism that has featured in much recent literature. However, post-mortem evangelism is not concerned with the moment of death, but the moment after death. This theory proposes that every person will have an encounter with Christ after death and thus all will hear the gospel message. Again it is claimed that this will not necessarily lead to universal salvation as not all will accept Christ. Sanders notes that this is not a new development in Christian thought, but: 'It became well known through the Alexandrian theologians Clement of Alexandria and Origen but fell out of favour after the time of Augustine'.[20] One recent advocate of this position is Nigel Wright. In *The Radical Evangelical: Seeking A Place to Stand* Wright suggests: 'In some condition beyond death, all who have been deprived of the opportunity for faith in Christ in life are given that opportunity by direct encounter with Christ'.[21] Although this would ensure that the gospel was heard universally, Wright warns that we should not 'assume that post-mortem evangelism must necessarily lead to universal salvation, as though people find it easier to believe once confronted beyond death with the living God'.[22] The theory of post-mortem evangelism does not necessarily entail further opportunities for character developing or purging, but only wishes to ensure that all have equal opportunity to hear the gospel and make their decision for or against Christ.

Some however have claimed that this life is insufficient for us adequately to develop our characters and make our decision for or against God. Hick proposes

---

[17] John Sanders, *No Other Name: An Investigation into the Destiny of the Unevangelized* (1992) Grand Rapids, Micigan: Eerdmans p.164.

[18] Ladislaus Boros, *The Mystery of Death* trans. Gregory Bainbridge (1965) New York: Herder & Herder p.110 quoted in Sanders, 1992 p.167.

[19] Sanders, 1992 p.167. He goes on to make some criticisms of the final option theory.

[20] Sanders, 1992 p.177.

[21] Nigel Wright, *The Radical Evangelical: Seeking A Place to Stand* (1996) London: SPCK p.99.

[22] Wright, 1996 p.99.

that after this life we encounter a further series of progressive lives.[23] These existences will be similar to this one in so far as they will be soul-making environments. Thus on this theory, the moment of decision could come at death for the rare individual who has already undergone the transformation into a 'child of God'. However for most people the moment of decision could occur in any one of their further lives and indeed it would seem that their lives can continue indefinitely until the decision for God is made. Thus Hick's theory of further lives after death does lead towards universal salvation. Although Hick allows that there could be regression as well as progression in any of the future lives Thomas Talbott argues that evil could not continue forever. In 'Providence, Freedom and Human Destiny' he asserts that:

> Though it is quite possible that someone should continue freely to choose the good for an indefinite period of time, it is not possible that someone should continue freely to choose evil; over the long run (by which I mean to include the afterlife) evil will always undermine and destroy itself.[24]

Thus Talbott assumes that given sufficient time evil would destroy itself and thus all would be able to reconcile themselves to God.

The moment of decision is significant in discovering whether all people ultimately have equal access to the good news of Christ and circumstances in which they are able to respond to it. The discussion of post-mortem evangelism, which is largely to be found in evangelical literature and the Roman Catholic idea of purgatory demonstrate a recognition of the inequalities of this life and the desire for our fates to be sealed on a more even footing.

Hell and Universalism - Some Definitions

In this section I will look at some definitions of different understandings of hell and universalism. All these categories are not exhaustive, they cover most of the major differences in positions and will be essential in evaluating the theories of hell and universalism which we shall be looking at.

Hell

The doctrine of hell has been particularly prevalent at different times throughout Church history,[25] and although the concept of hell has always existed in Christian thought, there have been many different understandings of what is meant by hell.

---

[23] See Hick, 1976 pp.200ff; 235ff and 465ff.
[24] Talbott, 1990 p.237.
[25] See bibliography for the history of hell.

This may be due, in part, to the fact that the doctrine of hell is not explicitly enshrined in the creeds of the Church. For many, hell is a place of eternal physical torment which punishes sinners for their wrong doings in this life. Augustine strongly defended this kind of doctrine of hell and it is arguably his position which has shaped western Christian thought. For others hell constitutes an eternal separation from God, or an exclusion from the company of saints. Those who believe in some sort of hell are often called separationists, referring to the fact that there will be an eternal separation of people in the afterlife. The view that after death the unrighteous will be annihilated, or allowed to pass out of existence has been proposed. As this too, is a separatist view I will discuss it in this section.

Strong View of Hell

The strong view of hell is the belief that God sends those who will not be saved to hell. Hell consists of some sort of eternal punishment, which could be either physical or mental. The strong view of hell is the most traditional one as fully developed by Augustine, and preached by many since. Talbott describes proponents of this view as 'conservative theists', people who consent to the view that 'God will irrevocably reject some persons and subject those persons to everlasting punishment'.[26] Kvanvig breaks the strong view of hell into four components:

> (H1) The Anti-Universalism Thesis: some persons are consigned to hell;

> (H2) The Existence Thesis: hell is a place where people exist if they are consigned there.

> (H3) The No Escape Thesis: there is no possibility of leaving hell, and nothing one can do, change, or become in order to get out of hell, once one is consigned there; and

> (H4) The Retribution Thesis: The justification for and purpose of hell is retributive in nature, hell being constituted so as to mete out punishment to those whose earthly lives and behaviour warrant it.[27]

Thus hell is created by God for the purpose of punishing the unrighteous. They will never escape hell and they will never cease to exist. They will endure the punishment of hell forever. The strong view of hell can envisage this punishment as being mental or physical. Mental punishment would generally be defined as being very aware of being separated from God and an outcast from the company of heaven. Mental punishment might also be thought to be a perpetual reliving of

---

[26] Talbott, 1990 (b) p.21.
[27] Kvanvig, 1993 p.19.

one's worst deeds. Physical punishment infers the continual infliction of some sort of corporeal pain on each individual in hell. Those who suppose that hell consists of physical suffering may well assume that there will also be mental suffering.

The strong view of hell does not necessarily entail that the punishments meted out are the same. This understanding of hell could allow for a scale of punishments which would be proportionate to the gravity of one's offences. Kvanvig claims that this makes a much more coherent understanding of hell. He writes: 'Although many Christians hold that all persons in hell receive the same punishment, this interpretation is not the only one possible. It is however the most demanding version to defend'.[28] Thus by incorporating what he calls the 'differential punishment view' the strong view of hell may escape some of the moral objections that even if some have behaved so as to warrant that level of punishment, not all who are nevertheless condemned to hell deserve so great a punishment. On this view, not all would receive the same degree of punishment and thus whilst hell would be horrendous for some, it would merely be unpleasant for others. However, what cannot be varied, on the strong view of hell is the duration of punishment. Kvanvig argues that this makes erroneous the scale of punishment theory.

> This version of the strong view of hell ignores the importance of the intentional realm for assigning punishment. Instead of consulting the intentional realm from the beginning of the process of assigning punishment, it refers to the intentional realm only after the basic sentence has been assigned.[29]

Thus the differential punishment view does not significantly change the issues and objections raised by the strong view of hell.

Proponents of the strong view of hell might deny that God desires the salvation of all people. Although this may answer some of the objections to the strong view theory, it certainly raises further questions. The argument has been offered that hell does not in anyway frustrate God's purposes and further that the salvation or loss of individuals is a matter of some indifference to God. For example, Joseph Bettis writes: 'God is good in himself and not because he does

---

[28] Kvanvig, 1993 p.25.

[29] Kvanvig, 1993 p.62. Kvanvig notes that there could be a third option to the equal punishment and differential punishment theories i.e. contingent equal punishment. That is, it just so happens that all punishments will be equal. Kvanvig explains: 'In essence, the contingent view holds that all humans, at some time or other, intentionally and maliciously strike at God in their actions and thereby deserve the sort of punishment described by the equal punishment version of the strong view of hell' p.61. This theory must appeal to what Kvanvig refers to as the 'status principle' (p.29); that is the understanding that harm is measured not just according to intention or actual damage done but according to the status of the being who is harmed. Thus harm to God, an infinite being, requires infinite punishment.

nice things (even giving eternal life) for men. God's love does not imply the salvation of any man'.[30] Peter Geach goes even further than Bettis.

> For God a billion rational creatures are as dust in the balance; if a
> billion perish, God suffers no loss, who can create what he wills with
> no effort or cost by merely thinking of it; the perishing of those who
> break his law is the natural penalty of their folly and can only
> redound to the praise of his Eternal Justice.[31]

Thus Geach claims that God is not sorry when some are lost, but that this brings God glory. Proponents of the weak view of hell generally claim that God mourns for those who decide eternally to reject God. According to Geach, God would barely even notice the fate of a billion beings separated from God forever. Many have objected to this sort of view and have affirmed the universal salvific will of God. I will be arguing that God's love does imply that God at least desires the salvation of every person. I will also assume that the fate of every individual is a matter of some importance to God.

Weak View of Hell

The weak view of hell states that God does not send people to hell, rather they send themselves there. Talbott calls advocates of this thesis 'moderately conservative theists'. He explains that they subscribe to the statement: 'Some persons will, despite God's best efforts to save them, finally reject God and separate themselves from God forever'.[32] In another article from the same year, Talbott refers to this as the Rejection Hypothesis. He describes this hypothesis very similarly to the view of the moderately conservative theist. He writes, 'some persons will, despite God's best efforts to save them, freely and irrevocably reject God and thus separate themselves forever'.[33] That individuals decide of their own free will to reject God is fundamental to the weak view of hell. The weak view of hell entails that God does love all people and desires their salvation but having given individuals the choice to accept or reject God, God must honour whatever choice they make. As Stephen T. Davies writes: 'Separationists like me do not deny that God desires the salvation of all persons and that Christ's atoning work was designed to rescue everyone'.[34] However they do deny that this necessarily leads to universal salvation because of human freedom.

---

[30] Joseph Dabney Bettis, 'A Critique of the Doctrine of Universal Salvation' *Religious Studies* vol.6 (1970) p.339.

[31] Peter Geach, *Providence and Evil: The Stanton Lectures 1971-1972* (1977) Cambridge: Cambridge University Press p.128.

[32] Talbott, 1990 (b) p.23.

[33] Talbott, 1990 p.227.

[34] Stephen T. Davies, 'Universalism, Hell and the Fate of the Ignorant' <u>Modern Theology</u> vol.6 no.2 (1990) p.176.

Most proponents of the weak view of hell would claim that hell consists of being separated from God. Because the weak view does not perceive hell as a punishment, but as an alternative to accepting God, it would be somewhat incongruous for this view to entail physical suffering. Rather the suffering entailed in the weak view of hell is a result of being separated from God even though individuals have freely chosen that end. Keith E. Yandell explains: 'To be in hell is to have no positive contact with God, to not be an object of efficacious divine compassion or a beneficiary of effective divine mercy'.[35] Thus those in hell are not necessarily suffering, but they are certainly not benefiting from the presence of God. Similarly, Davies writes:

> Hell is a place of separation from God. Not total separation, of course - that would mean hell would not exist. Furthermore, the biblical tradition denies that anything or anyone can ever be totally separated from God. But hell is separation from God as the source of true love, joy, peace and light.[36]

Thus whilst those who reject God cannot be entirely separated from God, they cannot experience the positive attributes of God. Once they are in this situation, there will be no good for them to choose and so their rejection of God will be eternal. The No Escape thesis is not necessarily a part of the weak view of hell, however most who hold this view claim that once in hell there will be no incentive for individuals to change their decision and they will continue to reject God.

Richard Swinburne holds a weak view of hell and claims both that it would be appropriate for God to punish an individual who had rejected their 'God-given capacity for moral awareness and choice and left himself as an arena of competing desires. He certainly deserves punishment, and God has a right to punish him'.[37] However he goes on to conclude: 'The *poena damni* is a loss of good, not an inflicted evil; and it is not so much a punishment inflicted from without as an inevitable consequence of a man allowing himself to lose his moral awareness'.[38] Thus whilst Swinburne claims that an individual choosing to reject God does in fact warrant punishment, what follows is a self-inflicted punishment and not one externally brought about by God. William Lane Craig claims that those who reject God condemn themselves.

> Those who make a well-informed and free decision to reject Christ are self-condemned, since they repudiate God's unique sacrifice for sin. By spurning God's prevenient grace and the solicitation of His Spirit, they shut out God's mercy and seal their own destiny. They,

---

[35] Keith E. Yandell, 'The Doctrine of Hell and Moral Philosophy' *Religious Studies* vol.28 (1992) pp.79-80.

[36] Davies, 1990 p.178.

[37] Richard Swinburne, *Responsibility and Atonement* (1989) Oxford: Clarendon Press p.181

[38] Swinburne, 1989 p.182.

therefore, and not God, are responsible for their condemnation, and God deeply mourns their loss.[39]

However, Craig goes on to state:

> Such persons who are not sufficiently well-informed about Christ's person and work will be judged on the basis of their response to general revelation and the light that they do have. Perhaps some will be saved through such a response; but on the basis of scripture we must say that such 'anonymous Christians' are relatively rare.[40]

Craig ostensibly subscribes to the weak view of hell. However it is not clear that Craig can demonstrate that according to his theory God does love all people and desire their salvation. Those who do not know Christ are not knowingly rejecting God's 'unique sacrifice for sin' so instead will be judged on the basis of the general revelation that has been available to them. It is not clear then how these individuals are self-condemned as they are not making Craig's 'well informed and free decision to reject Christ'. Thus it may be more accurate to state that Craig is actually advocating a strong view of hell because not all people will have the opportunity to be saved.

Some have argued that the differences between the weak and strong views of hell are only matters of detail and do not significantly alter the objections to hell. For example, Gordon Graham writes:

> If everlasting torment is so morally repellent as to be inconsistent with the idea of a loving God, it is equally inconsistent whether or not God is directly responsible for the administration of the torment, or indirectly responsible by creating a universe in which this is a possible outcome.[41]

This objection makes the valid point that not all advocates of the weak view of hell are willing to accept, that whether God sends people to hell or allows them to send themselves there, God is responsible for the existence of hell and for those who end up there. However, whilst moral objections to hell may not differ much according to the strong or weak view, for our purposes the weak view of hell is of greater interest. The weak view of hell is a popular modern understanding of hell and perhaps the most coherent. It is also the view which most closely relates to the question, are we free to reject God?

---

[39] William Lane Craig, '"No Other Name": A Middle Knowledge Perspective on the Exclusivity of Salvation Through Christ' *Faith and Philosophy* vol.6 no.2 (1989) p.176.
[40] Craig, 1989 p.186.
[41] Graham, 1988 p.483.

Annihilation and Conditional Immortality

The theory that the unrighteous will cease to exist after death has become popular in recent times. This is generally conceived as being an alternative understanding to the strong or weak view of hell. Instead of believing that hell consists of some sort of unpleasant, eternal existence, it claims that hell is ceasing to exist at all. Some offer this view, not as an account of hell but as another option altogether. Annihilation has recently become popular in evangelical theology, and indeed the ACUTE report claims that it is belief in annihilation and not universal salvation that is a threat to the evangelical consensus. They write: 'A far more immediate challenge to traditional evangelical understanding is posed by what has come to be known as conditional immortality or conditionalism'.[42] It is by no means uncontroversial, but the embracing of an annihilist position by John Stott[43] has opened a floodgate of discussion about the Biblical evidence for this position and brought it into the evangelical arena.

In 'Aquinas, Hell and the Resurrection of the Damned' Michael Potts names Richard Swinburne as a defender of annihilationism. Although Swinburne certainly defends the possibility of annihilation, it would be more accurate to say that he is ultimately agnostic about it and Potts notes in a footnote: 'Swinburne defends the plausibility of the annihilation of the damned, although he is open to other options'.[44] Swinburne suggests that if individuals choose to be annihilated rather than exist in hell, God might well allow them this choice and execute their decision.[45] This, however, is quite an unusual position. Most who profess belief in annihilation or conditional immortality claim that it is either an alternative to hell or it is the passing out of existence which constitutes hell.

Annihilation and Conditional Immortality refer to different concepts, arising according to whether or not one believes that the soul is immortal. For those who expect that the human soul is immortal, for a person to pass out of existence they would need to be actively annihilated. Those who believe that we can only remain in existence if God bestows life upon us may maintain that some will be kept in eternal life and some will be allowed to pass out of existence. It may appear that the issues raised here are different as they require different actions of God. However, Kvanvig argues that there is morally no difference between annihilation and conditional immortality.

Kvanvig explains that one might raise different objections to each position and suggests that it could be said: 'Even though holding that God intervenes to destroy some individuals would be problematic, holding that he merely fails to

---

[42] ACUTE, 2000 p.4.

[43] John Stott and David L. Edwards, *Essentials: A Liberal Evangelical Dialogue* (1988) Down Grove: Intervarsity Press.

[44] Potts, 1998 p.341.

[45] Richard Swinburne, *Providence and the Problem of Evil* (1998) Oxford: Clarendon Press p.201.

intervene in order to preserve in existence certain individuals is not problematic'.[46] However Kvanvig is not convinced that these two options are actually morally different. He comments that this view 'does not take into account the doctrine of divine conservation'.[47] Kvanvig continues: 'Hence, there are not two versions of the annihilation view to distinguish'.[48] As far as Kvanvig is concerned, the distinction is not even between an active or passive action of God. The doctrine of divine conservation means that God must actively allow every event and state of affairs to occur, because without God's active participation there would be nothing. God cannot passively allow things to happen because only by God's positive input can there be any states of affairs or events. Swinburne would be in agreement with Kvanvig's doctrine of divine conservation, as he too maintains that we continually owe our existence to God choosing to keep us alive. This leads Swinburne to a conditional immortality rather than an annihilationist position. He writes: 'God will give eventually to such souls as he keeps in being after death new bodies'.[49]

Conditional immortality or conditionalism became popular amongst those who were repelled by graphic descriptions of suffering in hell as a less offensive alternative. However whilst this view may avoid some of the objections to the strong view of hell, it cannot adequately respond to the problem of hell. Tony Gray comments that conditional immortality only changes what hell is, it does not justify it. He writes: 'whether the damned are annihilated or not, the problems of morality and arbitrariness remain'.[50] Thus whilst conditionalism may not fit into many descriptions of hell, it is susceptible to many of the same objections. Charles Seymour in 'Hell, Justice and Freedom' uses the phrase 'doctrine of hell' as a generic term to refer to that which is common to all views of hell. He explains: 'I define this generic doctrine as the belief that it is logically and epistemically possible that some persons will experience an everlasting existence each of whose moments is on the whole bad'.[51] Although broad, this distinction does not include conditionalism. Further discussions of conditionalism in this book will on the whole be distinct from discussions of hell. However general criticisms of hell may also apply to conditionalism.

---

[46] Kvanvig, 1993 p.69.

[47] Kvanvig, 1993 p.70. He defines the doctrine of divine conservation such: 'every created thing, that is, tends toward nonexistence, and only by God's power does anything that exists continue to exist. If so, however, there is no distinction to draw between annihilation by omission and annihilation by commission'.

[48] Kvanvig, 1993 p.70 .

[49] Swinburne, 1989 pp.179 -180.

[50] Gray, 1996 p.288.

[51] Charles Seymour, 'Hell, Justice and Freedom' *International Journal for Philosophy of Religion* vol.43 (1998) p.70.

Universalism

Universalism is the name given to belief in universal salvation or apokatastasis, the belief that all people will finally be reconciled with God. Although the universalist position has gained ground in recent times, it is by no means a new one. The most famous of the Church Fathers to be thought of as an universalist is probably Origen who taught the final restoration of all things.[52] The Fifth Ecumenical Council at Constantinople in 553 A.D. condemned universalism and specifically the position of Origen. However Origen was not the only Church Father to hold some sort of doctrine of universal salvation.[53] Like many doctrines, there is not one, cohesive universalist position but many different positions all of which conclude that all people will eventually be saved. As Bauckham writes:

> The problem of universalism cannot be reduced to a simple choice of alternatives. Only the belief that ultimately all men will be saved is common to all universalists. The rationale for that belief and the total theological context in which it belongs vary considerably.[54]

There could be many different categories of universalist positions, but in this section it will suffice to look at some of the main distinctions between different positions.

Pluralistic Universalism

Trevor Hart in 'Universalism: Two Distinct Types' distinguishes between Christian and Pluralistic universalism. Pluralistic universalism is the belief that all people are saved by whatever religious path is open to them. Thus salvation is not centred in Jesus Christ. The ACUTE report defines pluralistic universalism as the belief that 'conceives salvation as something that can occur 'outside' Jesus Christ, and is based on the premise that, in a world of many faiths God must distribute his saving purpose through other religions and philosophies'.[55] Universalism is not a necessary part of a pluralist position however. Hart writes that: 'Clearly a conviction that all must ultimately find salvation is helpfully bolstered by the view that their empirical refusal or failure to embrace faith in Jesus Christ makes no

---

[52] Although Origen is often cited as one of the earliest advocates of apokatastasis, Frederick W. Norris questions whether this is actually an accurate representation of Origen's position. Frederick W. Norris, 'Universal Salvation in Origen and Maximus' in Cameron (ed.) 1992 pp.36 - 37. Hans Urs Von Balthasar also questions this and concludes that Origen did not unequivocally proclaim universalism, but offered it as a point of discussion. See Balthasar, 1988 pp.59-62.
[53] See Balthasar (1988) p.63 for a discussion of the Church Fathers who supported universalism.
[54] Bauckham, 1978 p.49.
[55] ACUTE, 2000 p.27.

necessary difference to their eternal destiny'.[56] Thus whether pluralism leads to belief in universalism, or universalism to belief in pluralism they often go hand in hand.

John Hick is probably the most well known advocate of this position today. For Hick, belief in universalism (amongst other things) led to belief in pluralism. Hart notes that Hick's earlier works offer a less definite universalism. He writes: 'In Hick's earlier writings this optimistic universalism seems still to be wedded to a relatively orthodox Christian theology'.[57] Hick however does move on to a clearly pluralistic and more definite universalism. This has ultimately led him away from a Christian framework. His belief in universal salvation was born out of his belief in a God of Love, however Hick is now unwilling to proclaim that God of Love as it excludes other religions who do not share that understanding of God. Thus Hick is committed to the view that Christianity is one among many religions which are equally valid paths to salvation.[58] An advocate of pluralistic universalism could, of course, be a Christian in that he/she adhered to the teachings and practices of the Christian faith. However once the God of love has been abandoned this takes us beyond the broad Christian framework which I will outline at the beginning of chapter 4.

Christian or Inclusivistic Universalism

Christian universalists assert that all people will finally come to God through Christ. Christian universalism is sometimes called inclusivistic universalism. This position is held by inclusivists, as it entails the belief that all must be saved through Christ, but that those who do not now confess Jesus Christ as their Lord and Saviour will either have further opportunity to do so or will be saved by their response to the general revelation they have encountered. However, not all inclusivists believe in universal salvation. In fact it is probably a minority who do. Thus Christian universalism would constitute a strong inclusivist position. It may be referred to as inclusivistic rather than Christian universalism as some may hold that there can be no strictly Christian universalist position.

There are various understandings of how all people will finally come to know and accept Christ. One person who advocates a Christian universalism is J. A. T. Robinson. In *In The End ... God* Robinson defines universalism as 'the answer that God will be all in all because the whole world will be restored sinless to that relationship with Him in which and for which He made it'.[59] Robinson is certain that this end will be achieved through Christ, or at least through the body of Christ.

---

[56] Trevor Hart 'Universalism: Two Distinct Types' in Cameron (ed.) 1992 p.7.

[57] Hart, 1992 pp.7-8.

[58] Hick does actually state that not every religion is an equally valid path, he writes: 'Not by any means every religious movement - in the broad family-resemblance sense of 'religious' - is salvific: not Nazism, or Satanism, or the Jim Jones or the Waco phenomena.' John Hick, *The Rainbow of Faiths* (1995) London: SCM Press p.44.

[59] Robinson, 1950 p.108.

He explains: 'The Body of Christ is the only corporeity which is "eternal in the heavens". Not till a man has put on *that* will he know salvation; and not till *all* have found themselves in it, and everything is finally summed up in Christ, will this salvation be complete for any'.[60] He further asserts that 'the *telos* has been declared in the *fait accompli* of Jesus Christ'.[61] Thus for Robinson the ultimate salvation of all people can only come about because of the saving work of Christ.[62] Christian universalism affirms that Christ is the only means of salvation and yet all people will be saved. For some this conclusion is reached because the atoning work of Christ and God's salvific will lead them to believe that somehow eventually every person will come to know and be saved by Christ. For others, they may believe in universal salvation but not wish to abandon their belief in Christ. Therefore they develop a theory of universal salvation which places Christ at the centre.

As well as the distinction between Christian and pluralist universalism there are also different understandings of universalism.

Hopeful Universalism

Hopeful universalism is perhaps the most difficult universalism to classify. Holders of this position may not name themselves as universalists. The hopeful or optimistic universalist hopes that all people will eventually be reconciled with God, and believes that the message of the Gospel supports this hope, but they cannot affirm that it will be so. Hopeful universalists believe that God desires the salvation of all people and further that salvation is available to all people but cannot assert that this will be brought to fruition. This is usually because they claim that either human freedom or God's freedom mean that the outcome is unknowable. As has already been noted above, Hart claims that Hick in his earlier works could be classed as an optimistic universalist.

Karl Barth does not positively endorse universal salvation because he believes that God's freedom prevents us from being able to assert that will finally be the case. There has been much debate as to whether Barth can accurately be classed as a universalist or not. It would seem that the most appropriate definition of Barth's position would be hopeful universalism.[63] Schmitt observes that Barth

---

[60] Robinson, 1950 p.98

[61] Robinson, 1950 p.99

[62] For a discussion of Robinson's universalism see Harmon, 1993 p.160ff. Harmon is sympathetic to Robinson's position. However he ultimately rejects Robinson's position on the grounds that: 'Robinson cannot clear himself of the charge of being an advocate of divine coercion.' p.202. Similarly, Hart concludes that Christian universalism, and Robinson's version in particular, is more convincing than pluralistic universalism and is better able to respond to many of the generic criticisms made about universalism. Despite this he concludes that it must certainly be rejected. p.33.

[63] For detailed discussions and analysis of Barth's position see Karl Schmitt, *Death and After-life in the Theologies of Karl Barth and John Hick: A Comparative Study* (1985) Amsterdam: Rodopi. See also John Colwell, 'The Contemporaneity of the Divine Decision: Reflections on Barth's Denial of "Universalism" in Cameron (ed.) 1992.

does believe that all will be resurrected, and believes that because of the atonement all will be reconciled to Christ.[64] Thus as Schmitt remarks: 'Logically Barth is led to endorse universalism, but we also remind ourselves that logic does not control the teaching of Barth as much as faith'.[65] Therefore he is led to conclude:

> Barth remained reluctant to give support for apocatastasis, and that was principally because he wished to protect the freedom of God. Barth would neither constrain nor constrict God's options, even if the options would normally be considered favourable for His creature man.[66]

Daniel Strange defines this position as 'quasi-universalism'.[67]

J.A.T. Robinson objects to the hopeful or optimistic universalist position. He claims: 'Of all positions, though it sounds the most humble, it is in fact the most subtly unbiblical. For the New Testament never says that God *may* be all in all, that Christ *may* draw all men unto Himself, but that He *will*'.[68] Although Robinson finds this position offensive, there is a sense in which it is the most acceptable. Believers state only the hope that one day all people will be reconciled to God, thus wanting the best for all of their fellow humans and affirming the overwhelming grace of God, yet not explicitly denying the Biblical and doctrinal teaching on hell. Indeed it would seem curious for any Christian not to be a hopeful universalist to some degree. John Sachs in, 'Current Eschatology: Universal Salvation and the Problem of Hell' asks:

> Do I live here and now as one who hopes that all are being saved?
> Hope for the salvation of all requires that radical love and solidarity
> which Christians recognise on the cross of Christ. It expresses itself
> in active discipleship which labours for the universal communion of
> love and justice which God has always intended for the world.[69]

Sachs claims that to live as a Christian is to aim for the eventual salvation of all people and thus suggests that the Christian should be hopeful universalists.

Jan Bonda in *The One Purpose of God: An Answer to the Doctrine of Eternal Punishment* writes: 'The Church is called not to acquiesce in the perdition of fellow human beings - not one of them - since God himself does not passively accept that'.[70] Thus Bonda proposes that the Church should not only hope but also work for universal salvation. William Lane Craig who strongly defends the doctrine

---

[64] Schmitt, 1985 p.19.
[65] Schmitt, 1985 p.21.
[66] Schmitt, 1985 p.98.
[67] Strange, 1999 p.36.
[68] Robinson, 1950 p.102.
[69] Sachs, 1991 p.254.
[70] Bonda, 1993 p.66.

of hell writes: 'No orthodox Christian *likes* the doctrine of hell or delights in anyone's condemnation, I truly wish that universalism were true, but it is not'.[71] Craig then, although not a hopeful universalist, as he is certain that this would be a false hope, at least acknowledges that universalism would be desirable. Bettis comments that 'While universal salvation is always a possibility for God's free love, universalism as a theological proposition is unacceptable'.[72] Even the ACUTE report goes as far as to say: 'While rejecting universalism as a theological position, we would nevertheless emphasise that God's mercy might extend further than we can legitimately contemplate'.[73] Whilst they are not here embracing hopeful universalism, the compilers of the report are perhaps in some sympathy with those who are hopeful but not doctrinal universalists. Hans Urs Von Balthasar claims that not only should we hope for the salvation of all people, but that it is our duty to do so. Discussing Balthasar's position, Sachs writes:

> Balthasar maintains that to hope for one's own salvation and not for the salvation of all would be utterly un-Christian, since Christ died for all men and women. It is Christ's solidarity with all sinners that requires Christian hope to be universal in scope.[74]

Thus for Balthasar hopeful universalism is an inherently Christian position.

I believe that all Christians should at least *hope* that God will eventually reconcile all people to Godself, and therefore be hopeful universalists. However, whilst it is relevant to establish that hopeful universalism is a viable option for a Christian, and indeed a desirable one, I will be aiming to demonstrate the coherence of a position more certain than that of hopeful universalism.

Necessary or Hard Universalism

Necessary universalism asserts that because of the way the God has ordained the world, that all people must finally join the company of heaven, this is also sometimes referred to as hard universalism. Those who believe that all people are elected by God for salvation or predetermined to accept God could be classed as advocating necessary universalism. One such person is nineteenth century theologian Friedrich Schleiermacher. Schleiermacher claimed:

> Only in this limited sense, therefore - that is only at each point where we can make a comparison between those laid hold of by sanctification and those not yet laid hold of - ought we to say that God omits or passes over some, and that He rejects those He passes over ... [If] we proceed on this definite assumption that all belonging

---

[71] Craig, 1989 p.186.
[72] Bettis, 1970 p.340.
[73] ACUTE, 2000 p.34.
[74] Sachs, 1991 p.243. He is discussing Balthasar, 1988.

to the human race are eventually taken up into living fellowship with Christ, there is nothing for it but this single divine fore-ordination.[75]

Bauckham writes:

> [Schleiermacher] taught a predestination as absolute as that of Augustine and Calvin, but he rejected any form of *double* predestination - All men are elected to salvation in Christ, and this purpose of divine omnipotence cannot fail. In this respect Schleiermacher represents a 'Reformed' universalism, founded on the all-determining will of God.[76]

Thus Schleiermacher's universalism assumes not only that God desires the salvation of all people but also that humans do not have the option to alter or influence this fore-ordination.

Kvanvig explains: '*Necessary universalism* holds that it is not only true but also necessarily true that every human being will end up in heaven; that anyone be damned is simply impossible'.[77] Thus necessary universalism seems to entail the lack of human freedom, it is determined that all people will be saved. Hard universalism refers to the view that all people will be saved, however it may not imply quite the same determinism as necessary universalism. Jensen writes: 'Any view claiming that the salvation of all humans follows from the necessary attributes of God would qualify as hard universalism'.[78] Hard universalism asserts that universalism must be the outcome and thus is the same as necessary universalism, but does not put the same emphasis on it being predetermined. Jensen describes hard universalism as following from God's necessary attributes, therefore the emphasis is on it being the inevitable result of God's endeavours and relationships with humanity rather than simply God having determined that will be the case.

Jensen cites Thomas Talbott as a proponent of hard universalism, he writes: 'Talbott's conclusion seems to qualify as 'hard universalism' the view that no person *can* be finally lost, as opposed to 'soft universalism' the view that no person *will* be finally lost'.[79] Talbott writes:

> The picture is very simple: All paths ultimately lead to the same end, the end of salvation, but our choice of paths at any given instant may be a matter of our own free choice. This picture is not quite the same

---

[75] Friedrich Schleiermacher, *The Christian Faith* (1960) Edinburgh: T& T Clarke pp.548 - 549.

[76] Bauckham, 1978 p.50.

[77] Kvanvig, 1993 p.74.

[78] Paul T. Jensen, 'Intolerable But Moral? Thinking About Hell' *Faith and Philosophy* vol.10 (1993) p.236.

[79] Jensen, 1993 p.236. He cites Paul Helm as having come up with his distinction in, Paul Helm, 'Universalism and the Threat of Hell' *Trinity Journal* 4NS (1983) p.36.

as that of the grand chess master who is able to checkmate a novice regardless of the specific moves that the novice should make. It is rather a picture of the nature of moral evil and of the way in which, over a long period of time, moral evil inevitably destroys itself.[80]

Thus Talbott asserts that in the end sin and rejection of God are not viable options and so all people will eventually find their way to God. It might be objected that this is the same thing and that the difference between necessary and hard universalism is merely semantic. I will look at this issue in further chapters and hope to establish the importance of this distinction.

Contingent or Soft Universalism

Contingent universalism is so called because the ultimate reality of universalism is not necessary but given the states of affairs which actually exist, universalism is brought about. That is, it is possible that some humans could be eternally separated from God, but in the given circumstances, they will not. Kvanvig explains: '*Contingent universalism* holds that, although a person could end up in hell ...as a matter of contingent fact every human being will end up in heaven'.[81] Thus contingent universalism suggests that universalism would not pertain to any given world, and is not achieved by God determining it. Nor does it follow from God's attributes; rather it just so happens that given the creation of this particular world universalism will turn out to be true.

Kvanvig finds the idea of contingent universalism to be quite incoherent. He writes:

> If it would be wrong to send someone to hell, it makes no difference to the inconsistency between God's sending someone to hell and his perfect goodness whether people end up in hell in the actual world or only in other possible worlds. According to contingent universalism this irredeemably bad state of affairs does obtain in some (other) possible worlds. Hence, even if contingent universalism is true, it does not relieve us of the problem of hell. If hell is abhorrent, affirming contingent universalism will not solve the problem, it only modally masks it.[82]

Contingent universalism does not answer the problem of hell, but transfers it to a different possible world and thus the problem of hell being compatible with a good and loving God remains. Contingent universalism does not even assert the non-existence of hell but only maintains that no one will actually end up there. An argument sometimes offered in response to the problem of hell is that hell exists but

---

[80] Talbott, 1990 p.243.

[81] Kvanvig, 1993 p.74.

[82] Kvanvig, 1993 p.76.

it is empty. It would seem that this response could be classified as contingent universalism.

This view of universalism is also known as soft universalism. Jensen writes: 'Any view claiming that the damnation of some humans is logically and morally possible, but will never be actual, would qualify as soft universalism.'[83] Soft universalism does have one distinct appeal and that is that it could be described as 'free will universalism'.[84] One of the major criticisms of universalism which we will encounter in this book, is that it overrides human freedom, however with soft universalism this need not be the case. The adequacy of contingent or soft universalism will be further discussed, but it will ultimately be rejected because of the objections outlined above by Kvanvig.

The Free Will Defence

The Free Will Defence is significant for the problem of hell, as it is for the problem of evil. Simply, this defence claims that hell is a necessary conglomerate of human freedom. In order for the freedom we are given to be genuine, there must be an option ultimately to reject God. The exact form that the Free Will Defence takes depends upon one's understanding of both human freedom and God's knowledge. In this section I will introduce different types of freedom and knowledge and define the terms.

Human Freedom

Accounts of human freedom can be divided into three main categories, libertarian, compatibilist and determinist. There are of course more than three different accounts of human freedom, but generally they fit into one of these categories.

Libertarian or Strong Freedom

Libertarian, or strong human freedom is the belief that all of our actions are causally undetermined. Libertarian freedom is also called incompatibilism, as it is incompatible with causal determinism.[85] Thomas Talbott explains:

> What libertarians want to deny is simply that our free actions are causally determined, and their point is essentially this negative one: if it is causally determined that I will perform an action A, then it is causally impossible for me to refrain from A; and if it is causally

---

[83] Jensen, 1993 p.236.

[84] This definition is offered by Sanders, 1992 p.83.

[85] Strange notes that this type of freedom is also referred to as indeterministic freedom, contracausal freedom and categorical freedom. Strange, 1999 p.56.

impossible for me to refrain from A, then I am in fact powerless to refrain from A. But my doing A is a free act only if it is both within my power to do A and within my power to refrain from A; so if my doing A is causally determined, it is not a free act.[86]

Thus it is essential for libertarian freedom that our actions are not caused, otherwise they are not free. Swinburne holds a strong view of freedom and indeed it is this on which he rests his theory. According to Swinburne libertarian freedom is the greatest gift which God can give to us.[87] Swinburne further believes that in order for us to be truly free, our choices must be between good and bad and not just a range of good choices. Swinburne argues that: 'Free and responsible choice is rather free will ... to make significant choices between good and evil, which make a big difference to the agent, to others, and to the world'.[88] Therefore Swinburne claims that any human freedom which is causally determined or does not allow us to choose between a range of good and bad options is not in fact genuine human freedom.

Libertarian freedom generally entails the belief that our free actions are unknowable, thus libertarian freedom is incompatible with God's foreknowledge and middle knowledge. William Hasker explains:

> The incompatibilst claims that if God foreknows a person's action, then the action is not free. But, it is pointed out, if God foreknows that some person will freely choose a certain action, what follows is that the action will be done freely, which is the reverse of the conclusion desired by the incompatibilist.[89]

This is what Thomas Talbott describes as a modal confusion. He claims: 'Someone simply transfers the necessity of a conditional to its consequent, or the necessity of a disjunction to one of its conjuncts'.[90] Thus although many libertarians claim that this rules out God having simple foreknowledge, this is by no means an uncontroversial point and it will be crucial to this book to demonstrate that God can know what we will freely choose to do.

Compatibilist Freedom

Compatibilists believe that human freedom is compatible with some degree of causal determinism. This view is also known as soft determinism. Daniel Dennett notes that those who ascribe to this view typically claim in one way or another that

---

[86] Talbott, 1988 p.9.

[87] See Richard Swinburne, *Is There A God?* (1996) Oxford: Clarendon Press p.53.

[88] Swinburne, 1996 p.98.

[89] Hasker, 1985 pp.125-126.

[90] Thomas Talbott, 'Theological Fatalism and Modal Confusion' *International Journal for Philosophy of Religion* vol.33 (1993) p.65.

one acts freely and responsibly just so long as one does what one decides, based on what one believes and desires.[91] And such free actions are not incompatible with determinism. Richard Double explains: 'Traditional compatibilism's solution to the free will question was that freedom is the ability to act as one wishes. Since acting as one wishes is clearly compatible with determinism, freedom was seen as possible within a determined universe'.[92] Thus the distinction could be made that soft determinism allows that free acts are compatible with internal causes and hard determinism implies external causes.

Talbott describes what he believes would constitute a free act:

> I do something freely only if in some vague sense, the action in question is truly mine; and the action is truly mine only if, in some reasonably clear sense, it is not imposed upon me from outside, only if it is not causally determined by conditions external to myself and beyond my control.[93]

Thus this account of freedom could be described as compatibilst freedom as it is not determined by external but by internal factors. The compatibilist position is quite controversial and many claim that it does not constitute genuine freedom. However, many also claim that it is the most realistic account of human freedom. Plantinga notes that Anthony Flew claims that compatibilism is a coherent position. He writes: 'Flew's thesis, then is that there is no contradiction in saying of a man, both that all of his actions are causally determined and that some of them are free'.[94] Dennett suggests that compatibilism is a realistic account of human freedom. He writes:

> We can imagine a being that listens to the voice of reason and yet is not exempted from the causal milieu. Yes, we can imagine a being whose every decision is caused by the interaction of features of its current state and features of its environment over which it has no control and yet which is itself *in control*, and not being controlled by that omnipresent and omnicausal environment. ... yes, we can imagine a rational *and deterministic* being who is not deluded when it views its future as open and 'up to' it. Yes, we can imagine a responsible, free agent of whom it is true that whenever it has acted in the past, it could not have acted otherwise.[95]

---

[91] Daniel C. Dennett, *Elbow Room* (1984) Oxford: Clarendon Press p.83.

[92] Richard Double, *The Non-Reality of Free Will* (1991) Oxford: Oxford University Press p.27.

[93] Thomas Talbott, 'On the Divine Nature and the Nature of Divine Freedom' *Faith and Philosophy* vol.7 (1988) p.13.

[94] Alvin Plantinga, *God and Other Minds* (1967) London: George Allen and Unwin Limited p.134, see also p.31.

[95] Dennett, 1984 p.170.

The coherence of compatibilist freedom will be crucial to my argument and I believe that it is indeed the most realistic account of human freedom.

Determinism

The determinist position is not a popular one amongst philosophers today, implying as it does the sort of Calvinist predestination which has been so prevalent in Christianity. Indeed, Jensen notes that 'Calvin-bashing has become something of a cottage industry lately'.[96] Determinists believe that humans are not genuinely free but that their actions are causally determined. The general unpopularity of determinism means that most theories try to avoid endorsing hard determinism. Dennett explains:

> If determinism is true, then our every deed and decision is the inexorable outcome, it seems, of the sum of physical forces acting at the moment, which in turn is the inexorable outcome of the forces acting an instant before, and so on, to the beginning of time.[97]

This is so unpopular today because we do not want to believe that we have no control over our actions and states of affairs. Lucas writes that there are two specific reasons why determinism is found to be so objectionable:

> There are two reasons why we feel that determinism defeats responsibility. It dissolves the agent's *ownership* of his actions: and it precludes their being really explicable in terms of their *rationale*. If determinsim is true, then my actions are no longer really my actions, and they no longer can be regarded as having been for reasons rather than causes.[98]

Thus if our actions are determined, our moral responsibility is a delusion and we can do only that which we are determined to do.

However Lucas further notes that it is easy to confuse the issues relating to determinism. He writes that determinism can simply refer to the fact that all actions have causes, which is different to the claim that all actions are externally caused. He writes:

> It is easy to accept 'determinism' in some dilute sense, in which all that is being claimed is that there is some reason for every action, and then believe that one is committed to determinism in a strong sense, in which all our actions are causally determined by conditions outside

---

[96] Jensen, 1993 p.237.

[97] Dennett, 1984 p.1.

[98] J.R. Lucas, *The Freedom of the Will* (1970) Oxford: Clarendon Press p.27.

our control because occurring before our birth. ...Our starting point was the principle that every event has an explanation; which is not the same as, and does not imply, the contention that every event has a regularity explanation.[99]

Thus in discussing determinism, we must be careful to establish what sort of determinism we are referring to. The determinism that Lucas started with, could be included in the category of soft determinism or compatibilism, whilst the belief that all of our actions are externally caused is hard determinism.

God's Knowledge

The nature of God's knowledge is an important debate both in philosophy and theology. God is traditionally believed to be all-knowing and all powerful. God is also thought to be able to act freely, that is all of God's actions are uncaused. As Talbott writes: 'Nothing God does, after all, not even that which flows from the necessity of his own nature, is causally determined, and there are no causal conditions that prevent him from doing anything he chooses not to do'.[100] Thus God knows everything and can do anything. However many claim that this is not true. Alvin Plantinga has established that God being omnipotent does not mean that God is free to bring about any state of affairs.[101] There are some states of affairs which cannot be brought about even by God. Thus God's omnipotence must be redefined as meaning that God can do all that it is logically possible to do. A similar argument is made in relation to God's knowledge. Traditionally God is supposed to know all things but Swinburne for example, suggests that this too must be redefined to be understood as God knowing all that it is possible to know.[102] Talbott argues that God must know all true propositions, he writes: 'If God is essentially omniscient, then the person who is God necessarily knows all true propositions; and if therefore, this person does not know that a proposition p is true, then p is not true at all'.[103] Thus according to Talbott our future actions, which Swinburne defines as being unknowable, are not true. Swinburne claims that they are not yet true as they cannot be decided until they are carried out.

God's knowledge can be divided into three main categories, present knowledge, simple foreknowledge and middle knowledge. The first is uncontroversial and I will assume that God has present knowledge. However, there is much debate about foreknowledge and middle knowledge and I will outline these types of knowledge in this section. It is possible, as with Swinburne, to reject that

---

[99] Lucas, 1970 pp.54 - 55.

[100] Talbott, 1988 p.10.

[101] Alvin Plantinga, *The Nature of Necessity* (1974) London: Oxford University Press pp. 169-184. Referred to as 1974 (b).

[102] Swinburne, 1998 p.6.

[103] Talbott, 1990 p.231.

God has either of these sorts of knowledge. The sort of knowledge that God does have will be significant for this book to establish whether or not God can know what the outcome of individual lives will be.

Simple Foreknowledge

Simple foreknowledge is the belief that God knows what is going to happen, before it actually takes place. Either because God has some control over what is going to take place, that is God has determined it, or because God's knowledge means that God knows what creatures will freely choose to do. Swinburne holds that God does not have simple foreknowledge, that the undetermined actions of free creatures cannot be known in advance even by an omniscient being. Thus God being all knowing means that God knows all that it is logically possible to know and this does not include the free future actions of individuals. As Walls explains:

> Swinburne thinks that anything God foreknows is, in some sense, necessary. Thus, if God foreknows human choices, those choices are necessary rather than free. Indeed God's own choices cannot be free if God foreknows them. Consequently, Swinburne argues, we must either qualify the claims that God is perfectly free or we must qualify the claim that God knows all true propositions. Without qualification, the two claims are logically incompatible.[104]

Walls raises the objection to God not having foreknowledge that: 'If God does not have infallible foreknowledge of all future events, is he not likely to be surprised by some developments? Does this allow for the possibility that God might lose control of our world and fail to achieve his purposes?'.[105] Thus without simple foreknowledge God would be uncertain of the outcome of creation.

The view that God does not know what the outcome of creation will be, but chooses to take that risk has become proposed recently as the 'open view of God'. In the book *The Openness Of God*, Richard Rice writes:

> The traditional view of foreknowledge and predestination draws broader conclusions than the evidence warrants in three important ways. The fact that God foreknows or predestines something does not guarantee that it will happen, the fact that God determines part of history does not mean that he determines all of history, and the fact that God extends a specific call to certain people does not mean that he similarly calls all people.[106]

---

[104] Walls, 1992 p.47.
[105] Walls, 1992 p.47.
[106] Richard Rice, 'Biblical Support For a New Perspective' in Clark H. Pinnock (ed.), *The Openness of God: A Biblical Challenge to the Traditional Understanding of God* (1994) Carlisle: Paternoster Press pp.55 - 56.

This view accords with that of Swinburne, and claims that the open view of God is the most helpful understanding of God and also is best able to explain the nature of the world. Thus the view that God does not have foreknowledge is significantly popular in current debate. However we will return to this question in further chapters.

Middle Knowledge

The idea that God, as well as having simple foreknowledge also has middle knowledge, or knowledge of counterfactuals of freedom has been keenly debated over the last few years.[107] The idea was first developed by Luis de Molina a Jesuit Priest in the sixteenth century and hence this sort of knowledge is sometimes referred to as Molinism. Alfred J. Freddoso's translation of Part IV of Molina's *Concordia* was published in 1988 entitled *On Divine Foreknowledge*.[108] Freddoso explains in the introduction:

> Middle knowledge derives its name from the fact that it stands 'midway' between natural knowledge and free knowledge. Like natural knowledge but unlike free knowledge, middle knowledge is prevolitional, with the result that God has no more control over the states of affairs He knows through middle knowledge than He does over the states of affairs He knows through His natural knowledge.[109]

Freddoso adds the further explanation: 'Middle knowledge has as its objects *conditional* or *subjunctive* future contingents that stand "between" the actual and the merely possible'.[110] Thus God's knowledge of the counterfactuals of freedom is aptly termed middle knowledge.

The significance of God possessing middle knowledge for the question of salvation and damnation has more recently been explored by William Lane Craig.[111] Craig claims that God's middle knowledge allows God to ensure that all who would respond favourably to the gospel should they hear it, will in fact hear it in their lifetime. Craig claims:

> God knows via His middle knowledge how any possible free creature would respond in any possible circumstances, which include the offer of certain gifts of prevenient grace which God might provide. In choosing a certain possible world, God commits Himself, out of His goodness, to offering various gifts of grace to every person which are sufficient for his salvation. Such grace is not extrinsically efficacious

---

[107] For further discussions of middle knowledge see bibliography.
[108] Molina, 1988.
[109] Freddoso, 1988 p.47.
[110] Freddoso, 1988 p.47.
[111] See Craig, 1989.

in that it of itself produces its effect; rather it is extrinsically efficacious in accomplishing its end in those who freely cooperate with it.[112]

Thus Craig develops the theory of transworld damnation.[113] There are, he claims, some creatures who would reject God's gift of grace whatever world they existed in and thus would be lost in whatever world they had existed in. Thus Craig comments: 'If there were anyone would have responded to the gospel if he had heard it, then God in His love would have brought the gospel to such a person ... all who would respond to this gospel were they to hear it, did and do hear it'.[114] So according to Craig, middle knowledge gives God the ability to know who will in what circumstances respond favourably to the gospel. However because of transworld damnation, God cannot ensure that all people find themselves in a situation where they will favourably respond to the gospel, indeed according to Craig there is no such situation. Thus God having middle knowledge seems only to mean that God does not need to bother presenting the gospel to those whom God already knows will not respond favourably.

Talbott objects to Craig's theory and states that there is no point in God creating those whom God knows will reject the gospel. Talbott writes: '[If] God knows in advance which persons, or which combinations of persons are irredeemable, then he would simply not create those persons, or those combinations of persons, in the first place'.[115] Craig responds that it is not possible for God to create any imaginable world and therefore we must conclude that only worlds in which some are damned were possible for God to create.[116] God's middle knowledge although it is an additional knowledge of what would happen in alternative circumstances, does not actually give God any control over what would happen in those circumstances. Hasker writes: 'It is an absolutely essential feature of the theory of middle knowledge that the counterfactuals of freedom are not under God's control'.[117] So although God cannot control the counterfactuals of freedom, middle knowledge would clearly give God greater knowledge in deciding what to create and thus would, to an extent, allow God more control.

Thus the question of God's middle knowledge is relevant to the question of salvation and damnation as it allows God to know what the outcome of individual lives would be in every set of circumstances. Craig believes that it can excuse God of all responsibility for the lost as God has done the best that God can for them. However, the issue of middle knowledge is by no means uncontroversial, and I will return to this discussion in later chapters.

---

[112] Craig, 1989 p.179.

[113] Craig, 1989 p.184. This idea is based on Plantinga's transworld depravity, see Plantinga, 1974 (b) pp.184 - 189. I will discuss this further in chapter 6.

[114] Craig, 1989 p.185.

[115] Talbott, 1990 p.241.

[116] See Craig, 1989 pp.180 - 181.

[117] Hasker, 1991 p.385.

Conclusion

The debate about hell has been through many different phases. In this chapter I have outlined the main positions of separatists and universalists as well as different understandings of human freedom and God's knowledge. The current debate is largely concerned with the question of human freedom and whether we are free to reject God. Indeed it is the combination of the weak view of hell and libertarian freedom which comprises the most popular and successful defence of hell today. Indeed these two positions are essential to Swinburne's defence of hell. In the following chapter I will outline Swinburne's position before offering a critique of his defence of hell in chapter three. I shall then look at an alternative view, namely that of John Hick who rejects all defences of hell as well as the libertarian account of human freedom. I will then discuss some difficulties with Hick's position and finally in chapter six will rework Hick's defence of universalism to arrive at what I shall term 'firm universalism'.

Chapter 2

Richard Swinburne's Hell

Introduction

In this chapter I will examine Richard Swinburne's defence of hell. In order to answer the question 'Are we free to reject God?' I will look at four main areas of Swinburne's work. The moment of decision which for Swinburne is more a process of determining character, his defence of hell and consequent rejection of universal salvation and finally Swinburne's account of human freedom and God's knowledge. These two areas are crucial to Swinburne's defence of hell and his account depends upon his understanding of libertarian human freedom. It will be helpful to put these subjects into context by first looking at Swinburne's work and career and then what, for him, is the problem of hell.

Richard Swinburne

Richard Swinburne has become well known for his contribution to the philosophy of religion over the second half of the twentieth century. Since he began his academic career in the 1960s a constant stream of publications have given voice to his work in many areas of philosophical theology. Initially he was concerned with scientific philosophy, but his later works show a growing interest in questions raised by philosophy of religion.

Born in 1934, Swinburne was awarded a scholarship to read classics at the age of eighteen and then after a break for military service, studied philosophy, politics and economics at Oxford University. He went on to read for a philosophy degree, also completing a Diploma in Theology in 1960 and was Fereday Fellow at St. John's College, Oxford from 1958 until 1961. Swinburne then became Research Fellow in the history and philosophy of science at the University of Leeds from 1961 - 1963. During this time he studied science and its history. Swinburne then went on to the Philosophy department in the University of Hull from 1963 - 1972, with a year long break to take up the post of Visiting Associate Professor of Philosophy at the University of Maryland. He then moved to the University of Keele where he was Professor of Philosophy for twelve years. In 1985 Swinburne moved back to Oxford where he held the position of Nolloth Professor of the Philosophy of the Christian Religion. Throughout his career he has taken on a number of Visiting Lectureships in a variety of Philosophy and Theology departments in the UK, Australia, America and India.

Swinburne's first published article, 'Three types of Thesis about Fact and Value' was concerned with the use of language and specifically the relationship between verifiable, evaluative and non-analytic assertions. His first book *Space and Time* was published in 1968 and is, as the name suggests, an exploration of the relationship between space and time. Although Swinburne's approach to his work could be described as a scientific philosophy, his focus has changed from purely scientific understandings of the universe to aspects of Christian belief and the dogmas of faith. In his 'Intellectual Autobiography' Swinburne explains: 'There have been three major influences on my thinking. In order both of increasing time and of decreasing importance, they are the Christian religion, Western philosophy, and theoretical science'.[1]

One of the major focuses of Swinburne's career has been his attempt to prove that it is rational to believe that it is more probable than not that God exists. Swinburne has been determined to show that theism, and specifically Christian theism, is a coherent position and one that can be supported by logical argument. He explains that he was influenced by the philosophy he learnt as a young man. He writes: 'I disliked the Oxford philosophy of the 1950s for its dogmas, but I liked it for its tools of clarity and rigour, and it seemed to me that someone could use its tools to make Christian theology again intellectually respectable'.[2] In *The Coherence of Theism* Swinburne explains that his purpose in writing the book was to ask whether it is coherent to claim that God exists. He reaches the conclusion 'that the question of the coherence of the belief that there is a God cannot altogether be separated from the question of its truth'.[3] This is the first in a trilogy of books on this subject, along with *The Existence of God* and *Faith and Reason*. It is apparent that Swinburne's writing comes from a background of Christian faith, he writes:

> I came to believe it to be my Christian vocation to try and make a contribution to this process [of making Christian theology intellectually respectable]. I was going to become an Anglican priest, but I became a professional philosopher instead.[4]

However his writing style is quite impersonal and he does not really discuss his own experiences of faith.

Although Swinburne has an analytic approach to philosophy, his recent interests are not as conducive to this formulaic style of arguing as some of the subjects with which he earlier engaged. His most recent works show that he has become more interested in issues of Christian teaching, notably the problem of evil

---

[1] Richard Swinburne, 'Intellectual Autobiography' in Alan A. Padgett (ed.), *Reason and the Christian Religion: Essays in Honour of Richard Swinburne* (1994) Oxford: Clarendon Press p.1. Referred to as 1994 (b).

[2] Swinburne, 1994 (b) p.4.

[3] Richard Swinburne, *The Coherence of Theism* (1977) Oxford: Clarendon Press p.1.

[4] Swinburne, 1994 (b) p.4.

and theodicy and human freedom. Swinburne's position on some of the issues which I will look at in this chapter has changed over a period of time, as have the subjects of most interest to him. His most recent books have formed a tetralogy on the philosophy of Christian doctrine, which is made up of *Responsibility and Atonement*; *Revelation*; *The Christian God*; and *Providence and the Problem of Evil*. It is the first and final books of this set which will be of greatest relevance in examining Swinburne's understanding of hell. Eleanore Stump writes that Swinburne has set himself an enormous task in attempting to write on all areas of Christian doctrine, and indeed she notes that he is unique among philosophers for the breadth of his area of interest. She writes:

> Over the course of several books, Richard Swinburne has undertaken to produce a systematic philosophical defence of Christianity. While there are other philosophers who are engaged in defending one or another piece of traditional Christian philosophical theology, Swinburne is the only one to have embarked on a systematic treatment of all the major doctrines of the religion, and it is a mammoth undertaking.[5]

Swinburne describes himself as a follower of Thomas Aquinas, but believes that such a position entails defending Christianity in today's world, and not relying on Aquinas' defence for the thirteenth century. Swinburne explains:

> Each generation must justify the Christian system by using the best secular knowledge of its own day; which is why the true disciple of St Thomas cannot rely on the *summa* - he has to carry out Thomas's programme, using the knowledge of his own day.[6]

However, not everyone is appreciative of Swinburne's efforts to carry out this programme. Hick comments on Swinburne:

> My own view is that this new *summa* produced at the end of the twentieth century, is a vast anachronism, representing the thought forms out of which Christianity is developing rather than the kind of new thinking that is needed as we approach the twenty-first century.[7]

Swinburne's work is a reworking of Christian apologetics and, according to Hick, does nothing to advance Christian theology. However, the issues which Swinburne

---

[5] Eleanor Stump, 'Revelation and Biblical Exegesis: Augustine, Aquinas and Swinburne' in Alan A. Padgett (ed.), *Reason and the Christian Religion: Essays in Honour of Richard Swinburne* (1994) Oxford: Clarendon p.321. Referred to as Stump, 1994 (b).

[6] Swinburne, 1994 (b) pp.8 - 9.

[7] John Hick 'Is the Doctrine of Atonement a Mistake?' in Padgett (ed.), p.247.

discusses are still much debated in theology and philosophy of religion and his contributions add further fuel to the debate.

The Problem of Hell

Although the problem of hell has not been a major focus of Swinburne's work, in order to create a complete and systematic account of Christianity, he has paid it considerable attention. Although he does not subscribe to the traditional understanding of hell as a place of physical torment, he has defended a doctrine of hell in which the unrighteous suffer because they are eternally cut off from God. Thus for Swinburne the problem of hell is solved by reconciling a certain sort of hell with a good and loving God. In this chapter I will examine Swinburne's understanding of hell and the grounds on which he defends it as a coherent Christian doctrine.

Swinburne writes: 'A Christian theological system is, of course, an integrated web of doctrine; and the ground for believing some doctrines to be true is often that they follow from others which in turn have their justification in considerations outside the theological system'.[8] Swinburne's primary defence of the doctrine of hell is that it is necessitated by human freedom. He claims that we are created with strong or libertarian freedom and that freedom allows us to reject God should we choose to. Although the nature of human freedom is a question of importance to theologians, it is perhaps primarily a philosophical issue. Swinburne's justification for this libertarian freedom could be an example of a doctrine which comes from outside the theological system, but shapes the conclusions of theological questions. The doctrine of hell, like any other doctrine is, as Swinburne writes, 'an integrated web of doctrine' and in order to examine Swinburne's understanding of hell it will be necessary also to look at several other subjects: namely his understanding of purgatory and the moment of decision, his rejection of universalism and most crucially for Swinburne's defence of hell, his view of human freedom and God's knowledge.

The Moment of Decision

For Swinburne, the moment of decision is not a single moment which takes place at death, but is a lengthy process of decision making which gradually makes us the sort of people we are. Thus every moral or spiritual decision made throughout the earthly life contributes to the overall decision for or against God. According to Swinburne, it is how we determine our own character that constitutes our moments of decision. Thus for many the decision could be made long before death, however Swinburne suggests that this will not necessarily be the case for all people. Some people may need further time after death in order to confirm the choices they have

---

[8] Swinburne, 1989 p.123.

begun to make. Swinburne discusses the doctrine of purgatory and considers whether this could be the answer for those who have not sufficiently formed their character.

Shaping Character

Swinburne believes that throughout the course of our lives, we choose for or against God by choosing what sort of people we will become. He argues that the person who has allowed him/herself always to make bad choices has already decisively rejected God by rejecting the good, and after death will not reverse this choice, therefore God must honour that choice by allowing that person to go to hell. The person who has generally chosen good has chosen for God and therefore will go to heaven.

In *Faith and Reason* Swinburne denies that God will easily allow people to reject God.

> It is good that God should not let a man damn himself without much urging and giving him many opportunities to change his mind, but it is bad that man should not in the all-important matter of the destiny of his soul be allowed finally to destroy it.[9]

Swinburne claims that people do not generally damn themselves by single acts or by specific bad deeds but rather by adopting an attitude of ignoring the good. Swinburne explains:

> One mortal sin is not enough to produce total contempt for morality. Conscience will nag again; but repeated mortal sin will produce the state of total corruption. Sin is less serious in so far as the agent's choice is less deliberate (in so far as he is swayed by passion).[10]

Giving in occasionally, to one's strongest desires for what we know to be bad, is not how we condemn ourselves, and neither do we seal our fate by mistakenly making bad choices. However, constantly and deliberately choosing the bad and never fighting against desires for what we know to be wrong will eventually lead to a state of irreversible corruption.

This process happens throughout our life, allowing those who consistently begin to choose the bad to rectify this and vice versa. Swinburne explains: 'God chooses what choices to give us. And it is good that our bad choices and good choices should not form our characters with instantaneous effect. We need to show our resoluteness of commitment over a short period'.[11] Thus we need to be committed to our course of action, before we have decisively chosen for or against

---

[9] Richard Swinburne, *Faith and Reason* (1981) Oxford: Clarendon Press pp.154 - 155.
[10] Swinburne, 1989 p.176.
[11] Swinburne, 1989 p.200.

God. However, the option for future change is not unlimited and eventually our character will be confirmed and no future change will be possible. Swinburne writes:

> It is good that God should allow people that choice of forming their characters in such a way as not to be open to future change. For if God refused to allow someone to develop an irreformably bad character, that would be depriving her of an ultimate choice by an independent moral agent.[12]

Thus our freedom entails the choice to determine our characters irreversibly, and once this has happened we have made our choice for or against God.

Swinburne pre-empts the objection that although some people have consistently chosen the bad we have no reason to believe that they are beyond reform. He asks: 'Have we reason to suppose that such corruption may be total and (barring special divine intervention) irreversible?'.[13] Swinburne offers three reasons for supposing that this is indeed so. First, that we know ourselves how easy it is to become oblivious to certain aspects of good. Second, that we have seen this in evil people of the past, Swinburne gives the example of 'Nazi butchers'. Third such a person will 'have built up a strong desire ... to resist all such awareness'.[14] Swinburne holds that these reasons show conclusively that it is entirely possible for a person to reach a situation of irreversible corruption. Further he holds that the only action of a good and loving God is to honour this choice made by corrupt humans. 'A good God', he writes, 'will respect a considered choice of destiny'.[15]

Thus for Swinburne we do not need an encounter with God at death in order to choose for or against God, because through the choices we have made in our lives the decision is already made. Consequently those who have decisively chosen the bad will go to hell as a result of their free choice. However, not all who have chosen the good are ready for the Christian heaven and some have not yet finally shaped their character. Thus Swinburne suggests that there may be some sort of further stage in which those who have nominally chosen the good will be able to make this choice decisive.

Purgatory

Swinburne understands the traditional Roman Catholic teaching of purgatory to be an intermediate afterlife for those who are good, but not yet sufficiently good to enjoy the Beatific Vision with the saints in heaven. Thus those in purgatory would already have made their choice in favour of, or been chosen for, heaven, and once in purgatory they would lose their bad desires and develop their good desires.

---

[12] Swinburne, 1998 p.121.
[13] Swinburne, 1989 pp.177-178.
[14] Swinburne, 1989 p.178.
[15] Swinburne, 1998 p.198.

Swinburne suggests that the idea of purgatory could have a useful role in his theory. He comments: 'It seems to me that there is scope for the Christian tradition to maintain that not all fates are sealed at death. Some persons may have the opportunity in some further world to work out their ultimate destiny'.[16] He comments that in many ways, our task in this life would be manageable, if there was further time, in an afterlife, in which to complete our transformation to the good. Swinburne writes:

> If there is a possibility of further years after this life in which we can continue the process of sanctification (viz. in purgatory), then perhaps we can do enough in this life for God to give us those further years in which to complete the process.[17]

Thus one would only be required in the present life to show a tendency towards the good rather than firmly shape one's character for the good.

As well as the saints who are ready for heaven there could be a category of 'secondary saints' those who show promise but are not yet ready for the Beatific Vision. Swinburne explains:

> Those who die having pleaded the sacrifice of Christ with true repentance and apology, die forgiven by God. Although they do not merit the life of Heaven, God, who seeks man's eternal well-being in friendship with himself, would surely recognise their basic inclination of will towards the good manifested in that pleading, either by taking them straight to Heaven (removing from them in the process their bad desires) or by allowing them to reform their own character further, e.g. in Purgatory.[18]

Both this life and the life of heaven are gifts from God but Swinburne believes the life of heaven to be the greater of these two gifts. He suggests that God, being generous, would allow those who had appreciated the gift of this life but not used it to its best potential to have further opportunities to gain the greater gift of heaven. Thus the purpose of purgatory would not be to offer further opportunities for decision, rather it would offer those who have chosen the good the chance to confirm this choice and make themselves truly good in preparation for the life of heaven.

Swinburne suggests that in order to help those in purgatory with the process of settling their character for the good, there may be 'need for a further *poena damni* to give the opportunity for reform'.[19] Thus this purgatory would involve an environment in which we were still prone to bad desires. He comments:

---

[16] Swinburne, 1981 p.169.

[17] Swinburne, 1989 p.131.

[18] Swinburne, 1989 p.198.

[19] Swinburne, 1998 p.201.

'This intermediate state might involve suffering, for the same reason as the permanent state, through the frustration of wrong desires'.[20] This environment would enable those who want to choose whole-heartedly for the good to settle their character.

Swinburne concludes: 'Maybe, as in the Catholic version, purgatory is so arranged that its "inhabitants" cannot, in virtue of the good desires they have formed or kept intact on earth, ever finally lose the Vision of God'.[21] Thus those who enter purgatory will not be cast out to join those in hell. However neither is it guaranteed that they will participate in the Beatific Vision. Swinburne suggests that a further option for those who never sufficiently establish their good character would be to remain in purgatory. He acknowledges that this is a significant variation from the traditional doctrine, however, 'it would require little amendment to it [the doctrine of purgatory] to allow someone to refuse ever to be reformed sufficiently to make himself suited for Heaven'.[22] According to Swinburne, the addition of purgatory to the different fates after death does not actually allow further opportunity for deciding between heaven and hell. Those who go to purgatory have already nominally chosen the good and thus may, after settling this choice go to heaven. However purgatory does seem to allow the option of not firmly settling one's character for good or bad, in which case Swinburne changes the status of purgatory from an intermediary state to an eternal state for those of unsettled character.

Conclusion

For Swinburne the moment of decision does not come at the same time for all people. Some will, throughout their lives, consistently choose the good or the bad and thus firmly shape their character for good or bad. There are also those who choose a mixture of good and bad, but who, by the time of their death, have fixed their character in favour of one or the other. However there are some people who, by the time of their death, will not have fixed their character. If they have shown a preference for the good then Swinburne suggests that God will give them further opportunity in purgatory to fix their character for the good. For those who never confirm their character in this way, Swinburne proposes that they remain eternally in purgatory, thus for such people a decision is never really made.

Hell Versus Universal Salvation

Although Swinburne has consistently defended the idea of hell as an important part of Christian teaching, his defence of hell has taken various forms throughout the course of his career. Swinburne's primary defence of the doctrine of hell, and the

---

[20] Swinburne, 1998 p.201.

[21] Swinburne, 1998 p.201.

[22] Swinburne, 1989 p.197.

one that is presented in his most recent works, is that hell is necessary as a result of our strong human freedom. He claims that in order for our freedom to be serious, we must have the freedom ultimately to choose for or against God, and thus God should allow any who freely choose it to send themselves to hell. Swinburne's account of hell is not the traditional one and indeed he claims that it does not entail physical punishment but rather that the suffering results from individuals being separated from God. Thus Swinburne may want to add a fourth point to our three point problem of hell: 4) humans are strongly free. Or Swinburne might claim that because hell does not entail eternal physical punishment that the problem of hell does not arise, as such a hell would not be incompatible with a God of love. Although these two points constitute Swinburne's major, current defence of hell, he has three further minor defences of hell, namely that it is not a bad thing for people who do not desire heaven to be instead in hell. Second, that the threat of hell is effective as a deterrent and finally that the New Testament and Church Fathers teach an eternal separation of the good and bad. In this section I will look at these defences of the doctrine of hell and establish the particular sort of hell that Swinburne defends. I will also look at Swinburne's idea of the afterlife as compensation and his view of conditional immortality.

The Individual's Choice for Hell

Swinburne's main defence of the doctrine of hell is that it is necessitated by human freedom. Rather than contradicting God's goodness, Swinburne believes that it is in fact a sign of God's goodness that God is prepared to take human choices so seriously that God allows individuals to choose eternal separation from God. For Swinburne human free choices are the most important gift that God has bestowed upon us, and is an even greater gift because we can make such serious free choices as choosing whether finally to accept or reject God. Although many may claim that a good God should not allow individuals to reject God and so damn themselves, Swinburne contends that God would not be good, if having given us the gift of free will God then interfered with human choices.

In *Faith and Reason* Swinburne asks: 'Does God give the well-being of Heaven only to those who pursue the Christian way, and if so does not this seem ungenerous of him?'.[23] He responds to this:

> One might answer that man has no right to Heaven and God wrongs no one by not giving it to some men; but he has offered it to those who pursue the Christian way, and he will fulfil his promise. Man has the choice of whether to pursue the way or not; but he must take the consequence of not doing so.[24]

This is an early version of Swinburne's now much developed thesis that hell is

---

[23] Swinburne, 1981 p.147.
[24] Swinburne, 1981 p.147.

freely chosen by those who reject God and the offer of heaven. However Swinburne in subsequent works does not explicitly emphasise the choice for or against Christianity, but rather talks of choices between good and bad. In his first article specifically focusing on this subject, 'A Theodicy of Heaven and Hell' Swinburne writes:

> The crucial point is that it is compatible with the goodness of God that he should allow a man to put himself beyond the possibility of salvation, because it is indeed compatible with the goodness of God that he should allow a man to choose what sort of person he will be.[25]

He further argues: 'Free will is a good thing, and for God to override it for whatever cause is to all appearances a bad thing'.[26] Thus Swinburne here clearly formulates the argument that as free beings, we choose our own eternal destiny and that a good God who has given us that freedom will not interfere with those choices.

In *Responsibility and Atonement*, this defence of hell is an important part of Swinburne's argument. He writes: 'Human free will is not just free will: it involves what I may call a choice of destiny'.[27] Again Swinburne asserts that God, having bestowed the gift of freedom, cannot intervene with the choices which are made.

> He who seeks man's eternal well-being in friendship with himself would respect man's free choice and not force his friendship upon him. In giving to men the gift of free will, a creator is, I suggest under an obligation not to use force to change it when it is not to his liking.[28]

Swinburne believes that God has given individuals sufficient opportunity and encouragement not to reject God. He claims: 'Since any who do damn themselves will have had an initial vision of a good and a capacity to choose it freely, they will have been given God's gracious help, enough of it to avoid damnation if they choose'.[29] Thus it is clear that God, having given individuals a free choice of destiny cannot at any later point override this decision. Rather, according to Swinburne, it is good that God should honour this choice and allow individuals who continually choose for the bad to put themselves beyond the reach of salvation.

Indeed it is the freedom to make this choice which Swinburne considers to be the best gift which God has given to us. He writes: 'That our choices matter

---

[25] Richard Swinburne, 'A Theodicy of Heaven and Hell' in Alfred J. Freddoso (ed.), *The Existence and Nature of God* (1983) London and Notre Dame: University of Notre Dame Press p.52.

[26] Swinburne, 1983 p.49.

[27] Swinburne, 1989 p.178.

[28] Swinburne, 1989 p.180.

[29] Swinburne, 1989 p.181.

tremendously, that we can make great differences to things for good or ill, is one of the greatest gifts a creator can give us'.[30] Again in *Providence and the Problem of Evil* he writes:

> To give someone free will makes it up to him what will happen. That is a great good and (from the view point of his creator, who does not make his choice for him) there is a certain chance of a further good that he will use it to choose the best.[31]

Swinburne argues that God is not responsible for those who do end up in hell, because God has given them the great gift of free will, and so obviously cannot control how it is used. He continues:

> It is good in itself (i.e. good for those agents) that free agents have such responsibility, even if the chance of their misusing it is so great and the resulting bad so great that on balance it is not a good thing that God gives agents such free will.[32]

The good of humans having free will, outweighs the bad that results from these free choices, even to the extent of outweighing the bad of some individuals freely choosing to spend eternity in hell.

Thus Swinburne argues that hell is a necessary consequence of serious human freedom and that having created us with this freedom it would be wrong for God to interfere to prevent anyone finally choosing to reject God. This defence of hell is dependent on Swinburne's account of human freedom which he claims is of the libertarian kind. This defence also relies on Swinburne's judgement that strong human freedom is of more importance than eventual salvation. I will challenge both of these assertions in the next chapter.

Hell as Poena Damni

Swinburne consistently rejects the traditional teaching of hell as a place of physical suffering. He explains:

> The tradition has been that the everlasting punishment consists of two parts: the *poena damni*, the penalty of the loss of God, the really heavy punishment; and also a *poena sensus*, a suffering of some sort represented pictorially as the 'flames of Hell'.[33]

Swinburne believes that many Christians today reject the idea of this dual

---

[30] Swinburne, 1996 p.103.
[31] Swinburne, 1998 p.87.
[32] Swinburne, 1998 p.88.
[33] Swinburne, 1998 p.197.

punishment and believe that the torment of hell consists only of being deprived of the vision of God. In 'The Christian Wager' he writes: 'Most Christians today think of Hell, not as the medieval place of literal fiery torment, but merely as a state of separation from God'.[34] Swinburne however does not just reject the concept of physical torment in hell because it is no longer a popular explanation of the fate of the wicked. He holds that although there will be a separation of fates in the afterlife, eternal physical punishment is not compatible with a good and loving God. In *Faith and Reason* he writes:

> No doubt the bad deserve much punishment. For God gave them life and opportunity of salvation but they ignored their creator, hurt his creatures, damaged his creation, and spent their lives seeking trivial pleasures for themselves. But for God to subject them to literally *endless* physical pain ... does seem to me to be incompatible with the goodness of God. It seems to me to have the character of a barbarous vengeance; whatever the evil, a finite number of years of evil-doing does not deserve an infinite number of years of physical pain as punishment.[35]

Again in *Responsibility and Atonement* Swinburne writes:

> God being good, would not punish a sinner with a punishment beyond what he deserved; and I suggest that, despite majority Christian tradition, literally everlasting pain would be a punishment beyond the deserts of any human who has sinned for a finite time on Earth.[36]

Swinburne emphasises that the *poena damni* is not so much a punishment inflicted by God, but rather is the result of one's actions. He writes: 'The *poena damni* is a loss of good, not an inflicted evil; and it is not so much a punishment inflicted from without as an inevitable consequence of a man allowing himself to lose his moral awareness'.[37] Indeed it seems that a hell inflicted on the sinner by God as punishment would challenge Swinburne's belief in God. He writes: 'Unending, unchosen suffering would indeed to my mind provide a very strong argument against the existence of God. But that is not the human situation'.[38] Although Swinburne is not specifically referring here to the traditional doctrine of hell, that doctrine would fulfil the criteria he suggests for a strong argument against the existence of God.

Swinburne does not intend by rejecting the idea of physical torment to dilute

---

[34] Richard Swinburne, 'The Christian Wager' *Religious Studies* vol.4 (1969) p.222.

[35] Swinburne, 1981 p.171.

[36] Swinburne, 1989 p.181.

[37] Swinburne, 1989 p.182.

[38] Swinburne, 1996 p.107.

the doctrine of hell. He believes that the experience of *poena damni* will be a severe one and indeed that the permanent loss of the presence of God is the worst thing that could possibly happen to a person. Indeed he claims:

> For the totally corrupt there must be the *poena damni* (i.e. damnation), the penalty of the loss of the vision of God, a penalty of far greater importance than any *poena sensus* ... as Augustine, himself a firm advocate of eternal sensory punishment for the wicked, pointed out.[39]

Despite this, Swinburne does not totally move away from the idea of hell as a punishment. In *Faith and Reason* he discusses the case of a man who has been part of the Christian community only to increase his business opportunities. He writes:

> Heaven is a place for the generous and a man who sought only to increase his trade would not get there. Worse, if the Christian religious system is true, he will suffer for his hypocrisy. For he could only gain business for his trade by worship if he pretended to have other purposes for worshipping; and if there is any truth in the Christian doctrine of judgement, he will be punished therefore.[40]

Here, Swinburne suggests that wrong behaviour will be punished by God. Despite his defence of hell as being the choice of the individual, in his more recent works Swinburne still writes of hell as a punishment. In *Responsibility and Atonement* Swinburne writes that the totally corrupt being, 'certainly deserves punishment, and God has a right to punish him'.[41] Thus although Swinburne claims that hell is a result of the choices of individuals, he also refers to hell as a punishment which is inflicted upon individuals and not just a state chosen by them. This tension is not resolved by Swinburne and I will return to this point in the following chapter.

Further Defences of Hell

The combination of hell being a result of one's own free choices and the rejection of hell as a place of physical torment result in a weak view of hell.[42] However Swinburne also has three further defences of the doctrine of hell. The idea of hell as a deterrent, and appeal to the traditional doctrine of hell do not necessarily strengthen Swinburne's main defence as they seem to support the strong view.

---

[39] Swinburne, 1989 p.182. See also Swinburne, 1998 p.197 where Swinburne describes the *poena damni* as being the 'heavier' punishment.

[40] Swinburne, 1981 p.139.

[41] Swinburne, 1989 p.181.

[42] The weak view of hell is defined in chapter 1, it does not in anyway suggest that Swinburne's belief in hell is weak in the normal sense of weak; indeed it is apparent that Swinburne's belief in hell is, in its normal sense, strong.

However the third defence, that hell is in fact the best option for some is a development of his weak view of hell, yet one which changes the nature of hell even further from the traditional doctrine.

Hell as the Traditional Teaching of the Church

Although Swinburne rejects the idea of eternal fires of hell, he does believe that there will be an eternal separation of fates, and he believes that this is the teaching of the New Testament. In *Faith and Reason* Swinburne writes that the Biblical information about the afterlife is far from cohesive.

> The New Testament certainly warns that the fate of many is sealed at death for good or ill, and that a man should live his life conscious that his own fate is likely to be sealed. But it can hardly be said to contain a rigid and explicit doctrine of the fates of all categories. A healthy agnosticism on some of the issues would seem suitable for the Christian tradition.[43]

In *Responsibility and Atonement* Swinburne gives a brief account of the representation of hell in the New Testament and given by the early Church Fathers. He writes that the 'New Testament writings seem to me ambiguous on the issue of whether the punishment of the wicked is an everlasting sensory one'.[44] However he continues more emphatically: 'They are fairly unanimous that the end of life marks a permanent division between the good and the wicked'.[45] Thus Swinburne claims that we can learn from Scripture that there will be an eternal separation of the sheep and the goats, but not the details of what these separate lives will consist.

    This has not been the standard view, however. He remarks: 'Most Christian theologians of subsequent centuries have had a fairly definite doctrine of eternal sensory punishment of the wicked'.[46] One of the most notable amongst these was Augustine, who Swinburne notes: 'was firm in his own belief in the eternal sensory punishment of the wicked'.[47] It was in medieval times, Swinburne asserts, that the view that the wicked would endure eternal, physical pain was most prevalent. 'The First Council of Lyons (AD 1245) declared that those who died without penitence in mortal sin would be "crucified forever in the fires of eternal Hell."'[48] Although Swinburne claims to have the weight of Biblical teaching and

---

[43] Swinburne, 1981 p.169.

[44] Swinburne, 1989 p.183.

[45] Swinburne, 1989 p.183.

[46] Swinburne, 1989 p.183 He notes that a significant exception to this was Origen: 'Who claimed that all men would eventually be saved'. This view was also taken on by Gregory of Nyssa and to a lesser extent by Gregory Nazianzen.

[47] Swinburne, 1989 p.183.

[48] Swinburne, 1989 p.184. His information is from Denziger, *The Church Teaches: Documents of the Church in English Translation* (1955) London and St Louis: B. Herder Book Company p.839. He is keen to note that Aquinas differed slightly in claiming: 'This

Christian tradition on his side, it seems that the latter at least has been geared to asserting a strong view of hell. Therefore it is questionable how beneficial this tradition is to Swinburne in defending a weak view of hell.

Hell as a Deterrent

Traditionally the purposes of punishment have been thought to be prevention, deterrence, reform and retribution.[49] Swinburne claims that whilst eternal separation from God cannot achieve prevention or reform and is not retributive, it is valuable as a deterrent.[50] In *Providence and the Problem of Evil* he explains: 'Poena damni will not serve any purposes of prevention or reform, but if it is known to or suspected by others that may be the fate of those who sin continually, it can certainly deter those others'.[51] Swinburne claims that the threat of physical punishment will be an even more potent deterrent.

> The threat of *poena sensus* will ... be a more powerful deterrent to the hard-hearted who have little love for God, than the threat of *poeni damni*. The former threat may - and through the centuries so often has - started the hard-hearted on the road to sanctity.[52]

Thus he believes that the traditional Christian view of hell is useful for encouraging people to choose the good in order to avoid the eternal physical suffering which it threatens. Swinburne further claims that if God has threatened to punish those who will deserve it, then God must also act on that threat. In *Responsibility and Atonement* he writes: 'It is perhaps good that God should exercise that right if, in order to provide men with a disincentive to sin, he has vowed previously that he will punish sinners'.[53] In *Providence and the Problem of Evil* Swinburne again cites the purpose of deterrence as providing God with 'reason to vow to punish in the next life (temporarily or permanently) those who sin in this life'.[54]

The deterrent of hell is, for Swinburne, a good thing and he believes that behaving better because of the fear of hell is also a good thing.

> While to avoid the pains of hell is always a good reason for doing anything at all, including worshipping God or giving to the poor, there are other and better reasons for doing the latter things. But if it

---

physical punishment was not of infinite intensity; and, like all other thinkers, he also held that it varied in intensity for different sinners'. He refers to Thomas Aquinas, *Summa Contra Gentiles* (1924) London: Burns, Oates and Wathburn, III, 145 and Thomas Aquinas, *Summa Theologiae* (1929) London: Eyre and Spottiswood, 1a. 2ae. 87.3.

[49] For a discussion of the purposes of punishment see Swinburne, 1989 chapter 6.

[50] See also Walker, 1964 pp. 40-42 on the deterrent value of hell.

[51] Swinburne, 1998 p.198.

[52] Swinburne. 1998 p.199.

[53] Swinburne, 1989 p.181.

[54] Swinburne, 1998 p.199.

> is very difficult to get yourself to give out of love for the poor, it is
> good to remind yourself that by giving you avoid the pains of hell.[55]

Swinburne is not concerned that the motive for charitable giving, if it is done to avoid the pains of hell, is hardly altruistic. However he does not claim that this giving in itself constitutes virtuous behaviour. He writes: 'Threats are a useful spur to virtue, not because they immediately produce virtuous action, but because they weaken the power of desires which inhibit the pursuit of virtue'.[56] Swinburne holds a fairly low view of humanity and believes that humans are most likely to do good with the aid of deterrents and promises of rewards. He pre-empts the objection that God should not have made us so weak in the first place, with the response that this weakness allows us 'by our own choice to form our characters, and to allow others to help us to do so. That can only happen if we do not have a firm character to start with'.[57] Thus Swinburne's defence of hell as being of benefit to humans as a deterrent to making bad choices is dependent on his understanding of human nature and his assertion that the freedom to shape our own characters is the best gift that God could have given to us.

Hell as the Best Option for Some

In his most recent works Swinburne has claimed that for those who do not desire the good of heaven, and thus end up in hell, hell is not a bad thing. He argues that if individuals do not want the good of heaven, it cannot be a bad thing for them not to have it. In *Is There A God?* Swinburne writes that a selective Beatific Vision would only be a bad state, 'if those deprived of that vision desire it all the same. If some do not desire it, it would not be a bad thing if they do not have it'.[58] Those who have not made themselves good people will not desire the Beatific Vision and the good pursuits of heaven and thus it will be no loss for them to be excluded from heaven. In *Providence and the Problem of Evil* Swinburne writes:

> If someone does form their character in such a way as to be
> unalterably bad and if that involved their having no residual desire
> for the good which they cannot choose, they do not then desire the
> Vision of God; and so it is not a bad thing that they do not get it.[59]

He continues: 'There may also be those who never had a desire for the good (i.e. the morally good) in the first place, and there would be nothing bad in them not obtaining the Vision of God'.[60] And again he writes: 'It will only be a bad thing that

---

[55] Swinburne, 1989 p.168.

[56] Swinburne, 1989 p.168.

[57] Swinburne, 1998 pp.188-189.

[58] Swinburne, 1996 p.120.

[59] Swinburne, 1998 p.121.

[60] Swinburne, 1998 p.121.

those in that condition [of incorrigibly rejecting the good] should be deprived of the Beatific Vision if they still desire to have it'.[61]

Swinburne writes in a passage discussing the fate of a bad individual:

> There would be no point in giving him the 'vision' of God, for he could not enjoy it ... the wicked cannot be happy in doing actions or experiencing states whose value arises form their moral goodness. Moral goodness is so central to what God is that only one who valued that would wish to adore God.[62]

Thus Swinburne maintains that the life of heaven is extremely desirable. However it is the desire for it that makes it worth having. For those who do not desire heaven, they would not enjoy being in heaven and so there is nothing bad about them being excluded from the company of heaven. For such people who have moulded their characters so as to prefer the bad, hell is a better and more suitable option. Therefore Swinburne argues that existence in hell is not a bad thing, but indeed for those who have chosen to be excluded from heaven, the state of being in hell is actually good.

Afterlife as Compensation

It is integral to Swinburne's theodicy that no life will be on balance, bad. As that does not always seem to be the case in this life, Swinburne claims that the afterlife will provide compensation for those whose lives have consisted of more bad than good. All peoples' lives are different and they experience varying degrees of good and bad. Swinburne acknowledges this and comments: 'This would only be "unfair" if the bad states were too bad or not ultimately compensated'.[63] Swinburne affirms that those who have very bad lives will receive their compensation in heaven.[64] He suggests that if there are any human lives which are on balance bad, 'God would be under an obligation to provide life after death for the individuals concerned in which they could be compensated for the evils of this life, so that in this life and the next their lives overall would be good'.[65]

However Swinburne does not think that every life will need the opportunity for compensation in the afterlife. Discussing the fate of people who die at an early age, Swinburne writes:

> There seems nothing wrong in God sending unbaptised babies to Limbo rather than Heaven. Babies do not have a character capable of

---

[61] Swinburne, 1998 p.197.

[62] Swinburne, 1989 p.182.

[63] Swinburne, 1998 p.236.

[64] Swinburne, 1998 p.239.

[65] Richard Swinburne, 'Theodicy, Our Well-Being and God's Rights' *International Journal for Philosophy of Religion* vol.38 (1995) p.91.

enjoying Heaven, any more than do goldfish. There is nothing wrong
in God creating lesser beings capable of lesser joys, or keeping such
in being rather than making only persons fitted for the highest joys.[66]

In *Responsibility and Atonement* he similarly comments: 'Elimination seems not an
unjust fate, again on the grounds that there is no formed character worth preserving
to eternity, nor enough good deeds worthy of reward'.[67] Thus those who have only
a very short earthly existence are not to be compensated in the after-life.

There is a difficulty then, in Swinburne's claim that the afterlife will serve
as an equaliser for the injustices of the earth, and that is that the opportunity for
compensation will not be given to all people. A further difficulty may be that this
view of the afterlife is incompatible with Swinburne's weak view of hell, and would
more logically be part of a strong view in which God decided the fates of
individuals. I will return to these difficulties in the next chapter.

Conditional Immortality

In *The Evolution of the Soul* Swinburne argues at length for the dualistic position
that every human is made up of both body and soul. Although he claims that
dualism is no longer a popular philosophical position, in *Is There A God?* he
writes: 'I find these arguments (of an entirely non-theological kind) in its favour
inescapable'.[68] It is then the soul which Swinburne supposes remains, or is kept by
God, in existence after death.[69] Swinburne does not believe in the immortality of
the soul as the early Greeks and many others have done. He comments: 'I suspect
that one factor which influenced the Fathers and scholastics to affirm eternal
sensory punishment was their belief in the actual immortality of the soul'.[70] Their
belief that the soul would remain in existence eternally ruled out for them the
possibility, entertained by Swinburne, of conditional immortality.

In 'The Christian Wager' Swinburne comments: 'Not all Christians believe
that anyone will go to Hell, some Christians would say that the culpable non-
Christian merely ceases to exist'.[71] In *Faith and Reason* Swinburne seems uncertain
as to what fate awaits the wicked after death. He writes that the bad:

> Might cease to exist after death. They might cease to exist after some
> limited physical pain as part of the punishment for their wickedness.
> Or they might continue to exist forever, pursuing trivial pursuits ...

---

[66] Swinburne, 1981 p.170.

[67] Swinburne, 1989 p.197.

[68] Swinburne, 1996 p.77.

[69] For Swinburne the soul is the essential part of a person, he writes: 'It is the soul which is
the initiator of intentional action and is the subject of conscious experience, and is the
vehicle of character', 1989 p.179.

[70] Swinburne, 1989 p.184.

[71] Swinburne, 1969 p.222.

perhaps not even realising that their pursuits were trivial.[72]

In *Responsibility and Atonement* Swinburne asks: 'What is the point of keeping a totally corrupt being alive? He has lost the centre of his being. There would be no point in giving him the "vision" of God, for he could not enjoy it'.[73] Thus if the soul is not immortal but immortality is part of the gift bestowed upon good human souls by God after death, Swinburne holds that it would be reasonable to conclude that God would simply not keep in existence those who were not, through their own bad choices, capable of joining the saints in heaven. He goes on to assert: 'God certainly does not owe every human soul an eternal life'.[74] Indeed Swinburne writes:

> There is no obligation on God to keep any man alive in a world to come. Yet should he keep the totally corrupt man alive forever ... he will give him only those pleasures whose enjoyment involves no recognition of the moral goodness of what is enjoyed.[75]

In *Providence and the Problem of Evil*, Swinburne, in line with his belief that we choose our own destiny through our free moral decisions, suggests that individuals can decide whether or not they wish to continue in existence. He writes: 'God would not impose permanent, intense suffering on wrongdoers who do not want to go on existing'.[76] Thus those who are not to be admitted to the company of saints in heaven may choose to pass out of existence altogether. Again, he writes:

> The only way in which God could eliminate the bad state of it [a residual desire for the good] not being satisfied would be by eliminating the bad themselves, and maybe that is what God would do with the incorrigibly bad - but surely only if that is what, after long consideration, they strongly desire.[77]

Swinburne does not come down unequivocally on the idea of conditional immortality. Although he suggests that those who do not go to heaven will instead pass out of existence, he is far from adamant that this will be the fate of all of the unsaved, and indeed he does not seem wholly convinced that it will be the fate of any. Certainly in his most recent book, *Providence and the Problem of Evil,* he suggests that immortality could be a choice for those who will not join the company of heaven. Swinburne believes that if God chose, or allowed individuals themselves to choose to end their existence, this would not be a wrong act of God.

---

[72] Swinburne, 1981 p.172.
[73] Swinburne. 1989 p.182.
[74] Swinburne, 1989 p.196.
[75] Swinburne, 1989 p.182.
[76] Swinburne, 1998 p.201.
[77] Swinburne, 1998 p.198.

Rejection of Universalism

Swinburne is very dismissive of the universalist position and does not engage in a discussion of it but rather comments that it is an untenable position. For example, in 'The Christian Wager' he writes: 'Some few Christians would maintain the rather unbiblical view that all men go to heaven eventually'.[78] Similarly in 'A Theodicy of Heaven and Hell' he claims that universalist doctrine 'is not that of the New Testament'[79] Swinburne's most extensive discussion of universalism is in *Responsibility and Atonement*. Here he discusses the evidence of the New Testament and gives a very brief background to universalism. As we have seen Swinburne claims that universalism is not a Biblical position. He writes: 'That the wicked have permanently a status quite other than that enjoyed by the blessed ... seems a crucial central point of the great biblical parables of judgement such as the parable of the sheep and the goats'.[80] However he goes on to note: 'There are even occasional passages which seem to imply that the division of the sheep and goats is only a temporary one'.[81] Swinburne however does not discuss the implications of this and is resistant to the idea that eventual universal salvation has any place in New Testament teaching.

Although there has been a fairly definite doctrine of eternal sensory punishment of the wicked throughout Christian history, Swinburne acknowledges that there have also been some who have disagreed with this consensus.

> The best-known exception was Origen, who claimed that all men would eventually be saved, and his view remained to exert a considerable influence over the next three centuries. Gregory of Nyssa advocated Origen's view, and Gregory Nazianzen toyed with it. St Basil acknowledged that most ordinary men of his day believed that the sufferings of hell were only of finite duration; and St Augustine acknowledged the diversity of opinions on this matter which were current in his day.[82]

Swinburne is unconcerned however by these dissentions and goes on to say: 'Protestant reformers stoutly defended eternal sensory punishment. But the last two centuries have, of course, witnessed a large-scale rejection of this view, at least among Protestants and Anglicans'.[83] Again, in *Providence and the Problem of Evil* he writes of universalism:

---

[78] Swinburne, 1969 p.222.

[79] Swinburne, 1983 p.39.

[80] Swinburne, 1989 p.182.

[81] Swinburne, 1989 p.183.

[82] Swinburne, 1989 p.183. He cites St Augustine, *The Enchiridion of Augustine - to Laurentis* trans. J. F. Shaw London: Religious Tract Society.

[83] Swinburne, 1989 p.184.

That position was virtually unknown in earlier times. That humans who fall outside the limits stated above in their widest sense will not be saved has been the traditional Christian view (although it has been allowed that just maybe in fact every human falls within the limits in their widest sense).[84]

Swinburne here suggests that there may be a place for hopeful universalism in Christian tradition. However he does not discuss this idea and goes on to confirm his rejection of universalism as a minority position. He writes: 'Christian tradition has ... affirmed fairly universally (until the last two centuries, when a contrary minority position developed) that there is everlasting punishment for impenitent sinners'.[85] Thus Swinburne does not discuss universalism in any great detail. However it may be that he does not feel he needs to argue directly against universalism, as he is in effect doing this by arguing in favour of an alternative position.

God's Universal Salvific Will

Despite his clear rejection of the universalist position, both as a tenable position for today's Christian and as a significant position within Christian tradition, Swinburne does affirm that God has a universal salvific will. In *Faith and Reason* he writes:

> God seeks the salvation of all; but he will not pressure any, and so he will at most give encouragement and opportunity for men to seek their salvation. Although he desires that men seek their salvation he will not necessarily give the maximum encouragement to some without prayer from others, for he desires to be guided by the prayers of others.[86]

---

[84] Swinburne 1998 p.119. The limits he refers to are a list of those whom Christianity has believed to be saved. Obviously believers who have had a good life and death are the first category; those who have been baptised but died in infancy; Jews who lived good lives before the advent of Christ and arguably those who have lived a good life but have not heard the gospel convincingly - Swinburne suggests that they can be included because they will be open to the gospel when they hear it after death. Swinburne, 1998 p.119.

[85] Swinburne, 1998 p.197. The assertion by Swinburne that universalism has developed in the last two centuries is a questionable one. Although it may have gained ground in the last century, we have already seen Swinburne's outline of Church Fathers who taught universalism. For a more detailed account of Church Fathers with universalist views see Balthasar, 1988 pp.59 - 63. For evidence that the universalist position was widespread by the 1600s see Walker, 1964.

[86] Swinburne, 1981 p.158. Swinburne believes that it is the task of those who are already part of the Church to lead others into salvation. In *Faith and Reason* he writes that the saints in heaven have work to do '(by intercession or other means) in bringing others into the sphere of God's love', Swinburne, 1981 p.132. He goes on to say that by being a good

Although Swinburne is emphatic that God desires the salvation of all people, he does not believe that this desire will bring about universal salvation. In *Responsibility and Atonement* Swinburne writes that God: 'Seeks man's eternal well-being in friendship with himself'.[87] Thus he is clear that God's purpose for people is that they live in communion with God.

That Swinburne believes God desires the salvation of all is particularly apparent from his discussion in *Providence and the Problem of Evil.* He writes that God, being good, desires to be in a good relationship with humans. 'A good God, for his sake and for theirs, will seek to have creatures rightly related to himself. He will seek for those creatures who have the capacity to do so to know him, interact with him and love him'.[88] Swinburne goes on to assert that relationship with Godself, was the purpose of creating humans. He writes, 'Blessedness with the saints in the life of God himself, in adoration of the good and ever promoting that good further, is, according to the Christian revelation, what God, our loving parent, had in mind in creating us'.[89] Finally Swinburne states even more emphatically that God's desire is that all humans should finally join the company of heaven. He writes that God, 'seeks to take us to himself in Heaven, a marvellous world with a vast range of possible deep goods, including the good of being able to choose to reject the good'.[90]

Conclusion

Swinburne defends a weak view of hell, where the unrighteous are not sent to eternal punishment by God, but rather choose to separate themselves from the God whom they have rejected. Swinburne is certain that hell will not consist of eternal physical punishment, as has traditionally been claimed, and indeed for those who have chosen against heaven, it will in fact be in their best interests to be in hell. Sinners who do not have the desire to live in hell may be annihilated, but there will clearly be an eternal separation from God and the company of heaven. Swinburne suggests that as well as allowing us serious human freedom, hell may serve the further purpose of deterring us from sinning. Swinburne's claim that the afterlife will be compensatory is somewhat at odds with his main defence of hell because he denies that many will have the opportunity to receive compensation. Swinburne argues that the universalist position has not been that of the majority of Christians and is not taught by the New Testament. Consequently he rejects this position with

---

example and helping them, we can help others towards salvation, Swinburne, 1981 p.138. In 'A Theodicy of Heaven and Hell' Swinburne is more emphatic about our duty towards others: 'if men, in a particular church, are to make known the possibility of heaven, there must be those who otherwise would live in total ignorance of that possibility. It is good that the fate of men should depend in small part on the activity of other men - that men should carry the enormous responsibility of the care of the souls of others', Swinburne, 1983 p.51.

[87] Swinburne, 1989 p.122.

[88] Swinburne, 1998 p.111.

[89] Swinburne, 1998 p.122.

[90] Swinburne, 1998 p.250.

little discussion. Swinburne does however believe that God has a universal salvific will but denies that this will lead to ultimate universal salvation. I will look at challenges to Swinburne's rejection of universalism and defence of hell in the following chapter.

Human Freedom

There are many different accounts of human freedom, and it is already clear that strong or libertarian freedom is essential to Swinburne's defence of hell. However, in order to defend this account of freedom, Swinburne rejects the traditional idea of predestination and defends the idea of epistemic distance, which means that we are created without full knowledge of God. I will look at these two subjects and then Swinburne's defence of libertarian freedom. He further claims that our free choices must be between good and bad and not just between different varieties of good in order that we have moral responsibility which is an important part of libertarian freedom.

Predestination

Swinburne claims that there are three ways of understanding the concept of predestination. First, the Calvinist understanding that before each human was created God had already decided whether they would be with the blessed in heaven or condemned to an eternal hell. Second he discusses the view that: 'God predestines to salvation only those who, he foresees, will partly of their own free will do good works'.[91] Although Swinburne has no specific moral objection to this theory, he writes: 'there do seem to be substantial philosophical difficulties in supposing that God can have now complete foreknowledge of that which is not yet determined'.[92] Instead Swinburne understands an acceptable interpretation of predestination to be: 'The doctrine that God predestines in the sense of "intends as their destiny" the salvation of all men; and he helps them towards that salvation, but he does not force it upon them'.[93]

Although God gives sufficient grace to all for salvation, Swinburne holds that this grace cannot on its own suffice for salvation.

> If the grace of God were always sufficient for salvation without human effort, and without that grace none can be saved, then it would follow that all who were not saved were not saved solely as a result of being deprived of grace enough to make salvation possible for them, i.e. God would have reprobated them.[94]

---

[91] Swinburne, 1989 p.1947
[92] Swinburne, 1989 p.194
[93] Swinburne, 1989 p.194
[94] Swinburne, 1989 p.193.

Swinburne cannot accept that this would be the case. Thus it is the combination of grace and human effort which gains salvation. God cannot determine who will or will not contribute their own effort, because of the free choices God gives us. Thus God cannot predetermine who will ultimately join the company of heaven and who will be permanently separated from God. Thus Swinburne rejects the traditional doctrine of predestination and claims only that God desires the salvation of all people, therefore I will return to this discussion in the following chapter.

Epistemic Distance

Swinburne believes that were we to be fully aware of the presence of God, and thus of the character of God we would have no choice but to love and worship God. The magnitude of God's presence would render our free choices with regard to God meaningless. God, who wants us freely to come to accept or reject God, does not want to force God's presence upon us and thus creates us at what has come to be called an epistemic distance from Godself.[95] This means that there is a gap between ourselves and God with regard to what we know about God. God has chosen not to make us unequivocally aware of God's presence so that we have the choice whether or not to seek God. Indeed for Swinburne, it is an essential proof of God's goodness that God allows us to choose in this way, rather than forcing God's presence upon us. In *Is There a God?* Swinburne writes: 'Like a good parent, a generous God has reason for not foisting on us a certain measure of knowledge and control, but rather for giving us a choice of whether to grow in knowledge and control'.[96] This distance between humans and God allows us not only freely to choose for or against God, but gradually to discover God ourselves should we choose to. Swinburne claims that this is a generous gift from God and one which is immensely important to our freedom.

In *Providence and the Problem of Evil* Swinburne writes that if we were created with an automatic awareness of God:

> We will be in the situation of the child in the nursery who knows that mother is looking in at the door, and for whom, in view of the child's desire for mother's approval, the temptation to wrong doing is simply overborne. We need 'epistemic distance' in order to have free choice between good and evil.[97]

The only way Swinburne can see that a strong awareness of God would not control our behaviour in this way, would be if we had a stronger desire to do wrong than for approval from God. He writes: 'If our desire to hurt others is strong enough, we

---

[95] Hick first uses this phrase. See chapter 4 for a discussion of Hick's explanation of epistemic distance.
[96] Swinburne, 1996 p.53.
[97] Swinburne, 1998 p.206.

will have a serious temptation to yield to the desire even if we believe that God is watching us'.[98] Swinburne of course does not suggest that this would be a satisfactory solution and he concludes:

> Just as it is good that we desire the love of God, so it is bad if we are naturally malicious and lack natural affection. Yet it is not logically possible that God give us both a strong awareness of his presence and a free choice between good and evil at the same time as giving us a strong desire for his love and some natural affection for our fellows.[99]

Thus Swinburne argues that the only way in which God could make us genuinely free, without making our overriding desires bad ones, is by creating us at an epistemic distance from Godself.

As we have seen, Swinburne believes that good people who have had the wrong beliefs in this life will be given the right beliefs before they join the company of heaven. This will involve a removal of the epistemic distance as right beliefs, according to Swinburne entail knowledge of the Christian God. Thus whilst epistemic distance is essential to our freedom in this life, it seems that it may not be a good which it would be appropriate to preserve in the next life.

Libertarian Freedom

In *Is There A God?* Swinburne discusses the scientific arguments for free will. He explains that in this context what he means by free will is: 'Our purposes are not fully determined by our brain states or anything else. It does not seem to us that way, as we choose, that it is up to us how we choose'.[100] But, one might ask: 'Is not the brain an ordinary material object in which normal scientific laws operate?'. Swinburne responds that it is not an ordinary material object: 'Since - unlike ordinary material objects - it gives rise to souls and their mental lives'.[101] But Swinburne continues: 'Even if the brain is governed by the same laws as govern other material objects that could still be compatible with humans having free will'. That is because: 'Quantum Theory shows that the physical world on the small scale is not fully deterministic'.[102] So Swinburne concludes from this discussion that:

> When humans form their purposes to think of this or that or behave in such and such a way, they thereby cause those small changes unpredictable by science which in turn cause the thought and behaviour. In this way, humans can exercise free will without their doing so involving any violation of the physical laws which govern

---

[98] Swinburne, 1998 p.206.

[99] Swinburne, 1998 pp.206 - 207.

[100] Swinburne, 1996 p.91.

[101] Swinburne, 1996 p.91.

[102] Swinburne, 1996 p.91.

the brain.[103]

Thus Swinburne believes that science supports his understanding of human free will.

The free will defence has been of great importance to theodicy, and Swinburne believes: 'Almost all Christian theologians have affirmed that humans have "free will" - the only exceptions are a few of the classical Protestant theologians'.[104] However, not all Christian theologians have affirmed, what is to Swinburne's mind an acceptable doctrine of free will. He writes: 'There is reason to suppose that some Christian theologians who affirmed "free will" were affirming free will only in the compatibilist sense, and not in the libertarian sense'.[105] Swinburne understands compatibilist free will to mean: 'That someone has free will on this sense if they do what they want and value (and do not act in consequence of psychological or physical pressure) even if they are fully caused to want and value what they do'.[106] So, the crucial difference between compatibilist free will and libertarian free will according to Swinburne is: 'An agent may have compatibilist free will even if God (or any other cause) causes him (via causing him to want and value what he does) inevitably to make the choices he does, while he cannot have libertarian free will if God (or any other cause) causes him to make the choices he does'.[107] Thus he comments: 'if the only free will humans have is compatibilist free will, there will be no distinction to be made between God allowing some human to do a bad act, and causing him to do it'.[108] If this is the case then the free will defence, Swinburne would argue, contributes nothing to theodicy as it only succeeds in showing that God is directly responsible for all wrong acts.

Swinburne thus opts for strong free will or as he calls it, libertarian free will. By this he means that whatever action an agent does: 'Is not fully caused - either through some process of natural causation (i.e. in virtue of laws of nature) or in some other way (e.g. by an agent such as God acting from outside the natural order)'.[109] So whatever causes might be at work in the universe Swinburne emphasises: 'It will remain possible either that the agent will do the action in question, or that he will refrain from doing it'.[110] Swinburne suggests that in this understanding of free will, he is in company with:

> All Christian theologians of the first four centuries [who] believed in human free will in the libertarian sense, as did all subsequent Eastern Orthodox theologians, and most Western Catholic theologians from

---

[103] Swinburne, 1996 p.93.
[104] Swinburne, 1998 p.33.
[105] Swinburne, 1998 p.33.
[106] Swinburne, 1998 p.33.
[107] Swinburne, 1998 p.34.
[108] Swinburne, 1998 p.34.
[109] Swinburne, 1998 p.33.
[110] Swinburne, 1998 p.33.

Duns Scotus (in the fourteenth century) onwards.[111]

Despite this strong doctrine of free will, Swinburne does acknowledge that our freedom as created beings is limited. As humans, Swinburne concedes, we do not have perfect freedom. We are persuaded by our body being tired to rest[112] and in other ways bound by our physical make up. However Swinburne emphatically claims that our taking rest, for example, is the result of our free choice.

Swinburne's defence of hell and much of his theological theory is dependent on his belief that humans have libertarian freedom. He claims that on any weaker understanding of human freedom, we would not be genuinely free and thus rejects compatibilist human freedom. However it is not clear that this libertarian account of freedom is the most accurate description of human freedom. In the next chapter I will look at some criticisms of Swinburne's account of freedom.

Good World

In discussion of human freedom and theodicy the question is often asked whether it would be possible for humans to have free choices but from a range of different goods rather than from a range of good and bad. I will refer to this proposed world as the Good World. Swinburne is adamant that the choices which we make must be morally significant and he rejects the coherence of the Good World as a world in which people are genuinely free. He believes that human free will is dependent on us also having moral responsibility. Swinburne claims that we can only be responsible for our actions if they are not caused externally, that is if we have the sort of strong freedom which he describes. In *Responsibility and Atonement* he writes, a person will only have moral responsibility 'if he has "free will" in the traditional and obvious sense that his will is free from necessitating causes'.[113] He continues: 'An agent with free will but no moral beliefs could not be held morally responsible for his actions'.[114] Thus our free will alone, is not enough to make us strongly free and does not succeed as a theodicy nor Swinburne argues, does it allow us to make a significant contribution to the world. It is only the combination of free will and moral responsibility, which makes us able to contribute effectively to the world. Swinburne writes: 'The glory of humans is not just their very serious free will, but the responsibility for so much which that free will involves'.[115]

Free will for Swinburne then cannot be a choice between two equal goods. In *Is There A God?* he explains: 'Free and responsible choice is rather free will ...

---

[111] Swinburne, 1998 p.35. He notes that Augustine, 'at any rate in his later writing [seemed] to believe that humans have only compatibilist free will'. And that Aquinas was 'ambivalent on the issue'.

[112] Swinburne, 1977 p.144.

[113] Swinburne, 1989 p.51.

[114] Swinburne, 1989 p.51.

[115] Swinburne, 1989 p.106.

to make significant choices between good and evil, which make a big difference to the agent, to others, and to the world'.[116] Thus the freedom which we exercise as humans affects our environment and other people. We therefore, in having this libertarian freedom, have significant responsibilities. Swinburne writes:

> If my responsibility for you is limited to whether or not to give you a camcorder, but I cannot cause you pain, stunt your growth, or limit your education, then I do not have a great deal of responsibility for you. A God who gives agents only such limited responsibilities for their fellows would not have given much.[117]

Thus God allows us important choices between what is morally good and what is morally bad, rather than simply between varying degrees of good. It is good, Swinburne suggests that God should allow us this degree of freedom, and that God should be prepared to take the risk entailed, of humans choosing what they know to be evil. He writes: 'A good God ... will delegate responsibility, in order to allow creatures a share in creation, he will allow them the choice of hurting and maiming, of frustrating the divine plan'.[118] And he will do that through giving them libertarian free will. Thus Swinburne rejects the idea of the Good World and places great importance on moral responsibility which, combined with our free will gives us not only free choices but serious free choices which may have serious consequences.

Conclusion

We have seen that libertarian free will is intrinsic to Swinburne's understanding of God, and humans. Swinburne holds that humans are not determined by their brain-states and their actions are not caused by physical necessities. Neither are we made with an immediate awareness of God as this would impinge upon our freedom to choose between bad and good. Humans are not merely free to choose between different types of goods, as this would not constitute a serious freedom, but also have a moral responsibility which means we are answerable for the choices we do make. There are several difficulties with Swinburne's account of human freedom and it will be essential to my argument to show that his understanding of libertarian freedom is not the only account of genuine human freedom.

God's Knowledge

It is obviously relevant to any theological theory to establish what sort of knowledge God has. What God can and cannot be held responsible for depends on

---

[116] Swinburne, 1996 p.98.
[117] Swinburne, 1996 pp.99 - 100.
[118] Swinburne, 1996 p.100.

what sort of knowledge God has and this is particularly important for theodicy and the problem of hell. Swinburne claims that God has only present knowledge and this contributes to his thesis that hell is compatible with a good and loving God. God having present knowledge is uncontroversial. However Swinburne rejects the view that God has two types of more controversial knowledge, foreknowledge and middle knowledge.

Foreknowledge

There are two main objections to the idea of God having foreknowledge. The first depends on one's understanding of God being eternal. If one believes that God is eternal in the sense of being out of time, the idea of foreknowledge will be meaningless, as obviously God cannot have fore – knowledge if all moments are out of time for God. The second objection is that if humans are free, even God cannot know what their as yet unmade, free choices will be. Swinburne's rejection of God's foreknowledge relies upon the second objection.

In *Is there a God?* Swinburne describes the two understandings of eternal. The first explanation is that God is eternal 'in the sense that he exists outside time'. Swinburne continues: 'In his one timeless "moment", he simultaneously causes the events of AD 1995 and in 587 BC. In his one timeless moment also he knows simultaneously (as they happen) what is happening in AD 1995 and in 587 BC'. He then comments: 'For myself I cannot make much sense of this suggestion'.[119] The other way of understanding eternal is as everlasting. 'God is eternal in the sense that he has existed at each moment of past time, exists now, and will exist at each moment of future time.' Swinburne comments that this is clearly how the Biblical writers understood 'eternal' and he also thinks that it is a preferable definition. 'I prefer the understanding of God being eternal as his being everlasting rather than as his being timeless. He exists at each moment of unending time'.[120] Thus Swinburne clearly rejects the idea of God being timeless.

The second objection to foreknowledge then, is the one which causes Swinburne to reject that God has foreknowledge. In *Responsibility and Atonement* Swinburne firmly argues that if determinism is false there is no way that even God can know what is going to happen.

> [God] will not necessarily know anything that will happen unless it is already predetermined that it will happen. For there is a logical inconsistency in supposing that any being knows necessarily what is yet to happen when that has yet to be determined (i.e. when it is not already fixed by its causes).[121]

Again in *Providence and the Problem of Evil* Swinburne asserts:

---

[119] Swinburne, 1996 p.9.

[120] Swinburne, 1996 p.9.

[121] Swinburne, 1989 p.3 .

> No one (not even God) can know today (without the possibility of mistake) what I will choose to do tomorrow. So I suggest that we understand God being omniscient as God knowing at any time all that is logically possible to know at that time. That will not include knowledge, before they have done it, of what human persons will do freely.[122]

For Swinburne it does not make sense to understand God's omniscience as entailing knowledge of all things, including future actions and decisions by free creatures. Swinburne's definition of God's omniscience, as God 'knowing all that it is logically possible to know at that time' means that he can believe that God is omniscient, and yet maintain that God does not know future action of free beings. Swinburne is advocating an 'open view' of God whereby God does not control the future of the world, but rather responds to the events bought about by the choices of free creatures.

Swinburne acknowledges that this is not the only understanding of God's omniscience. In *Providence and the Problem of Evil* he discusses Plantinga's writing on the omniscience of God. Swinburne notes that Plantinga holds that God necessarily knows what choices free people will make, that is, God knows without the possibility of a mistake.[123] For Plantinga, God being omniscient entails God knowing all true propositions. Swinburne notes that Plantinga 'combines this with the view that God is not timeless but everlasting and so knows now how people will choose tomorrow'.[124] Thus for Plantinga God has foreknowledge even of free choices which have not yet been made. Swinburne objects that if God already knows what these choices will be, and God cannot be wrong, that these choices are not actually free but already determined. Thus for Swinburne God's foreknowledge is incompatible with free beings.

Middle Knowledge

In *Providence and the Problem of Evil* Swinburne also discusses the possibility that God has middle knowledge. He notes that Plantinga holds that God has middle knowledge, that is, God does not just know how people will choose in each circumstance but God also knows what the result would have been of any possible choice that could have been made. Swinburne explains that with the benefit of this knowledge, God, 'knew all the worlds which he could create and in which circumstances governed by which (deterministic or probabilistic) natural laws he could place them; and also which free choices each of them would make in

---

[122] Swinburne, 1996 p.8.

[123] Swinburne's discussion on Plantinga is based on Plantinga, 1974 part 1 and Plantinga, 1974 (b) ch. 9.

[124] Swinburne, 1998 p.128.

different circumstances'.[125] Swinburne suggests that given this knowledge, God 'would only create beings and put them in circumstances in which (he foresaw) they would freely choose the good'.[126] Plantinga's argument against this position is that there may be what he calls 'universal transworld depravity', in other words, there is no possible world God could have made in which all people would freely choose the good. He does not insist that this is in fact the case, but attempts to point out that God having middle knowledge does not necessarily mean that God could have created a world in which people always freely chose the good. Swinburne cannot accept this argument and comments that Plantinga must prove that all creatures would do some wrong in some circumstances, if his theory is to be given credibility.[127]

Although Swinburne does not believe that God has middle knowledge because the world is not as it would be, had God created it with the benefit of that knowledge, he has a further objection to middle knowledge. Swinburne questions whether a counterfactual of freedom can have any truth value. He notes that Robert Adams suggests that there are no counterfactuals of freedom with truth value, that is ones which are either true or false.[128] Plantinga argues that it is a coherent proposal and indeed that, as Swinburne explains: 'Often we can have a justified belief about what is the truth -value of some counterfactual of freedom'.[129] However Swinburne refers to William Hasker who raises the question: 'What makes it true?'.[130] Swinburne argues that if the world were deterministic:

> Its laws of nature would make it the case that there would be a certain outcome ... and it would be the fact that they operated which would provide the truth-conditions of the counterfactual. But if it is a counterfactual 'of freedom' there are no such laws.[131]

So the laws of nature cannot make it true, and neither Hasker argues, can the agent make it true. The fact that it is a counterfactual means that the agent in question has not had the opportunity to act upon it and thus Hasker concludes that it is not a 'a counterfactual "of freedom" at all, for she is the agent with whose freedom it was supposedly concerned'.[132] Swinburne concludes: 'The defender of counterfactuals of freedom may urge that nothing else makes the counterfactual true; it is just "barely true"'.[133] Thus Swinburne concedes that a counterfactual of freedom could

---

[125] Swinburne, 1998 p.128.

[126] Swinburne, 1998 p.129.

[127] Swinburne, 1998 p.130. He is referring to Plantinga, 1974 (b) pp.184-189.

[128] Swinburne, 1998 p. 130. He is referring to R. M. Adams, 'Middle Knowledge and the Problem of Evil' *American Philosophical Quarterly* vol. 14 (1977) pp. 109-117.

[129] Swinburne, 1998 p.131.

[130] Swinburne, 1998 p.131. He is discussing William Hasker, *God, Time and Knowledge* (1989) Ithaca: Cornell University Press pp. 39-52.

[131] Swinburne, 1998 p.131.

[132] Swinburne, 1998 p.131.

[133] Swinburne, 1998 p.131.

have truth-value. However he argues that Plantinga is still wrong, because he supposes that God has 'incorrigible knowledge of the truth-value of a counterfactual of freedom'.[134] Swinburne argues: 'No one can foreknow incorrigibly the future free actions of an agent in circumstances which *will* be realized'.[135] Thus Swinburne uses his arguments against foreknowledge also to reject middle knowledge.

Conclusion

Swinburne rejects that God has either foreknowledge or middle knowledge. He believes that they are both incompatible with libertarian human freedom and thus according to Swinburne God has only present knowledge. In the following chapter I will discuss the coherence of both foreknowledge and middle knowledge and whether foreknowledge and middle knowledge exclude any genuine human freedom. In chapter 6 I will discuss what it means for God to have middle knowledge.

Conclusion

Swinburne defends a weak view of hell, according to which individuals through their own decisions make themselves bad people who choose to reject God and thus opt for hell. Those who have not sufficiently formed their characters may have further opportunity to fix them in purgatory, but only if they have shown some preference for the good. Swinburne maintains that hell does not consist of eternal physical punishment, and indeed he is not certain that there is any suffering in hell. If there is suffering, it is a result of being separated from God but as Swinburne maintains this is the individual's free choice he claims that hell may be, for those who have chosen it, the best option. For those who have rejected God and do not wish to continue in existence, Swinburne suggests that God will allow them to be annihilated. Thus Swinburne's view of hell is very different to the traditional strong view of hell and some of the defences of hell which he employs do not actually strengthen the weak view of hell.

Swinburne dismisses universalism as he believes not all people have made the choices to be fitted for heaven. However there are several difficulties with this account which I will look at in the next chapter. Swinburne is adamant that humans have strong libertarian freedom and indeed his defence of hell is dependent upon this doctrine. Swinburne believes that we were created at an epistemic distance from God to allow for this strong freedom and that God has only present knowledge. He rejects foreknowledge and middle knowledge as being incompatible with human freedom. Thus according to Swinburne we are free to reject God and he supposes that many will.

---

[134] Swinburne, 1998 p.131.
[135] Swinburne, 1998 p.131.

Chapter 3

Evaluation of Swinburne's Hell

Introduction

It is clear that Swinburne's account of human freedom is the corner stone of his defence of hell. In order for his theory to succeed not only must his libertarian freedom be viable, but also compatibilst freedom must be shown to be untenable. In this chapter I will return to the subject areas looked at in the previous chapter in order to discuss some critiques of Swinburne's view of hell. Having established the problematic areas of Swinburne's thesis, we will see whether or not Swinburne's version of what Thomas Talbott has termed the Rejection Hypothesis[1] succeeds.

The Moment of Decision

It is clear that the moment of decision is significant in any defence or rejection of hell. Although Swinburne does not propose a moment of decision, but rather suggests that we make our decision through deciding what sort of people we will become, he does propose a cut off point. That is a time when one has decided definitively for or against God and consequently will go to heaven or hell or, according to Swinburne, to purgatory. Purgatory is the exception to Swinburne's claim that we will decide our future states because he does suggest that some will end up in Purgatory and does not rule out the possibility that they may remain there eternally. Swinburne argues that we shape our character irreformably by the decisions we make in this life. The lost person is one who so consistently chooses bad that they reach the point where they are no longer able to choose good. Swinburne proposes that for those who do not definitely shape their character they may remain eternally in purgatory. This is contrary to the traditional doctrine of purgatory and makes a third eternal resting place with heaven and hell.

Shaping Character

Swinburne's account of shaping character and thereby choosing final destinies involves a point at which one has made one's decision and is no longer able to change it. However the objection is made to this thesis that it is not clear that there

---

[1] 'Some persons will, despite God's best efforts to save them freely and irrevocably reject God and thus separate themselves from God forever'. Talbott, 1990 p.227.

does come a point when the good can no longer be chosen, and Swinburne's evidence for this fails to be convincing. If this proves to be a valid criticism of the premise that individuals can put themselves beyond the choice for good and consequently choose hell, then Swinburne's defence that the individual chooses hell fails.

Despite his certainty that some will end up in hell, as a result of making themselves consistently bad people, in *Faith and Reason* Swinburne admits that he has never known this to happen.

> Far be it from me to say that that has happened to any man whom I have ever met; there is a lot more latent capacity for good in most people than appears on the surface. Nevertheless it is a possibility that a man will let himself be so mastered by his desires that he will lose all ability to resist them.[2]

However, in *Responsibility and Atonement*, Swinburne suggests that we have sufficient reason to believe that some people will lose all capacity for good. Although we are, as Swinburne claims, aware how easy it is to become 'oblivious to certain aspects of good'[3] that is very different to becoming permanently oblivious to all aspects of the good. Swinburne cites as an example of this state 'Nazi butchers'.[4] Whilst there is no doubt that these people committed great atrocities, there is no reason to suppose that they were incapable of choosing all aspects of good or that they had built up a strong desire to resist all awareness of good. Even a person who does many evil acts may also perform some good acts. If such a person were still capable of one small act of good, would a God who desired their salvation not take this to be a literally 'redeeming feature'?

Swinburne states that it would only be bad for individuals to be 'deprived of the Beatific Vision if they still desire to have it'.[5] He discusses the case of the incorrigibly bad who have some residual desire for the good. He comments, 'clearly it is a bad thing if it is not satisfied'. However Swinburne continues:

> If their residual desire for the good remains through the choice of the incorrigibly bad humans, God will respect that too; and the bad state that their desire for the good is unsatisfied will be the known consequence of their own considered choice.[6]

Thus those who have made themselves incorrigibly bad but hung on to a residual desire for the good will not have the opportunity to develop that desire. It will at

---

[2] Swinburne, 1981 p.154.
[3] Swinburne, 1989 p.178.
[4] Swinburne, 1989 p.178.
[5] Swinburne, 1998 p.197.
[6] Swinburne, 1998 p.198. Swinburne goes on to suggest that in order to eliminate the bad state of this unsatisfied desire for the good, God could eliminate the bad themselves.

best be unsatisfied and at worst be eliminated. This is because, Swinburne argues, God should not interfere in the freely made choices of individuals. 'A good God', he writes, 'will respect a considered choice of destiny'.[7] So God, having given us free will is unable to help the person who has made him/herself incorrigibly bad. However Swinburne does not suppose this to be the case for those who have made themselves good. In *Responsibility and Atonement* he writes that God:

> Would surely complete the process of character formation which the saint sought to achieve on earth ...[God] will finally remove his imprisonment to desires which he fully rejects by judging them bad and fighting against them. God will give him a firmly fixed good will, and firm desires to do what he rightly believes to be good.[8]

Thus the person who has made him/herself good receives God's assistance to complete this process. Swinburne would argue that this does not challenge human freedom because it is merely a completion of the choice made by the individual. How can a God without foreknowledge know that this is the agent's final choice in shaping character? The agent might choose to stop fighting his remaining bad desires and reject the good he had previously chosen. By giving the agent a firmly fixed good will, God takes away the agents freedom to make this choice. We may respond that this is a good action of God, to fix the will of an agent who has been choosing good and finally free him of imprisonment to desires and thereby allow the agent to be ready for heaven. Swinburne would presumably argue that God does exactly the same for the agent who has consistently chosen bad, by freeing the agent of his remaining good desires in order that they will not remain unfulfilled, thus making the agent thoroughly bad and unfit for heaven. The difficulty is that God is not treating people in the same way: the good agent is being offered salvation whilst the bad agent is condemned to hell. Although this is based on the state of their characters at the time, and presumably, for a significant previous period, a God without foreknowledge cannot know that there is no hope for the persistently bad agent, until God takes away the agent's residual desire for good and thereby condemns him to hell. Thus whilst it is obvious why a God who desires the salvation of every individual would intervene on behalf of the good agent, God's actions toward the bad agent are harder to fathom.

Although it is reasonable to assume that those who have made themselves good deserve God's help in completing this process, there is clearly a point at which it is acceptable for God to intervene. However if God can intervene because the person has chosen the right path, why cannot God intervene when a generally bad person chooses good and so fix their character at that moment for the good? Swinburne would, of course, say that such a person has not chosen that character for him/herself and therefore God would override their free choice by fixing their character at this point. However God, who according to Swinburne, does not have

---

[7] Swinburne, 1998 p.198.
[8] Swinburne, 1989 pp. 186 - 187.

foreknowledge, does not know what shape future free choices will take. The bad person with a residual desire for good, is surely demonstrating the potential to turn from bad choices so far made and begin to choose good. God cannot know whether or not they are going to do that, and thus by fixing their destiny at that moment, denies them any further opportunity to develop the good, which residual or not they still have.

Swinburne's claim that a person condemns him/herself to hell through consistently choosing the bad and loosing all knowledge of the good only works for those who have made themselves thoroughly bad. However it is not clear that this is an accurate representation of even a very bad human. Swinburne states that the incorrigibly bad person cannot enjoy the moral good of any situation, but there is no evidence that this is necessarily the way bad people become. To return to Swinburne's example of the 'Nazi butcher' whose actions were very bad, perhaps even the worst human behaviour imaginable. However there is no evidence to support Swinburne's claim that he was irredeemably bad. For instance they may still have loved and cared for their families and friends and put their needs before their own. Let us suppose this to be the case, this Nazi butcher then is not incapable of choosing all aspects of good as Swinburne supposes. Whilst this does not make him a good person, this remaining good is surely grounds for hoping that the good may ultimately triumph over the persistent bad in such a person.

A further difficulty arises when we try to establish at what point one's desire for the good is only residual, or one's bad desires merely mar a persistently good character. Is the Nazi butcher's concern for his family only a residual good in an otherwise bad person or is it a good desire that means his character is not yet firmly shaped in one way or the other? For Swinburne's theory to work, a point must be established whereby good desires are no longer part of one's character but merely residual desires. This raises the problem of arbitrariness. At what point does God give up on a person with a persistently bad character and decide that their remaining good desires are only residual and so remove the remaining good from such a person? If even the most persistently bad people have some residual desire for the good it is hard to understand why a God who desired their salvation would settle their future decisively by removing further opportunities for change. Given that, according to Swinburne, God does not have foreknowledge, it is even harder to see why God would make such a decision.

It is not clear that an individual, no matter how many choices he has made for bad, ever becomes incapable of choosing good. Kvanvig argues that Swinburne overlooks the possibility that one could still choose good with divine aid.

> The fact that one has lost the power to choose the good does not logically imply that at present one cannot choose the good. All that might follow is that the power to choose the good would require some sort of divine intervention to restore what has been lost.[9]

---

[9] Kvanvig, 1993 p.101.

He continues that in order to defend his argument Swinburne must opt 'to maintain that it is not the choosing of the good that is metaphysically impossible, but rather the choosing of the good *without divine intervention*'.[10] Swinburne asks: 'Have we reason to suppose that such corruption may be total and (barring special divine intervention) irreversible?'.[11] He does not state a specific reason for barring special divine intervention, so we must assume that he rules this out on the grounds that it would infringe human freedom. However we need not suppose that this intervention takes the form of God compelling a person to make a certain choice.

Rather suppose that the bad person has the Gospel presented to him/her and as a consequence decides that he/she has been wrong in the choices he/she has made. Thus the previously bad person resolves to follow the teaching of the New Testament and ask for God's guidance when making choices. This would presumably result in the bad person making a significant number of good choices. Indirectly this constitutes a divine intervention. Swinburne cannot deny the possibility of such an event without denying the transforming power of the gospel message. Indeed this is the account of conversion we hear in the New Testament. The New Testament records the stories of many individuals who had supposedly put themselves beyond the good, but by encounter with the living or risen Christ had their lives turned around. Indeed it seems to be the promise of the Gospel that an encounter with Jesus has the power to turn around even the most hardened heart. It is indefensible in the light of the Gospels to maintain that divine intervention would be inappropriate or necessarily contrary to human freedom. Indeed, it is clear that Swinburne assumes that at a certain point, namely when one's character is firmly shaped, it is appropriate for God to intervene.

Thus for the condition of the damned to be irreversible, God must put them or allow them to put themselves beyond the reach of the Gospel and thus beyond the reach of salvation. Kvanvig concludes:

> In the end, Swinburne must hold that at some point God simply abandons persons to the consequences of their free actions, for nothing in his account explains how, once it becomes impossible for a person to choose the good, the issue of place of residence for eternity is closed. Yet Swinburne never argues for the moral acceptability of this abandonment, and thus his reasoning is incomplete.[12]

Swinburne denies that God has foreknowledge and thus cannot claim that God knows that those who have consistently chosen the bad will continue to do so. Neither does Swinburne claim that the criterion is the state of one's character by the time of death. He proposes further opportunities after death to shape character firmly. Rather Swinburne's emphasis is on the final determining of character.

---

[10] Kvanvig, 1993 p.101.

[11] Swinburne, 1989 p.178.

[12] Kvanvig, 1993 p.101.

Without foreknowledge, God can never be certain that a character is finally determined, for even if there is no latent capacity for good in a person at that time, there is no reason to suppose that this could not be found at some point in the future, as with the conversion scenario. Talbott argues that Swinburne does not ultimately succeed in moving the responsibility for hell away from God onto the individual. He writes:

> Suppose that for fifty years God were to act towards Smith in exactly the way he would act towards someone he loves, and suppose that God were to do so in the full knowledge that forever afterwards he would act towards Smith in unloving ways. Could we then say that God loved Smith for a while? - that for a while he intended to promote the best interest of Smith? Surely not. In the case of God, it surely is a necessary truth that God loves a person at one time (in the New Testament sense of *agape* love) only if he loves that person at all subsequent times.[13]

According to Swinburne God would not know that in the future God would act in an unloving way towards Smith. However the point is still relevant that God's love is limited with respect to a particular agent if after a certain period God removes their remaining desire for the good and thus puts them beyond the reach of salvation. It is hard to see how Swinburne can support his claim that God loves all people and desires their salvation when he also proposes that after a certain point God will reject some people. Some would claim that a character can only be properly finally determined when it has chosen for God. As Sachs writes, 'as long as human freedom tries to refuse God, it fails to reach the finality for which it is created for this finality comes not from human freedom in itself, but from and in God'.[14] Hick argues along these lines and I will discuss this in the following chapters.

Swinburne's claim that God wills the salvation of all and that there is a time when salvation is no longer offered to some people is problematic. For his account of shaping character and thereby choosing one's eternal fate to succeed, Swinburne must concede that a time comes when salvation is no longer available to those who have preferred the bad. Swinburne cannot claim that this is their own doing as a God without foreknowledge does not know whether they will repent in the future and thus according to Swinburne, God who desires the salvation of all people, at some point takes back the offer of salvation from those whom God assumes to be irreformably bad. Therefore Swinburne's claim that individual's choose their ultimate fate fails as those who have chosen bad have the offer of salvation withdrawn and thus are condemned to hell without the possibility of future reformation of character.

---

[13] Talbott, 1990 (b) p.26.
[14] Sachs, 1991 p.252.

Hell

As we have seen Swinburne offers several defences of hell. Although Swinburne appeals to the tradition of hell within Christianity to support his argument, the theory of hell that he proposes is so different from the traditional view that it is difficult to see how this actually supports his argument. Swinburne makes several unorthodox claims about hell, the most significant being that hell is a result of the free choice of the individual. A minor defence of hell which stems from this is Swinburne's claim that for some people hell is the best option. Levine comments on this:

> Swinburne's surprising suggestion is that it is in the bad person's best interest *not* to be in heaven. (Whatever else one may say of Swinburne's account this view is not part of any classical Christian doctrine - and is indeed opposed by such doctrines.)[15]

Thus Swinburne completely moves away from the traditional concept of hell as punishment. It seems inappropriate for Swinburne, who emphasises the joy of heaven and the happiness of knowing God as well as God's universal salvific will, to claim that it would be in any person's best interest not to partake of the life of heaven. Surely if, as Swinburne says, God intends heaven to be the destiny of all people,[16] then it would be in no person's best interest not to be part of that company. By redeveloping hell in order to provide an acceptable defence of the doctrine, it is apparent that Swinburne is unable to defend the traditional doctrine of hell. Thus Swinburne's defence of hell is a defence of a very different view of hell to the one traditionally taught by the Church.

In this section I will discuss objections to Swinburne's major defences of hell. His most crucial claim is that hell is the result of the individual's choice and I will look at some difficulties with this claim before discussing Swinburne's view of hell as *poena damni*, his account of compensation in the afterlife, and finally the coherence of his agnostic conditional immortality.

The Individual's Choice for Hell

I will discuss two objections to the theory that hell is a result of individual's choices. The major objection is that no one would rationally choose in favour of hell. The further objection is made that our freedom in this instance is at the expense of God's own freedom.

One may well ask why, given a choice, anyone would make a firm decision in favour of hell. Thomas Talbott asks this question:

---

[15] Levine, 1993 p.520.
[16] Swinburne, 1989 p.194.

> What could possibly qualify as a motive for such a choice? As long
> as any ignorance, or deception, or bondage to desire remains it is
> open to God to transform a sinner without interfering with human
> freedom; but once all ignorance and deception and bondage to desire
> is removed, so that a person is truly 'free' to choose, there can no
> longer be any motive for choosing eternal misery for oneself.[17]

He claims that the sort of influences which would encourage a person to choose hell
make those people incapable of free choice. Talbott further claims that God should
release people from such influences to allow them to make a properly free choice.
Whilst Talbott admits that the individual may well be responsible initially for
allowing him/herself to become enslaved to such desires, he writes:

> However *responsible* one might be for one's ignorance and one's
> bondage to desire, no choice that such ignorance or bondage
> determines is truly free (in the libertarian sense); and if one is free
> from the kind of ignorance and bondage that is incompatible with
> free choice, one could never have a motive to choose eternal misery
> for oneself.

Thus Talbott can see no reason for a truly free person, to choose hell. However
there are two major objections to Talbott's claim. First it is objected that God
would not free a person from bondage to desires, as this would involve overriding
the freedom of that individual. Second, just because a choice for hell is not rational,
or does not seem so to Talbott, that does not mean such a choice would not be
made by a free being.

Jerry Walls suggests that whilst our libertarian freedom remains, it is
entirely possible that some people will choose to go to hell.

> The choice of hell is psychologically possible because we are able to
> deceive ourselves ... God cannot always remove our (self-imposed)
> deception without interfering with our freedom. If God allows us to
> retain libertarian freedom, some illusions may endure forever.[18]

Thus Walls concludes that unless God interferes with our freedom, a choice for hell
could be made. However Talbott believes that God would rather override human
freedom than allow any to be lost.

> Even if such a choice were perfectly coherent ... it would be the kind
> of evil which a loving God would be required to prevent; his failure
> to do so would be inconsistent not only with his love for the person

---

[17] Talbott, 1990 (b) p.37.
[18] Walls, 1992 p.133.

who might make such a choice, but with his love for all other persons as well.[19]

Thus for Talbott, even if an individual did choose hell, God could not allow that to be the last word but must reconcile them to Godself, even if that involved overriding their freedom. This debate thus becomes concerned with the respective values of salvation and freedom and I will return to this discussion below.

Even if we concede that God would allow some to send themselves to hell, would any person make that choice? Craig argues that although a choice for hell might be irrational that does not make it unlikely. He claims that Talbott over-estimates the human response to God.

> Even omnipotent love can be spurned if that love requires worship and submission of one's will. Talbott might insist that such a motivation is irrational - but so what? Is it not possible that the will to self-autonomy be so strong in some persons that they will act irrationally in preferring self-rule to God's rule?[20]

Talbott cannot see that there is any reason to favour hell, but Craig suggests that reluctance to submit to God's will could be one reason to make this choice. Holten similarly argues: 'A choice for hell is not in the first place a choice for unpleasant experiences (eternal misery), but the alternative to being saved by God'.[21] That is, choosing hell is not necessarily a positive choice in favour of eternal misery but a positive rejection of God. Craig argues that Talbott's response to the choice for hell demonstrates that Talbott does not take the human condition seriously and does not have a proper doctrine of sin.

> I should say that he greatly underestimates both human depravity and human capacity to sin. Admittedly, it seems insane that some people should resist every solicitation of the Holy Spirit and every offer of God's grace and perhaps even prefer damnation to submission to God's will, but that is the mystery of iniquity, a measure of the depth of human depravity.[22]

It is clear that Craig does not take a very optimistic view of humanity and neither does he suppose that God's grace will necessarily be efficacious. Talbott is more optimistic about the choice of each individual and thinks that an individual free of bondage to desire would choose God. Talbott assumes that unless one was ruled by such desire, not only would there be no reason to reject God, but neither would there be any desire to reject God. Craig assumes that some people's desire for self

---

[19] Talbott, 1990 (b) p.40.
[20] Craig, 1991 p. 302 .
[21] Wilko van Holten, 'Hell and the Goodness of God' *Religious Studies* vol. 35 (1999)p.48.
[22] Craig, 1991 p.303.

rule would be stronger than the desire for God. Although Craig may point out that this is the case with some people now, there is no reason to suppose that in the final reckoning this will be so. As Talbott writes: 'God wills for me exactly what, at the most fundamental level, I want for myself'.[23] Thus Talbott suggests that each person in fact desires God and to be in a relationship with God, and thus will not ultimately choose to reject this. Swinburne argues that those who have made themselves bad people and thereby chosen to reject God no longer desire this. However, if we have an inherent desire for God, as Talbott suggests, would it be possible to extinguish this completely? Although Swinburne suggests that it would it is not clear that this is the case. Our response to the offer of salvation from God will be crucial to this theory. Hick argues that all people were made with a desire for God and I will discuss this issue in the following chapter. If after further discussion we can conclude that everyone would ultimately respond favourably to God's offer of salvation, because, as Talbott claims, that is what they actually desire, then any free choice for heaven or hell must result in universalism.

Craig claims that one may reject God assuming that there will be further opportunities to change one's mind and be reconciled with God.

> *S* need not resolve at *t* never to be reconciled to God in order for his rejection to be in fact final. On the contrary, he may kid himself into thinking that his rejection is merely for the present, that later he shall appropriate God's salvation unaware that because (b) is true he has forfeits his salvation forever.[24]

On this view however, it seems to remain a possibility that *S* may at some later time bring it about of his own accord that *S* freely repents of sin and so is reconciled to God. On this account it seems as though *S* has been tricked into finally rejecting God, assuming that there will be further opportunities to reverse this decision. A God who desires the salvation of all would surely not hold *S* to his decision, given that it was not the answer he finally wanted to give. On this account God would be like a quiz master who can only accept the first answer even when the correct one is later offered. Further, Craig's premise that 'there is nothing within God's power to do' to reconcile *S* with God seems blatantly false in this case. All God needs to do is wait until such time as *S* chooses to appropriate God's salvation. The claim that an individual could reject God without realising the decisiveness of his/her choice has no place in an account of hell which also claims that God desires the salvation of all and further that hell is the free choice of the individual. For in this instance

---

[23] Thomas Talbott, 'Craig on the Possibility of Eternal Damnation' *Religious Studies* vol.28 (1992) p.500.

[24] William Lane Craig, 'Talbott's Universalism' *Religious Studies* vol. 27 (1991) p.299. The premise he refers to is: (b) There is nothing both within God's power to do and consistent with the interest of all other created persons that would (weakly) bring it about, either at *t* or subsequent to *t*, that *S* freely repents of *S*' sin and is thereby reconciled to God.

the individual's choice is to reject God in the short term but to be reconciled to God in the long term and therefore that would be the choice that God had to accept.

A further difficulty with Swinburne's defence that individuals make their own choice for or against hell is that it gives individuals choices that they expect God to make. Moltmann argues that this both gives too great a significance to human decisions and makes us the means of our own salvation.

> Anyone who faces men and women with the choice of heaven or hell, does not merely expect too much of them. It leaves them in a state of uncertainty, because we cannot base the assurance of our salvation on the shaky ground of our own decisions.[25]

The claim that hell is a result of our own free choice moves away from the traditional teaching of Christianity. Moltmann continues:

> The logic of hell seems to me not merely inhumane but also extremely atheistic: here the human being in his freedom of choice is his own lord and god. His own will is his heaven - or his hell. God is merely the accessory who puts that will into effect ... If God has to abide by our free decision, then we can do with him what we like. Is that the love of God?[26]

Moltmann argues that such a defence of hell reduces God simply to being the one to carry out our wishes and makes us responsible for the joy, or otherwise, of eternal life. Moltmann seems to suggest that on this account God is like a parent who allows its child so much freedom that it plays only a passive part in the child's life and bows to his/her every whim. Indeed it is not even apparent in this situation that the parent cares for the child. Thus Moltmann would argue that Swinburne has wanted to ascribe so great a freedom to human beings that he has done so, not only at the cost of God's freedom but also at the cost of our relationship with God.

Swinburne's defence that hell is chosen by the individual fails, as he can provide no compelling reason why any individual would choose hell. In the following chapter I will look at another response to this in the form of Hick's argument that we are made with an inherent desire for God and thus would not ultimately choose to reject God. The further objection is made that by giving individuals freedom to decide upon their own future state, Swinburne reduces God to our accessory. Thus this defence of hell is far removed from the traditional, strong view of hell and significantly alters the role of both humans and God in determining individual fates in the afterlife.

---

[25] Jürgen Moltmann, 'The Logic of Hell' in Richard J. Bauckham (ed.), *God Will Be All in All - The Eschatology of Jürgen Moltmann* (1999) Edinburgh: T & T Clark p.45.
[26] Moltmann, 1999 p.45.

Hell as Poena Damni

As we have seen, Swinburne rejects the idea of hell as eternal physical punishment. He claims instead that hell is the state of being separated from God. Thus Swinburne assumes that the punishment of hell as *poena damni* avoids the challenges to God's morality that arise when hell is conceived of as *poena sensus*. However Swinburne also claims that the *poena sensus* is the more serious punishment. [27] Levine writes:

> If Swinburne sees the deprivation of the happiness of heaven as the 'all-important punishment', then in claiming that God opts for distributing that punishment rather than the milder one of endless physical pain he sees God as choosing the more important and significant punishment. But given that Swinburne sees the less important punishment (i.e. endless physical pain) as incompatible with the goodness of God; is there not a presumption in favour of the view that the harsher more significant punishment is also incompatible with the goodness of God?[28]

Swinburne has indeed made a difficulty for himself here. If the less serious, physical punishment is incompatible with the goodness of God, it seems apparent that a more serious punishment must also be incompatible with such a God. However Swinburne may contest that there are grounds for rejecting physical suffering which do not apply to the view of hell as separation.

Perhaps Swinburne would claim that physical suffering, in this case, has no rehabilitative purpose. However an eternal separation from God does not allow for reform or rehabilitation and so cannot be justified on this basis. Alternatively Swinburne may claim that an eternal physical punishment is greater than any human sin could warrant. However if this is in fact the less serious punishment, Swinburne cannot defend the punishment of separation in this way. The defence most likely to be offered by Swinburne is that no individual would choose to subject him/herself to eternal physical torment but may choose to reject God eternally. Eternal physical punishment must be inflicted by God on the sinner, whereas eternal separation is the result of a sinner's own choice. However there are two difficulties with this claim. First, we have seen that Swinburne cannot escape the criticism that it is God who finally sends the sinner to hell by removing the opportunity for further change. Therefore the punishment of separation is still inflicted by God. Second, it could be argued that even if an individual chooses to reject God, the punishment of eternal separation is still disproportionate to the crime of consistently choosing bad and consequently rejecting God.

---

[27] Swinburne, 1981 p.171.

[28] Michael Levine, 'Swinburne's Heaven: One Hell of a Place' *Religious Studies* vol. 29 (1993) p.530.

Although Swinburne believes that the doctrine of hell can be defended on the grounds that it is the result of an individual's own free choice that she is consigned to hell, it could still be claimed that an eternal separation from God is too severe a consequence of such a choice. Even if a person, of her own free will, decisively rejects God and positively chooses separation from God, it may be that she later repents of this decision. She may realise that this choice was a result of her self-centredness and desire the opportunity to accept, and live in communion with, God. On Swinburne's account, no second chance would be forthcoming. So although the sinner is living with the consequences of her free choice, at the point when she regrets her decision or would like to alter her choice, the separation becomes a punishment and not a choice. Swinburne may argue that a sinner, having chosen hell would be unable to repent of this decision as God would have removed any her residual desires for the good and thus nothing in her environment or within herself would turn her towards God. Again, it is not clear that this does not amount to a punishment. The sinner is deprived of her remaining good desires and therefore deprived of the libertarian freedom which Swinburne so highly prizes. Thus the sinner is abandoned to an eternity totally devoid of all good. It seems that this too is a punishment disproportionate to the crime. Even the sinner who has chosen this end for him/herself arguably deserves the opportunity, after a period of this separation to be given the choice between bad and good and the chance to accept God.

The defence of hell as *poena damni*, even combined with Swinburne's claim that the individual chooses hell, does not avoid the element of punishment in the doctrine of hell. Although there is no physical punishment in Swinburne's account it is not clear that separation from God, which he claims to be a more serious state, can avoid the moral problems which a God who inflicts eternal physical punishment faces. Ultimately Swinburne cannot claim both that hell as *poena sensus* is not a state a good God would allow, but also that the more serious punishment of *poena damni* is compatible with a good God without creating an inconsistency in his defence of hell.

Afterlife as Compensation

As part of his theodicy, Swinburne suggests that suffering in this life should be compensated in the afterlife. He does not claim that all suffering requires compensation but specifically those lives which on balance contain more bad than good. Swinburne believes that it would be contrary to a good God to allow a person to experience more bad than good, but as this happens, the compensation must come after death. According to Swinburne, God would not know that this would be the outcome of any life and thus God is unable to avoid the creation of an overall bad existence. Thus God must alter the balance of such a life through the compensatory afterlife. I will discuss two difficulties with this account: first that the compensatory afterlife is incompatible with other elements of Swinburne's theory and second, that the notion of the afterlife as compensation is inappropriate.

An obvious example of a life which on balance has been bad rather than good would be a child, born into a hostile environment and alive only for a short time. There is little opportunity in such a life for good experiences, but only suffering and an early death. Therefore we might assume that this is a prime example of a life which deserves compensation. However this is not Swinburne's claim. He suggests that those who die in infancy or with severe mental deficiencies, will not require compensation as they are not sufficiently developed to warrant the status of a person who has undergone suffering. Swinburne argues that instead these people may well pass out of existence as 'there is no formed character worth preserving to eternity'.[29] Thus although such a life may, on balance, be bad, it will not be compensated because the character has not been sufficiently formed.

Let us take a second example of a woman who has lived in extreme poverty and the constant threat of violence to herself and her family. Her entire life has been a battle for survival and she has seen most of her family and friends killed by starvation or war of which they wanted no part. She dies in her thirties, thus having fulfilled Swinburne's criteria of forming a character. However her experiences have led her to believe that if there is a God, it is a cruel and uncaring God and she rejects God finally and decisively so, according to Swinburne, condemning herself to hell. Again the compensatory afterlife is denied to one whose life has, on balance, been bad. Thus it seems that Swinburne's compensatory afterlife is not available to those we might suppose to be obvious candidates, and indeed whose situations might persuade us that there should be compensation for a life which has been, on the whole, bad.

It may be argued that the woman has a good character and has rejected only a caricature of God, and not the true God. Thus she may have the opportunity to accept or reject the true God and consequently receive compensation or send herself to hell. However Swinburne makes no provision in his scheme for individuals to experience the true God before making their decision. Indeed given his claim that full knowledge of God would leave us unfree and unable to reject God, such a provision would drastically change Swinburne's theory of hell. Even if the woman was offered the chance to accept the true God, the compensation of the afterlife would still not reach the individual who died in infancy. It would seem that Swinburne's compensatory afterlife is only to compensate those who have formed good characters and consequently accepted God. That is, those who will anyway join the company of heaven. Thus the compensatory afterlife offers little compensation. As part of his theodicy Swinburne's appeal to the afterlife for compensation fails. Consequently Swinburne's defence of hell leads to the situation where some lives will be, on balance, bad. A situation he claims a good God would avoid.

The further objection is raised that Swinburne is wrong to describe the afterlife as compensation. Hick writes:

---

[29] Swinburne, 1989 p.197.

Evaluation of Swinburne's Hell   79

Swinburne speaks of the joys of heaven as compensating for suffering endured in this world. There are good and bad points in anyone's life, and 'the compensation for bad periods may for some of them come after death' [*Providence and the Problem of Evil* p.239]. At this point some theodicists will want to propose an amendment, substituting fulfilment for compensation - fulfilment of the best potentialities of our nature in a completion of the soul-making process which is taking place through our free responses to the mixture of happiness and misery, pleasure and pain, success and failure, achievement and disaster that characterises our life in this world.[30]

The emphasis on fulfilment rather than compensation is perhaps today a more popular account of the after life and is a much more positive one. Salvation is understood to be about transformation, allowing people to become fitted for heaven. Frances Young writes:

The New Testament at its deepest level is about transformation. That transformation means the forming of Christ, the image and glory of God, in each believer as part of the transformation and renewal of the whole of God's creation.[31]

Salvation, as Hick writes, is about the transformation from 'self-centredness to Reality-centredness'.[32] The life after death allows individuals to complete this transformation, and thus no question of compensation arises, but each individual fulfils the potential with which they were created. Further, it would seem more appropriate to young deaths if they were to have the opportunity to fulfil the potential which has been denied them in this life. Compensation is very subjective, and it is hard to imagine how it could be calculated who would receive what amount of compensation. Individual fulfilment would give purpose to every life however stunted or short-lived it was on earth.

In the following chapter I will discuss Hick's theory of the afterlife, or afterlives as the fulfilment of the potential of each person, or in more 'Hickian' language, the transformation into children of God. It would appear that Swinburne cannot maintain both the compensatory value of the afterlife and his defence of hell, as his claim that only those who have formed a sufficiently good character will enjoy a good afterlife renders the compensatory afterlife meaningless.

---

[30] Hick, 2000 p.58.

[31] Frances Young, 'Salvation and the New Testament' in Donald English (ed.) *Windows on Salvation* (1994) London: Darton, Longman and Todd p.29.

[32] John Hick, *The Second Christianity* (1983) London: SCM Press p.86.

Conditional Immortality

Swinburne considers the idea of conditional immortality, which he concludes may be an option for those who will not be joining the company of heaven and who do not want to remain in existence. I will discuss several criticisms of Swinburne's account of conditional immortality in order to show that the option of allowing some to pass out of existence does not strengthen his defence of hell.

Swinburne does not really reach any conclusions about the idea of conditional immortality, but leaves it open as a possibility should the damned choose it over eternal existence in hell. However Walls believes that this passing out of existence would seriously challenge the strong freedom which Swinburne claims we have. He claims that the sort of serious freedom insisted upon by Swinburne, requires that one lives eternally with the consequences of one's choices.

> Freedom, in its most significant form, requires that we live with the consequences of our choices, at least our decisive choices. Our choices are far more significant if the consequences are eternal and inescapable rather than merely temporal, or, like the choice of annihilation, eternal but escapable because not experiencable.[33]

Walls thus argues that those who have rejected heaven should not also have the opportunity to reject hell. The serious libertarian freedom held by both Swinburne and Walls conflicts over the idea of conditional immortality. Walls believes that our choices are only serious enough if they have eternal, inescapable consequences, whilst Swinburne maintains that we are so free that God would even allow us to pass out of existence if that is what individuals choose. Swinburne himself seems unresolved as to whether the idea of conditional immortality is beneficial to his argument, and his theory does not in any way rest on it. This disagreement between Walls and Swinburne highlights that however serious our freedom is, it is restricted, either by our ultimate choices being limited to eternal heaven and eternal hell, or by us making choices with escapable consequences, and thus making them less serious choices.

Walls further argues that no person would in fact choose to pass out of existence altogether.

> It can be plausibly maintained that the damned may not desire extinction. And if they do not, this strengthens my previous claim that everyone gets what he wants. Some want a loving relationship with God and other persons in heaven, whereas some prefer to cling to their sins in hell, but none finally want total extinction.[34]

---

[33] Walls, 1992 p.136.
[34] Walls, 1992 p.137.

Walls pre-empts the objection that those who commit suicide in this life may well be examples of people who would wish to pass out of existence altogether. He writes:

> It does not obviously follow from the fact that some commit suicide in this life that the damned would prefer annihilation over existence in hell. Maybe the distorted pleasures of hell are sufficient from the viewpoint of the damned to make life in hell preferable to extinction.[35]

Indeed Swinburne claims that hell is the best option for those who are unfit for heaven, so it is hard to see why they would choose the further alternative of passing out of existence. Thus Walls raises two objections to the idea of annihilation or conditional immortality and he concludes:

> One can maintain that the seriousness of our moral freedom rules this [annihilation] out, or one can propose reasons for thinking the damned do not want extinction. Either way, one can uphold the traditional view that our final choice is between eternal heaven and eternal hell.[36]

For Swinburne either of these objections to conditional immortality would be problematic for his defence of hell. He takes great care to uphold our serious human freedom and responsibility, so Wall's claim that conditional immortality allows us to escape the consequences of our actions, is one Swinburne must take seriously. Further, having claimed that hell is the best option for those not in heaven, there is little reason, on Swinburne's account to suppose that any person would prefer the option of non-existence.

Swinburne entertains the notion that hell may consist of a finite period of physical suffering followed by annihilation.[37] However this seems to be the cruellest of all the options. Physical torment could have no rehabilitative purpose if it was to be followed by extinction, and it would seem unacceptable for a God of love to inflict physical torment only for the purpose of vengeance. This combination of punishments also ignores one of the common incentives for advocating conditional immortality, that non-existence is a lesser punishment than eternal physical torment. Those who believe in conditional immortality often assume that this would be a less severe punishment than eternal torment in hell.[38]

---

[35] Walls, 1992 p.137.

[36] Walls, 1992 p.138.

[37] Swinburne, 1981 p.172.

[38] See for example: Clark H.Pinnock, *A Wideness in God's Mercy: The Finality of Jesus Christ in a World of Religions* (1992) Grand Rapids, Michigan: Zondervan Publishing House pp. 156-157 and John Wenham, *The Enigma of Evil: Can We Believe in the Goodness of God?* (1994) Guildford, Surrey: Eagle Press p.75 ff.

However Kvanvig argues that annihilation is in fact a far more severe punishment than existence in hell:

> Nothing is to be gained in responding to objections to a penal theory by substituting metaphysical capital punishment for metaphysical life imprisonment; if anything, our views about capital punishment would suggest that the annihilation view assigns a more severe punishment than does the strong view. So if the strong view cannot offer an adequate response to the moral objection, neither can the annihilation view; if the strong view cannot solve the arbitrariness problem, neither can the annihilation view.[39]

Kvanvig thus claims that conditional immortality cannot avoid the moral questions raised by an eternal hell. Indeed rather than softening this problem, he claims that the alternative of non-existence creates a more serious moral challenge to the goodness of God. Annihilation after death, or after a period of punishment, does not provide a less problematic alternative to the doctrine of hell.

The objections to Swinburne's defence of hell are not resolved by the addition of the possibility of conditional immortality. Arguably this weakens Swinburne's account of serious human freedom and responsibility and also contradicts his claim that hell is the best option for those not in heaven. The option of conditional immortality does not strengthen Swinburne's theory, and does not avoid the challenges made against the doctrine of hell.

God's Universal Salvific Will

Swinburne believes that God has a universal salvific will, and yet claims that this will not bring about the ultimate salvation of all. However if God does not, as Swinburne claims have foreknowledge, Swinburne cannot know that universal salvation will not be the outcome. He writes: 'In claiming that God "seeks" man's eternal well-being, I make no assumptions about how far he will pursue his goal despite man's unwillingness to co-operate'.[40] As we have seen, Swinburne believes that some people will, as a result of their free choices, end up in hell. Although this is on Swinburne's account, certainly a possibility, Swinburne cannot affirm that this will be the outcome.

Although God desires the salvation of all people, Walls explains that this does not necessarily mean that universal salvation will come about. 'If God does everything he can to save all persons, short of destroying anyone's freedom, it may be that God can, consistent with perfect goodness, create some persons knowing they will never act in accordance with grace'.[41] According to Swinburne, God does not actually know that they will never act in accordance with grace, but he would

---

[39] Kvanvig, 1993 p.68. The 'strong view' he is specifically referring to is his four-point understanding of hell, Kvanvig, 1993 p.19.

[40] Swinburne, 1989 p.122.

[41] Walls, 1992 p.93.

say that this is the risk God takes in creating free beings. However, as he insists that neither we nor God can know how people will freely choose, Swinburne cannot assert that all people will not eventually choose in favour of God. Thus Swinburne's rejection of universalism is most relevant to necessary universalism, which claims that the universalist outcome is preordained. However it cannot equally apply to free will universalist positions and Swinburne can certainly not deny the possibility of a contingent universalism.

Swinburne's claim that God will only offer a finite period for individual's to shape their character and thus choose the good seems contradictory to God's universal salvific will. As Leslie Stevenson writes: 'If God's mercy is so great, if he wills the eventual salvation of every person, should he not always be prepared to grant a further chance for repentance?'.[42] Although Swinburne argues that some may have a further chance in purgatory, he is clear that those who have consistently chosen the bad will have no possibility of further chances for repentance. Stevenson acknowledges the sort of argument put forward by Swinburne. He writes: 'It may also be objected that if God is to respect our freedom, he cannot go on waiting for ever, hoping that the recalcitrant will eventually see the light'.[43] However he responds:

> Against this, I venture to cite Matthew 18:21-22, where Peter asks Jesus how many times he is to forgive his brother … and Jesus answers 'I do not say seven times but seventy times seven'. I take it that the moral is not that on the 491st offence we are at last allowed to give up this strenuous forgiving, but rather that we are never to stop. Like many of Jesus' gnomic or parabolic sayings, this appears to set a humanly impossible standard … But if this is what is require of us, how can God - who is supposed to exemplify the ideals of perfection to which we can only aspire - be anything less than always prepared to forgive?[44]

Swinburne would probably argue that forgiveness is irrelevant because God is simply allowing honouring the individuals' free choice and not punishing them. However by putting them beyond the possibility of future redemption God is denying them the option of forgiveness. A God who desired the salvation of, and who was prepared to keep forgiving, an individual would not put that person beyond the possibility of salvation because that person had over a significant period preferred to make bad choices. Thus although Swinburne claims that God has a universal salvific will, even allowing for the fact that it may not be efficacious because of free human choices, God does not act in accordance with the desire to save all people.

---

[42] Leslie Stevenson, 'A Two-Stage Life After Death?' *Theology* vol.CIV (2001) p.345.

[43] Stevenson, 2001 p.346.

[44] Stevenson, 2001 p.346.

Conclusion

Swinburne's defence of hell is centred around his claim that hell is the result of the individual's free choice. However it is clear that Swinburne must value freedom over salvation in the final reckoning and Talbott challenges this choice. Even if it is conceded that God would not override the free choice of individuals it is debatable as to whether any individual would choose hell, and in the following chapters we will discuss premises which would mean that no individual would freely choose hell. Although Swinburne claims that hell consists of *poena damni* and not *poena sensus* he does not escape the moral difficulties caused by the doctrine of hell as eternal physical punishment and neither does he do this by suggesting that some may prefer conditional immortality. Swinburne's account of the compensatory afterlife is incompatible with his defence of hell. Swinburne's minor defences do not succeed and he is dependent on the claim that hell is the free choice of the individual. Swinburne cannot affirm that there will not be a contingent universalism, even though he seems sure that there will not be a universalist outcome. If it can be shown that no individual would choose in favour of hell, then Swinburne's defence of hell fails.

Human Freedom

It is clear that Swinburne's defence of hell relies heavily on his account of freedom and the importance he places on it. Thus if it can be shown that a more limited form of freedom in fact constitutes a genuine human freedom then this will pose a serious challenge to Swinburne's position.

Epistemic Distance

Epistemic distance is essential to Swinburne's account of human freedom. Swinburne holds that if we were made with full knowledge of God's presence, this knowledge would compel us never to do anything wrong and indeed would create a situation in which humans would not be free to act as they choose. However not everyone agrees that epistemic distance is necessary, or that the difficulties which Swinburne supposes would arise without it would in fact come about.

The objection has been made that our choices would in fact be freer if they were based on full knowledge of God. Levine asks:

> Why would making things clear deprive people of choice? A more
> accurate description would be that if God made things 'crystal clear',
> then having the relevant information, people would better be able to
> choose. Swinburne's reasoning as to why God does not and should

not, make it 'crystal clear' to people that heaven exists is implausible.[45]

Richard Gale writes that: 'There is much more free play between belief and assessment of probabilities than Swinburne allows'.[46] He further comments that Swinburne has misrepresented the relationship between humans and their knowledge or lack of knowledge concerning God's existence. Gale suggests the initial acceptance of God's existence is only the first stage in trying to match one's will with God's will.

> I believe that Swinburne has created a needless difficulty for himself. First, he has mislocated the point at which creaturely free will enters into the relationship between man and God. It does not concern the freedom with which we believe that God exists, for it is dubious that in general we can believe at will, be it for conceptual or only causal reasons. Our free endeavouring, rather, concerns the efforts we make to adopt and adhere to a religious way of life, part of which is doing that which will help to self-induce a belief that God exists.[47]

Thus Gale suggests that awareness of God would not automatically compel us to choose good but would only be the first stage in developing a religious way of life. Similarly David O'Conner argues that Swinburne makes an invalid assumption that were we aware of God and therefore aware of good, this would result in us automatically choosing good.

> In effect this amounts to a version of the belief that to know what is good is to do what is good, circumstances permitting, and to know what is evil is to avoid that evil... it seems to me false to claim that knowledge of goodness entails virtue.[48]

O'Conner claims that if humans knew that God was watching them, and desiring them to do good, it does not follow that they would be unable to make any other choice. He suggests that people may still freely decide to choose the bad, despite their awareness of God and even despite the promise of punishment. He explains:

> We would know, in knowing God, not just about future punishments but also, because of God's goodness and justice, that no punishment would ever be excessive and furthermore that God would abide by certain other constraints in punishing us, for instance, that there

---

[45] Levine, 1993 p.529.

[46] Richard M. Gale, 'Swinburne's Argument from Religious Experience' in Padgett (ed.), 1994 p.40.

[47] Gale, 1994, p.40.

[48] David O'Conner, 'Swinburne on Natural Evil' *Religious Studies* vol. 19 (1983) p.69.

would be no reprisals against an evil-doers innocent family and so
on. We would know too that God's punishment would never take the
form of denying us the enjoyment of our evil acts or the pleasures of
their fruits, for that would be to deny us any rational possibility of
genuine choice on moral matters, removing as it would all reason or
incentive for evil-doing remaining after our loss of hope of escaping
punishment. Hence we would know that a rational God who places
the high value Swinburne mentions upon moral responsibility would
never punish in these ways.[49]

O'Conner argues that one could rationally decide to do a certain action knowing it
to be wrong and knowing that one would be punished for it. He claims that this is
within the realm of our own experience. 'Nor', he writes, 'in actual fact, does it fail
to happen that people do things, knowing they should not even when they are
certain of punishment'.[50] However, Swinburne is perhaps suggesting more than just
a moral compulsion to do good if we were fully aware of God. Although we would
be aware of what was good and what was not good without epistemic distance, it is
not simply this awareness that would compel us to choose the good. An awareness
of God may, as O'Conner suggests, still allow us rationally to choose the bad, even
with the knowledge we will be punished for it. However the point is that if we were
made with no epistemic distance between us and God, we would have no desire to
choose the bad.

    Swinburne's emphasis on the need for people to remain ignorant of God is
dependent on the premise that if we were aware of God we would lose our capacity
for choice. Not all agree that this would be the case, but both Swinburne and Hick
assume that this would be the result of our being created without epistemic
distance. If we could be fully aware of God without this leading to an
overwhelming desire for communion with God then we would indeed be better able
to choose from all of the relevant information. However Swinburne does not
believe this to be the case. Thus without this epistemic distance, which allows us to
gravitate at our own pace and through our free choices, we would find our end in
God immediately and thus would not have the period of soul-making and free
choice which Swinburne and Hick argue is so valuable.

    The Christian idea of relationship with God is based on the personal
recognition of God as creator and Lord rather than because we have full knowledge
of God. The words of Jesus to Thomas after his resurrection support this: 'Happy
are they who find faith without seeing me' [John 20: 29]. Similarly, the author of
the first letter of Peter writes: 'You have not seen him, yet you love him; and
trusting in him now without seeing him, you are filled with a glorious joy too great
for words' [1 Peter 1:8]. Thus the faith of those who believe without seeing is to be
celebrated and indeed brings its own rewards. The opportunity for faith rather than
knowledge is, Swinburne would argue, valuable for our development as human

---

[49] O'Conner, 1983 p.70.
[50] O'Conner, 1983 p.70.

beings and in order to come to a genuine relationship with God. Swinburne's claim that God has not unequivocally revealed Godself to us in our present existence is confirmed by our own experience of the world. Many people do not believe that God exists at all and those who do are not agreed on what exactly God is. If a clear unequivocal revelation of God was given to us in this world, this surely would not be the case. Thus Swinburne believes that epistemic distance offers an explanation of the world according to our experience, and allows that there is a good God who has good reason to create us without full knowledge of God. As Swinburne believes full awareness of God would significantly challenge our freedom, we would not be better able to make choices given all of the relevant knowledge. Indeed given this knowledge we would be unable to make choices at all.

Libertarian Freedom

As we have seen Swinburne argues that libertarian is the only genuine account of human freedom. In this section I will look at some difficulties with the libertarian account and the main alternative to libertarian freedom, compatibilist freedom in order to establish whether this is a coherent account of genuine human freedom. I will look first at problems with libertarian freedom before looking at compatibilst freedom in order to determine whether that can offer a satisfactory alternative.

Libertarian versus Compatibilist Freedom

One of the major criticisms of libertarian freedom is that it amounts to nothing more than randomness of choice. The difficulty with an account of human freedom that in fact describes random occurrences is that one cannot than be held morally responsible. We have seen that Swinburne attaches great importance to the moral responsibility of the individual. Talbott objects:

> If a person makes a choice, and nothing causes him to make that choice, his undetermined choice would be a mere chance occurrence or random event, and one could hardly be held responsible for a chance occurrence or a random event.[51]

If strong human freedom, or indeterminism by definition has no causes, then it does not allow us to be held responsible for our actions. Moritz Schlick explains:

> If we should conceive of a decision as utterly without any cause (this would in all strictness be the indeterministic presupposition) then the act would be entirely a matter of chance, for chance is identical with the absence of cause; there is no other opposite of causality. Could

---

[51] Thomas Talbott, 'Indeterminism and Chance Occurences' *The Personalist* (1979) p.253.

we under such conditions make the agent responsible? Certainly not.[52]

This conclusion is echoed by Norman Geisler:

> If indeterminism were true, then there would be events without causes. The universe would be irrational and unliveable. In fact, it would be nonmoral since there would be no way to determine who is responsible for an action which has no efficient cause.[53]

Talbott claims that the indeterminist position requires three clarifications. These are that there are 'causal influences upon, and causal conditions'[54] for choices even though they are not causally sufficient. A realistic account of human freedom, and especially one which also wants to maintain moral responsibility, cannot deny that there are causal influences and conditions for decisions: however it can insist that these causes are not sufficient. Thus Talbott's second clarification is that choices can have a point and a reason, but 'no causal explanation can be given of why we should choose to act from one reason rather than from another'.[55] The third clarification is that they are still *our* choices. Libertarians 'do not deny that such actions are determined in the trivial sense of being performed by a person. But they do deny that anything causes a person to perform them'.[56] That is to say they deny that any one thing determinatively causes a person to perform them.

Swinburne concedes that human freedom is not perfect and that actions do have causes, but the point is that they are not sufficient causes. The libertarian then must provide an account of freedom with a very specific degree of causation. Too much, and the type of freedom will become compatibilst or even determinist and too little and the freedom will be no more than randomness of choice, unable to make that agent morally accountable.

How significant then are the differences between the libertarian and compatibilist view of freedom. The libertarian is not able to claim, without qualification, that an action has no cause, only that it is not a sufficient cause. However the compatibilist claim is that whilst there are causes which lead to actions these actions are still the free choice of the agent. Thus the compatibilist must claim that although there is an explanatory cause for an action, the agent must have been able to refrain from doing this action. William Hasker claims:

---

[52] Moritz Schlick, *Problems of Ethics* (1939) Englewood Cliffs: Prentice Hall p.156, quoted in Talbott, 1979 p.253.
[53] Norman Geisler, 'God Knows All Things' in David Basinger and Randall Basinger (eds.), *Predestination and Free Will* (1986) Downers Grove, Illinois: Inter Varsity Press p.74.
[54] Talbott, 1979 p.254.
[55] Talbott, 1979 p.254.
[56] Talbott, 1979 p.254.

On the libertarian view, in order to be truly free she must have the 'inner freedom' either to act or to refrain, but on the compatibilist view she needs only the 'outer freedom' to carry out the decision either way she makes it - but the decision itself may be completely determined by the psychological forces at work in her personality.[57]

Does the compatibilist position allow that the agent is free to do any other action, or, more straightforwardly, to refrain from doing the action? Much discussion about human freedom has been based around the question of whether in a specific situation an agent could have done other than they did. In order more to fully establish the compatibilist position it will be helpful to consider this issue.

'Could Have Done Otherwise'

The objection is often made that the compatibilist cannot give any genuine meaning to 'could have done otherwise'. Walls argues that the compatibilist position must be rejected because, 'it remains doubtful whether compatibilists can give any meaningful sense to their claim that a person whose actions are determined is able to do other than he does'.[58] If we were predisposed always to choose the good, this would not entail a free choice because the agent could not have done otherwise. Richard Double comments:

> Libertarians seem to be committed to the idea that free agents not only control which choices they actually make, but counterfactually *would* control alternative choices *had* they manifested their categorical ability to choose otherwise.[59]

The compatibilist likewise assumes that the agent controls the choices they make, but the challenge to compatibilism is whether they could have chosen otherwise.

Daniel Dennett suggests that the question of whether the agent could have done otherwise is misleading. He writes: 'I will argue that *whatever* "could have done otherwise" actually means, it is not what we are interested in when we care about whether some act was freely and responsibly performed'.[60] Our concern, he contends, is that the agent is responsible for their actions, and we do not judge this on whether or not they could have done otherwise. Indeed he claims that 'it is seldom that we even *seem* to care whether or not a person could have done

---

[57] William Hasker, 'A Philosophical Perspective' in Clark H. Pinnock (ed.), *The Openness of God: A Biblical Challenge to the Traditional Understanding of God* (1994) Carlisle: Paternoster Press p.137.

[58] Walls, 1992 p.64.

[59] Double, 1991 p.15.

[60] Dennett, 1984 pp.131-132.

otherwise'.[61] Dennett gives the example of Martin Luther's claim, 'Here I stand, I can do no other'.

> Luther claimed that he could do no other, that his conscience made it *impossible* for him to recant. He might, of course, have been wrong, or have been deliberately overstating the truth. But even if he was, perhaps especially if he was - his declaration is testimony to the fact that we simply do not exempt someone from blame or praise for an act because we think he could do no other. Whatever Luther was doing, he was not trying to duck responsibility.[62]

So Dennett claims that 'could have done otherwise' is a red herring in the debate about freedom and responsibility. He further contends that an agent having been in a certain situation once, will never again be in the same situation where all the variables and influences are exactly the same.[63] Thus he concludes:

> If anyone is interested at all in the question of whether or not one could have done otherwise in *exactly* the same circumstances (and internal state), that will have to be a particularly pure metaphysical curiosity - that is to say, a curiosity so pure as to be utterly lacking in any ulterior motive, since the answer could not conceivably make any noticeable difference to the way the world went.[64]

Thus Dennett argues that whether or not the agent could have done otherwise does not decide whether or not they are morally responsible for the action. However C.A. Campbell writes that it must be:

> A condition of the morally free act that the agent could have acted otherwise than he in fact did ... if it is one's nature to act in that way, then the praise is offered perhaps not of that act in particular as in a sense the agent could have done no other, but in general to the agent that developed such a nature that he could only morally act in that way.[65]

---

[61] Dennett, 1984 p,133.

[62] Dennett, 1984 p.133.

[63] Dennett, 1984 p.137.

[64] Dennett, 1984 p.138 Stump notes that this and other works are not adequately dealt with by Swinburne who does not respond to the challenges which they pose for his position. She writes, 'Daniel Dennett's defense of compatibilism is dismissed in a short footnote, and the defense of incompatibilism provided by Peter van Inwagen, who might have been a valuable ally for Swinburne here, is discussed and rejected in just a couple of paragraphs in a note'. Eleanore Stump, *'Responsibility and Atonement* - Richard Swinburne' *Faith and Philosophy* vol. 11 (1994) p.322.

[65] C.A. Campbell, *On Selfhood and Godhead* (1957) Aberdeen: University Press p.162.

So, in Luther's case his statement would imply that because of the sort of person he was, or had become he could do no other, not that he could physically do no other.

Campbell is establishing a distinction between the agent having the theoretical ability to do otherwise and having the practical ability to do otherwise. In 'God Ordains All Things' John Feinberg discusses seven definitions of the phrase 'can do otherwise'. He concludes that the best definition is one where 'can do' means 'reasonably could'. He writes:

> In this sense, to say someone can do something means it is reasonable to expect him to do so under the circumstances, and to say someone cannot do something means only that under the circumstances it is unreasonable to expect him to do it.[66]

Luther had the theoretical ability to do otherwise but in the circumstances it was unreasonable to expect him to do otherwise. That we become the sort of people who, because of our characters cannot do otherwise, or cannot reasonably be expected to do otherwise is, according to Swinburne, one of the aims of shaping character. Talbott claims that one of our aims in becoming moral agents is to develop such a character. He writes of the view that:

> An action is free only if it is logically and psychologically possible for the person who performs it to refrain from it. The latter claim seems to me inconsistent not only with Christian theology, but with the widespread intuitions about the nature of moral character as well. In a very real sense, the measure of one's moral character – the measure of one's love for instance – is just the extent to which certain actions are no longer possible.[67]

We do not erode our moral freedom by becoming the sort of people who can only react in certain ways to situations, rather this is the aim of being a moral person.

This brings us to a distinction between two different levels of 'could have done'. Flew explains that there is a common and more fundamental sense in which the phrase can be used. He writes:

> Certainly in the less fundamental but more common senses of these expressions, we do say that people really had no choice or that they surely could not have done other than they did when it is our belief that, although in those more fundamental senses they did or they could, nevertheless there were in fact no alternative causes of action

---

[66] John S. Feinberg, 'God Ordains All Things' in David Basinger and Randall Basinger (eds.), *Predestination and Free Will* (1986) Downers Grove, Illinois: Intervarsity Press p.28. For the other six definitions see pp.27-28.
[67] Talbott, 1988 p.17.

open to them which they could reasonably have been expected to adopt.[68]

It could be argued that the fundamental sense is irrelevant as it is the common sense which actually causes us to act. Indeed this would provide a good description of compatibilist freedom. Whilst we have the fundamental ability to do otherwise, because of the sort of person one is and the different internal and external factors acting at a given time, one may realistically have no choice but to follow one particular course of action. So, fundamentally there are many courses of action that could be taken, and an individual is free to follow any of them. However, causal influences on people's behaviour may mean that those choices are limited, and even narrowed down to one, because the sort of person that they are, means that not all of those courses of action are realistic options for them.

Talbott notes: 'One might have the power to do something, even though it is psychologically impossible that one should want to exercise that power'.[69] Mark Linville argues: 'The libertarian is likely to say that a power that, for one reason or another, is necessarily never exercised, is not a power at all'.[70] However this power is not *necessarily* never exercised in the strict sense of necessary. We all have powers which for various reasons we do not exercise, and so become the sort of people who will not exercise those powers. Indeed this is exactly how Swinburne suggests we shape our character. By choosing certain sorts of actions we become the sort of people who cannot reasonably be expected to choose opposite sort of actions. Swinburne goes so far as to say that we will make ourselves incapable of choosing any other sort of action. However he is not proposing that we will at this point have sacrificed or been denied our freedom rather he recognises that this is the result of our freedom. Thus the compatibilist can give an adequate definition of 'can do otherwise'. According to the compatibilist account of freedom, the agent has the fundamental ability to do otherwise but not what Flew has described as the 'common' ability to do otherwise.

Does the libertarian, or more specifically Swinburne, claim that the agent always has the fundamental and the common ability to do otherwise? Swinburne cannot claim both that agents shapes his/her character so firmly that he/she becomes incapable of doing certain kinds of actions or making certain choices, *and* that every agent always has the ability to do otherwise in the common sense. Therefore Swinburne must concede that although the agent always has the fundamental ability to do otherwise, the agent cannot always do otherwise in the common sense. This is not because of external causes but because of internal causes, formed by the agent. However on this account, what is the difference between the libertarian and the compatibilst position? The answer seems to be very little. To return to Hasker's distinction, he claims that the libertarian must have

---

[68] Anthony Flew, 'Freedom and Human Nature' *Philosophy* vol. 66 (1991) pp.54 - 55.

[69] Talbott, 1988 p.17.

[70] Mark D. Linville, 'Divine Foreknowledge and the Libertarian Conception of Human Freedom' *International Journal for Philosophy of Religion* vol. 33 (1993) p.168.

'inner freedom' to act or to refrain, whilst the compatibilist needs only the 'outer freedom' to carry out the action even if it is determined internally. Perhaps these two descriptions are not as distinct as they first appear. The compatibilist recognises that the inner freedom is only a fundamental or theoretical type of freedom and thus claims that genuine freedom requires only the outer freedom to carry out actions. The libertarian of course also requires this outer freedom but claims that he/she also needs the inner freedom to choose his/her actions. Whilst the libertarian recognises that there will be causes influencing this decision, these causes do not determine the decision. However we have seen that whilst there may not be external causes determining each decision, there is one major internal cause which effectively determines decisions, namely the character of the agent. It is essential to Swinburne's theory that the agent forms his/her character to the extent that he/she is unable to do otherwise. Thus the inner freedom required by the libertarian can only be initial freedom to form character, and this is not substantially different from the freedom required by the compatibilist. The compatibilst position does not require this inner freedom because the compatibilst recognises that actions have internal causes. However it would seem that the libertarian must also concede that there are internal causes and therefore, like the compatibilist, the libertarian can only demand the outer freedom to carry out actions.

There is then a major difficulty with Swinburne's account of libertarian freedom. Swinburne cannot maintain both that we have strong libertarian freedom and that we shape our character to the point where we can 'do no other'. However, Swinburne cannot abandon his emphasis on the importance of shaping character without undermining his whole defence of hell. Neither can Swinburne abandon his libertarian freedom and still offer a coherent defence of hell. Swinburne relies on his doctrine of strong free will to show that God cannot guarantee, or even know if there will eventually be a universalist outcome. Walls writes:

> When libertarian freedom is consistently maintained, it will be recognised that God's ability to bring about certain states of affairs is contingent upon the choices of free creatures. In view of this, perhaps God cannot create a world in which everyone is saved, as the universalist supposes. Nor is it the case if some are lost, it follows that God is unwilling to save them. For God could be willing to save everyone, but unable to do so, while remaining properly omnipotent.[71]

However without libertarian freedom this defence fails and Walls acknowledges that this removes a major obstacle to universalism.

> Without libertarian freedom, it is difficult, if not impossible to make sense of the claim that some are damned even though God wishes to

---

[71] Walls, 1992 p.81.

save all people. For if human beings are not free in the libertarian sense it would seem to follow that if God wishes to save all, then all in fact will be saved. For if freedom is compatible with determinism, then God could save everyone and do it in such a way that everyone would freely choose salvation.[72]

It seems that not only is Swinburne's theory untenable, but a compatibilist account of freedom both provides a more accurate description of our human freedom and invalidates one of the major defences of an eternal hell.

Freedom versus Salvation

Even if Swinburne's account of libertarian freedom were coherent, a further challenge to his theory is that he prizes strong freedom over salvation. Talbott suggests that if an individual chooses to damn him/herself, then God would have a duty to intervene. He writes: 'The argument that a loving God would not interfere with human freedom has no relevance in a context where, *by hypothesis*, we are speaking of those who have already lost their freedom, who are prisoners of bad desires'.[73] Talbott assumes that anyone who had made a choice to be separated eternally from God, would do so because they had become committed to their bad, self-destructive desires. Thus they have already lost their freedom. Talbott asks, 'if those in hell are already in bondage to their desires and have already lost their freedom, in what sense would God be *interfering* with their freedom when he releases them from bondage?'.[74] Rather he suggests, God would be reinstating their freedom and thus allowing them to choose without being trapped into their bad desires. Even though individuals may have freely started on the path of bad choices, Talbott maintains that they are not free whilst subject to this bondage.

> However *responsible* one might be for one's ignorance and one's bondage to desire, no choice that such ignorance or bondage determines is truly free (in the libertarian sense); and if one is free from the kind of ignorance and bondage that is incompatible with free choice, one could never have a motive to choose eternal misery for oneself.[75]

Thus Talbott maintains that if God were to free individuals from these desires, thus reinstating not overriding their freedom, that no one would have reason ever to choose eternal separation from God.

If one accepts that Swinburne's account of strong libertarian freedom is the only description of genuine human freedom then one may accept that we are free to

---

[72] Walls, 1992 p.39.

[73] Talbott, 1990 (b) p.36.

[74] Talbott, 1990 (b) p.37.

[75] Talbott, 1990 (b) pp. 37 - 38.

reject God. However, one could ascribe to this view of freedom and yet assert that in the end God would override human freedom to ensure that none are eternally lost. Swinburne does not propose this as he believes God honours the freedom we have been giving by allowing us to send ourselves to hell, should we so choose. Walls comments:

> Swinburne seems to place more value on freedom than does Talbott, since he does not think it should be overridden, even to prevent someone from being damned. Since this dispute involves a basic value judgement, it must be recognised that there is no simple way to resolve it, and indeed it may represent a ground-level difference of intuition.[76]

Charles Seymour in 'On Choosing Hell' notes: 'Talbott believes that separation from God is in itself an evil great enough to make even the most prosperous life on the whole bad'.[77] Talbott maintains not only that this would render an individual's existence to be bad overall, but he also claims that God could have no reason for allowing this to happen. Seymour does not think that God, having created us as free beings would be prepared to interfere with our freedom in order for us to accept salvation. He concludes: 'Free choice is essential to our being and hence not even an omnipotent God can override it for the sake of bringing us to heaven'.[78] However Talbott further claims that 'we have every reason to believe that everlasting separation is the kind of evil that a loving God would prevent even if it meant interfering with human freedom in certain ways'.[79] Thus Talbott believes that even if freeing us from our bad desires did constitute overriding our individual freedom, God would be justified in doing that to bring about the greater good of salvation. However, he claims that releasing us from such bad desires does not override our freedom, but allows us to make a genuinely free choice. Talbott believes that salvation would eventually be the free choice of every person.

> In a sense all roads have the same destination, the end of reconciliation, but some are longer and windier than others. Because our choice of roads at any given instant is truly free in the libertarian sense, we are genuinely responsible for the choices we make, but because no illusion can endure forever, the end is foreordained.[80]

Thus for Talbott we can have a genuine human freedom and yet be assured that all will ultimately be with God.

---

[76] Walls, 1992 p.105.
[77] Charles Seymour, 'On Choosing Hell' *Religious Studies* vol. 33 (1997) p.251.
[78] Seymour, 1997 p.265.
[79] Talbott, 1990 (b) p.38.
[80] Talbott, 1990 (b) p.39.

Swinburne does not show that the importance of libertarian freedom ultimately overrides the importance of salvation and thus he does not show that God would not be justified in eventually overriding the freedom of an individual in order to bring about his/her salvation. As Walls points out, Swinburne makes a value judgement that freedom is more desirable than salvation but for God to have decided this would seem to be a hard-hearted approach to humanity and not a choice that is reflected in the New Testament. Further Swinburne vastly overstates the need for human freedom to be of the strong libertarian sort. He does not show that compatibilist freedom is not genuine freedom, and indeed it would seem that the latter sort actually describes more accurately the freedom we have as created beings.

Good World

Swinburne rejects the possibility of a Good World in which free beings choose between different goods. Swinburne's grounds for this are that we would not have serious freedom or moral responsibility if our choices were only between a variety of goods. Many argue that a good God would have created a good world; however Swinburne claims that the actual world does not challenge the existence of a good God. The gift of freedom and therefore the actual world is, Swinburne believes, a better world than a good world without freedom. However the objection is made that we could still have significant freedom and moral responsibility in a good world. Levine argues that in the actual world we have only a limited number of choices and yet Swinburne does not consider this to be a limitation on our freedom. Levine writes: 'If it is no limitation on our freedom to come into existence with a limited range of choice, then why is it a restriction on our freedom to come into existence with a further limitation on that range?'.[81]

Swinburne asserts that God is prepared to pay the price of the suffering and sin involved in the actual world, in order to give us serious freedom and moral responsibility. However many scholars have claimed that this price is both too high and unnecessary. Steven Boër in 'The Irrelevance of the Free Will Defence'[82] claims that it only matters that we can choose freely, and not necessarily that we succeed in effecting what we have intended to accomplish. Frank B. Dilley explains: 'What I shall refer to as the "Boër reform" is the suggestion that God could have allowed creatures to exercise free choices but have intervened with "coincidence miracles" to prevent all the intended evil from actually occurring'.[83] Thus individuals would still be able to desire and intend to do evil, but would fail in actually bringing about this evil. Boër believes that, in this way, God could allow humans to be free and also prevent evil states of affair occurring.

---

[81] Levine, 1993 p.527.
[82] Steven Boër, 'The Irrelevance of the Free Will Defence' *Analysis* vol.XXXVIII no.2 (1978) pp.110-112.
[83] Frank B. Dilley, 'Is the Free Will Defence Irrelevant' *Religious Studies* vol. 18 (1978) p.355.

Dilley raises several objections to the 'Boër reform'. He points out that 'to be free merely to intend and not to do robs free will of much of its needed significance.'[84] Further: 'To have good result from every sort of intention would seem also to rob good-intending of some of its point'.[85] It would seem to be a clear restraint on our freedom if we could not carry out the actions we had intended and would mean that we had no moral responsibility at all. The value of human freedom lies significantly in the fact that we are responsible for our own choices and decisions. If the Boër reform were implemented none of our actions would have consequences and thus we would not even necessarily know what is good and what is bad. Shooting a gun at someone if the bullet would never be allowed actually to reach them, would not be a bad action. Wishing harm to someone, would not necessarily be a bad desire because nothing could actually happen to them. If none of our actions resulted in bad, we would not be able to shape our characters in the way that Swinburne claims we do and thus we would be unable to make our ultimate choice for or against God. Thus the Boër reform would erode our understanding of good and bad and put us in an environment where some of our actions could not have consequences. This proposal of a good world is particularly incompatible with Swinburne's theory as it destroys the aspects of the actual world which he considers to be most valuable.

Conclusion

Swinburne maintains that the only way in which we can be genuinely free is if we are created at an epistemic distance from God and indeed it does seem that without this distance we would not be free to form our own characters. However Swinburne's claim that we are strongly free does not provide an accurate description of our human freedom and he fails to show that compatibilst freedom does not provide a genuine account of human freedom. Indeed Swinburne cannot uphold both the strong libertarian view of freedom and his account of shaping character. Swinburne claims that we cannot live in a world where we will always choose good and be genuinely free and it is apparent that whether or not this is actually possible, it is not the nature of the actual world. It is clear that Swinburne's defence of hell is dependent on his account of libertarian freedom and thus his defence fails.

God's Knowledge

The type of knowledge which God has is clearly important to this debate. As we have seen Swinburne rejects God having foreknowledge and middle knowledge and holds that God has only present knowledge. In this section I will look at arguments against foreknowledge and middle knowledge.

---

[84] Dilley, 1982 p.357.
[85] Dilley, 1982 p.358.

Foreknowledge

As we have seen there are two major objections to the idea of God's foreknowledge. I do not intend to discuss the argument that God is out of time and therefore cannot have foreknowledge as Swinburne does not accept this account of God's eternity and for the purposes of this book we will assume God being eternal refers to God being everlasting. The other major objection to foreknowledge is not that foreknowledge is incoherent, but that it is incompatible with free creatures. Swinburne is adamant that God does not have foreknowledge, because human free choice means that God's knowledge could turn out to be wrong. Obviously Swinburne does not want to describe an omniscient God who could be proved wrong. Fouts comments: 'An incorrect foreknowledge is an obvious contradiction. Swinburne's fear here is not so much that God will fail to be future omniscient, but that humans will not be free'.[86] Neither God having incorrect foreknowledge or humans not being free would be acceptable to Swinburne, and Walls explains that one or both of these must be qualified:

> Swinburne thinks that anything God foreknows is, in some sense, necessary. Thus, if God foreknows human choices, those choices are necessary rather than free. Indeed God's own choices cannot be free if God foreknows them. Consequently, Swinburne argues, we must either qualify the claim that God is perfectly free or we must qualify the claim that God knows all true propositions. Without qualifications the two claims are logically incompatible.[87]

Thus Swinburne opts to limit the omniscience of God, and asserts that God being omniscient only means that God knows all it is possible to know at a given time.[88] Therefore there must have been no point in time when God had foreknowledge. Fouts comments that for Swinburne, our 'freedom is not just a matter of God not knowing the future, but rather a matter of God *never* knowing the future up to the time of any particular free action'.[89] Thus Swinburne is forced to argue that God has never had knowledge of the future and that there is no aspect of the future that God can know infallibly, including God's own actions.[90] Thus God chooses to limit God's knowledge of what God will do in the future. However, there is an exception

---

[86] Avery Fouts, 'Divine Self - Limitations in Swinburne's Doctrine of Omniscience' *Religious Studies* vol. 29 (1993) p.22.

[87] Walls, 1992 p.47.

[88] Swinburne, 1996 p.8.

[89] Fouts, 1993 p.24.

[90] See Swinburne, 1977 p.173ff. 'A being may be perfectly free and know everything - except which free choices he will make and what will result from the choices he will make'. Swinburne, 1977 p.176.

to this. God will still know the events that God's nature demands. Swinburne qualifies that these events are not in fact free.

Some have argued that God not having foreknowledge leads to a weak view of God. Sutherland claims:

> If, as Swinburne hints, a belief in free human action which is not either trivial or compatible with *determinism* is legitimate, then a consequence of this is that what God knows about the future will progressively diminish as human technology increases.[91]

The more humans develop and take control over things which would traditionally have been thought to be in God's control[92] the further God will be pushed out of the picture. Walls raises a similar concern. He writes, 'if God does not have infallible foreknowledge of all future events is he not likely to be surprised by some developments? Does this allow for the possibility that God might lose control of our world and fail to achieve his purposes?'.[93] A God who does not know what is going to happen in the future is not the God of traditional Christian belief. This would particularly be problematic for the view that God has a plan and purpose for every human life, and that God will use those who offer their life in service to God. If God is not in control of the world and does not know what will happen in the future, it is difficult to see how God could bring this about.[94] However Michael Robinson notes that Swinburne claims: 'God retains total control over the future. Since God is omnipotent and free, whatever events unfold in the future He is able to control. Indeed, at any moment, God may choose to abolish the universe completely. The deity remains sovereign into the future'.[95] Thus Swinburne suggests that although God does not know what will happen in the future, nothing could happen that would be beyond God's control as God is omnipotent. However it does mean that God could fail to achieve his purposes and even though God is omnipotent, if God chooses not to override our freedom there is nothing God will be able to do to bring these purposes about. So although God retains control in the sense that God could abolish the universe completely as Robinson suggests, without foreknowledge God does not have the power to bring about God's purposes in creation.

---

[91] Stewart R. Sutherland, *God, Jesus and Belief: The Legacy of Theism* (1984) Oxford: Basil Blackwell p.58.

[92] For example, genetic engineering, nuclear weapons, global warming could all have huge implications for the world, but because they are 'controlled' by humans, God cannot know what the consequences of these things will be.

[93] Walls, 1992 p.47.

[94] This is of course the understanding of both process theism and the open view of God. See Pinnock (ed.), 1994. See also Swinburne, 1977 p.177 on this subject. For a process theology view see A. N. Whitehead, *Process and Reality* (1929) Cambridge: Cambridge University Press or Charles Hartshorne, *A Natural Theology For Our Time* (1967) Illinois: Open Court p.25ff.

[95] Michael Robinson, 'Why Divine Foreknowledge?' *Religious Studies* vol.36 (2000) p.253.

Talbott claims that God's knowledge of the outcome of the universe is not dependent on God having foreknowledge.

God's providential control of history in no way depends upon his foreknowledge of future contingencies. He in fact knows each of us from the beginning and which free actions each of us will perform, but the power he has to accomplish his loving purposes does not rest upon such knowledge; it rests upon the nature of the universe he has created, the nature of choices that created persons face, and the self-corrective nature of moral evil itself.[96]

Thus Talbott claims that God does have foreknowledge but that this is not the reason that God can guarantee the desired outcome of creation despite us having free choices. Rather God has designed the world such that all roads will ultimately lead to God. However it is not clear that Swinburne could adopt a similar argument to show that God's purposes will eventually be fulfilled. Talbott's description of the influences at work in creation seem to constitute a compatibilist theory which, of course, Swinburne denies. Therefore Swinburne cannot appeal to this defence, because of his emphasis on the unknown variable of choices by agents with serious freedom. For Swinburne, even though God may have put these mechanisms in place in creation, there is still no assurance that humans will respond to them as God hopes. Therefore the act of creation is a huge risk for God, according to Swinburne and God has no way of ensuring that God's purposes will ever come about, as God will never resort to overriding human freedom.

The objection is made that God's foreknowledge does not destroy human freedom as Swinburne claims. Just because God knows that I am going to do something, does not mean that God has caused me to do it. Hasker writes:

Sometimes we ourselves know what another person is going to do (say, in anticipating a friend's reaction to some situation which has arisen), and we do not suppose that our knowing this is incompatible with their acting freely – so why suppose such an incompatibility when it is God who knows?[97]

However Kvanvig argues that this objection is 'inadequate because it confuses the problem of foreknowledge with the problem of divine knowledge'.[98]

To claim that God is essentially omniscient implies that God is absolutely certain about everything which He believes - and that certainty entails that God bears a very different relation to the future than we do, for we cannot be certain in the relevant sense of much

---

[96] Talbott, 1990 p.244.

[97] Hasker, 1985 p.124.

[98] Jonathan Kvanvig, *The Possibility of an All-Knowing God* (1986) Houndmills: Macmillan p.73.

more than our own present mental states … Thus whatever there is to be said regarding the incompatibility thesis, the thesis that God's foreknowledge is incompatible with human freedom, it cannot be dismissed by considering the case of ordinary foreknowledge - which is quite unlike God's foreknowledge.[99]

Thus Kvanvig draws a distinction between ordinary foreknowledge and divine foreknowledge. The sort of foreknowledge we have, Swinburne is happy to attribute also to God: that is ordinary or fallible foreknowledge. Michael Robinson writes: 'Swinburne points out that while God cannot certainly know future free acts of humans, He can predict very accurately such actions'.[100] However Swinburne denies that God has infallible foreknowledge. He argues that any beliefs God holds must be right beliefs and thus if God believes we will do a certain action, we are committed to that course of action.

However, the further point is made that the objection to foreknowledge is often wrongly understood. William Hasker writes: 'Another frequent objection against incompatibilism is that this view wrongly assumes that God's prior knowledge of what a person will do *causes* the subsequent action'.[101] However Hasker continues that this is not the claim of the argument. He explains that incompatibilists on divine foreknowledge 'merely assert that it is impossible that God should believe that an event will happen and yet it not occur'.[102]

> Probably the most common answer makes a point of the claim that God's knowledge of what Clarence will do does not cause Clarence to eat the omelette. This may be true, but it is irrelevant to the argument as presented, which does not make any claim to the effect that God's beliefs are the cause of human actions.[103]

Similarly William Alston argues that God's foreknowledge is not the cause of an action.

> Contemporary thinkers who suppose that God's foreknowledge rules out human free choice do not typically suppose that divine foreknowledge causes us to act as we do. They think, rather, that since God is necessarily infallible the fact that God believes at t_1 that Jones will do x at t_2 by itself necessarily entails that Jones will do x at

[99] Kvanvig, 1986 p.73.

[100] Robinson, 2000 p.253. He is referring to Swinburne, 1977 p.181.

[101] Hasker, 1985 p.125.

[102] Hasker, 1985 p.125.

[103] Hasker, 1994 p.149. Hasker is referring to the much used illustration, does God know whether or not Clarence will have an omelette for his breakfast tomorrow.

t_2 and hence is, by itself, logically incompatible with Jones refraining from doing x at t_2.[104]

Even when this objection is understood in this way, and avoids the obvious refutation that my knowing someone will do a certain action is not the cause of them doing the action, it still does not demonstrate the incompatibility of human freedom and divine foreknowledge. The knowledge that Jones will freely choose a certain action, prior to Jones making that choice does not mean that Jones does not act freely. The freedom of an action is not determined by the time at which one decides upon a particular course of action, neither is it determined by the point when that decision is known. Thus God knowing in advance how an agent will freely decide may mean that there is no doubt that will be the future action of the agent, but it is not committing the agent to any action which is not a result of the agent's free choice.

Further, divine foreknowledge is only incompatible with a libertarian understanding of human freedom and we have seen that Swinburne does not satisfactorily demonstrate that libertarian freedom offers a more coherent and genuine account of human freedom than compatibilist freedom. According to compatibilist freedom an action is the result of various internal influences, thus an action has causes all of which are known to God. Consequently God knows in advance the decision that will be made by any agent. This does not cause the agent to make this decision or mean he/she is committed to any action which is not the result of his/her own choice. It is simply to acknowledge that on omniscient God knows what will happen in the future even given the variable of limitedly free beings.

Swinburne's claim that God chooses not to have foreknowledge in order to allow humans serious freedom results in God having no control over the outcome of creation. However Swinburne does not convincingly show that God must sacrifice foreknowledge in order to allow us to be free. Whilst foreknowledge may be less compatible with strong libertarian freedom than with compatibilst freedom, we have seen that libertarian freedom does not provide a realistic account of human freedom. Divine foreknowledge does not exclude compatibilst freedom and Swinburne does not adequately dismiss either of these positions.

Middle Knowledge

Swinburne does not actually challenge the coherence of either middle knowledge or foreknowledge he is only concerned to demonstrate that they are incompatible with human freedom. Therefore, although Swinburne does not believe that God has middle knowledge he does concede that counterfactuals of freedom may have truth-value. This is an essential question in the debate about middle knowledge. If counterfactuals do not have any truth-value then the concept of middle knowledge

---

[104] William P. Alston, 'Divine Foreknowledge and Alternative Conceptions of Human Freedom' *International Journal for Philosophy of Religion* vol. 18 (1985) pp.20 - 21.

is meaningless. Thus in order to proceed with further discussions regarding middle knowledge in the following chapters it will be necessary first to establish the coherence of middle knowledge. Swinburne briefly discusses the debate over the truth-value of counterfactuals and concludes that it is possible that no one gives a counterfactual of freedom truth-value, but it is 'barely true'.[105]

David Basinger proposes this defence of the truth of counterfactuals. He claims that they simply are true, they do not need to be brought about by God or the agent.[106] William Hasker in 'A refutation of Middle Knowledge'[107] claims that somebody must make a counterfactual true. He asks: 'Who or what is it (if anything) that brings it about that these propositions are true?'.[108] Hasker uses the illustration of a research student, Elizabeth, and whether or not she will accept a particular grant if it is offered to her. He argues that it is not God who brings about the truth of counterfactuals.

> For in many cases, if not all, it will be God who brings it about that the antecedent of the conditional is true (for example, he might in some way influence Elizabeth's advisor to recommend her for the grant), and it is hard to avoid the conclusion that it would be God who bought it about that the action described in the consequent was performed, which contradicts the assumption that the act is done freely.[109]

The other obvious candidate for bringing about the truth of a counterfactual, is the agent. However Hasker also dismisses this answer. This leads to the further difficulty that the agent, in this case Elizabeth, is not responsible for her actions.

> On the proposed view, Elizabeth is not responsible for the fact that, if she were offered the grant, she would accept it ... Nor, we may assume, is she responsible for the truth of the antecedent, i.e. for the fact she is offered the grant. And if she is not, then the theory of middle knowledge ends up by undermining one of its essential purposes, that of preserving the freedom and responsibility of the human agent.[110]

---

[105] Swinburne, 1998 p.131.

[106] David Basinger, 'Middle Knowledge and Classical Christian Thought' *Religious Studies* vol. 22 (1986) p.421.

[107] William Hasker, 'A Refutation of Middle Knowledge' *Nous* (1986) pp. 545 - 557.

[108] Hasker, 1986 p.547.

[109] Hasker, 1986 pp.547-548.

[110] Hasker, 1986 p.553.

Clearly the agent is not normally responsible for the truth of the antecedent, in this case Elizabeth is not responsible for being offered the grant.[111] If the agent is neither responsible for the counterfactual then the agent does not control the consequent. In this case the agent is not responsible for his/her own actions. Clearly, then, this is not an acceptable defence of middle knowledge and in order for a defence of middle knowledge to retain the freedom and responsibility of the agent, it would seem that the agent must give truth-value to counterfactuals of freedom.

The agent must be responsible for the counterfactual and therefore for the consequent, otherwise a counterfactual of freedom cannot refer to what I would freely do in a situation I am never actually going to be in. Hasker asks:

> How might it be possible for the agent to bring it about that a given counterfactual of freedom is true? It would seem that the only possible way in which the agent might do this is by performing the action specified in the consequent of the conditional under the conditions specified in the antecedent.[112]

The agent makes the counterfactual true by actually doing it. If this is the case, then only counterfactuals that are actualised can ever be true, and strictly these counterfactuals are not known through middle knowledge, as counterfactuals that will be actualised are known by God through foreknowledge. Thus Hasker rules out the truth-value of counterfactuals known only by middle knowledge. However, the actualised counterfactual is true even before it is brought about by the agent doing it. Is its truth-value acquired from the fact that the counterfactual *will* be actualised and is therefore true? A discussion in philosophy of religion has concerned the correspondence theory of truth. As Craig explains: 'All that the view of truth as correspondence requires of future tense statements is that the realities described *will* exist'.[113] Therefore the counterfactual that will be actualised is always true simply because the agent will perform the action described. However Craig continues:

> Similarly, at the time at which counterfactual statements are true, it is not required that the circumstances or actions referred to actually exist. The view of truth as correspondence requires only that such actions *would* be taken if the specified circumstances *were* to exist.[114]

---

[111] Indirectly Elizabeth may bring about the truth of the antecedent by being the best qualified candidate etc.; however this is not really relevant to the purpose of this discussion.
[112] Hasker, 1986 p.548.
[113] William Lane Craig, *The Only Wise God* (1987) Grand Rapids: Baker Book House p.140. For some of the issues raised in the debate over the correspondence theory of truth, see Ruth Garrett Millikan, 'The Price of Correspondence Truth' *Nous* vol.20 (1986) pp.453-468.
[114] Craig, 1987 p.140.

Therefore the counterfactual that is never actualised is true because it accurately describes what an agent would do in a particular circumstance. The fact that the described situation is never faced by that agent does not affect the truth of the counterfactual. In this case the counterfactual corresponds to a state which *would* be true rather than one which *will* be true. Gray writes:

> We can conclude that counterfactual propositions are true in so far as they express what *would* happen. It does not matter that we cannot determine the truth-value of these propositions, as a future-tense proposition carries a truth-value which is present, even before we can verify it.[115]

Thus a counterfactual, even one which will not be actualised has a truth-value as it corresponds to a state which would be true, were that agent to face that situation.

Hasker suggests that other than actualising the counterfactual, the agent could do something which would ensure the truth of the counterfactual, should the situation arise.

> In order to bring it about that the counterfactual is true, the agent must do something which excludes the possibility of her failing to perform that action under those conditions. But if she were to perform some other action which would guarantee that the specified action would be performed (e.g., if Elizabeth were to do something in advance which would make it impossible for her to reject the grant) then this other action would deprive her of freedom with respect to the specified action, which contradicts the assumption that she is free with respect to the specified action.[116]

However this is not the case. Suppose a condition of being short-listed for the grant is that you must agree to accepting the grant should you be offered it. By agreeing to this, Elizabeth effectively makes it impossible that she reject the grant if it is offered to her. Hasker claims that this means she is not free with regard to the question of whether or not she will accept the grant. However Elizabeth is no less free in relation to the grant, in this scenario than if this were not a condition of being short listed. All that changes is that Elizabeth exercises her free choice about whether or not to accept the grant earlier in the process than she may have otherwise done. Making a choice sooner rather than later cannot sensibly be considered a restriction upon our freedom, otherwise we would be freer the less decisions we made and the later we made them and this cannot be the case. It is not

---

[115] Gray, 1996 p.300. Gray does ultimately reject middle knowledge, see pp.306-307 and pp.332-333.

[116] Hasker, 1986 p.548.

relevant at what point one exercises one's freedom in relation to a particular issue
in order to establish whether one is free in relation to that issue.

Thus a counterfactual has truth-value by corresponding to what the agent
would do, if she were in that situation, and therefore the counterfactual is given
truth-value by the agent. What the agent would do in a given situation depends
upon the character and free choice of the agent. However a further difficulty with
the agent giving counterfactuals truth-value is that in order for middle knowledge to
be useful, God must know the counterfactuals before creation. Craig writes:

> Whatever God knows, He has known from eternity, so that there is
> no temporal succession in God's knowledge, nonetheless there does
> exist a sort of logical succession in God's knowledge in that His
> knowledge of certain propositions is conditionally or explanatorily
> prior to His knowledge of certain other propositions. That is to say,
> God's knowledge of a particular set of propositions depends
> asymmetrically on His knowledge of a certain other set of
> propositions and is in this sense posterior to it.[117]

On this account, God knows counterfactuals of freedom prior to creation and thus
this knowledge assists God in creation. Craig explains:

> Whereas by His natural knowledge God knew what any free creature
> *could* do in any set of circumstances, now in this second moment
> God knows what any free creature *would* so in any set of
> circumstances. This is not because the circumstances causally
> determine the creature's choice, but simply because this is how the
> creature would freely choose.[118]

Thus a God with middle knowledge knows in advance how any free creature would
choose in any situation and not just in the situations they will actually encounter.

Thus Swinburne and Basinger's claim that counterfactuals can be true
without being made true by anyone, is rejected in favour of the view that it is the
agent who gives truth to counterfactuals. Swinburne also claims that counterfactuals
cannot be free if God already knows them. However, as with foreknowledge, God
knowing an event in advance is not the cause of that event and therefore middle
knowledge does not invalidate the freedom of counterfactuals. Freddoso admits that
the 'argument of how God has middle knowledge is arguably the weakest link in
the Molinist chain'.[119] However it seems that if the correspondence theory of truth
is employed a counterfactual does have truth-value, and therefore the coherence of
God's middle knowledge can be defended. Having established that God is able to

---

[117] Craig, 1989 p.177.
[118] Craig, 1989 p.177.
[119] Freddoso, 1988 pp.52-53.

use knowledge of counterfactuals in creation, I will discuss in chapter 6 how middle knowledge could have allowed God to create a free world with a certain outcome.

Conclusion

Swinburne is quite right that God knows all that it is logically possible to know, however what can be known is a much wider category than Swinburne has allowed. Swinburne further claims that God cannot have foreknowledge or middle knowledge if the agent is to be genuinely free, however he does not adequately defend this view and it is not clear that God knowing a free action before it is done affects the freedom of the action. Thus Swinburne's grounds for claiming that God does not have foreknowledge or middle knowledge are rejected and therefore God's position in relation to the outcome of creation changes. With foreknowledge and middle knowledge God cannot be surprised by any future events and therefore has a greater control at the point of creation.

Conclusion

In order to constructively reject Swinburne's claim that hell is the free choice of the individual it will be necessary to defend the view that we are made with a desire for God and thus would not ultimately chose to reject God. This is Hick's position and I will look at this in the following chapter.

There are then several difficulties with Swinburne's defence of hell. He fails to show that individual's decisively shape their character in the way he claims they do or that any individual would finally choose hell. Swinburne, by denying God's foreknowledge cannot justify his claim that there will not ultimately be a universalist outcome. However the most significant problem is with his account of human freedom. Not only does he fail to show that compatibilst freedom is not a genuine human freedom but his own account of libertarian freedom is incompatible with his view of shaping character and his defence of hell fails if either of these are removed. Further Swinburne's account of libertarian freedom is ultimately unrealistic and once qualifications are added to it, it is not far removed from the compatibilst freedom which he firmly rejects.

Chapter 4

John Hick's Universalism

Introduction

In this chapter I will look at Hick's rejection of hell and defence of universalism. For Hick the moment of decision is of great importance to his theory and is an important justification for his account of final universal salvation. The problem of hell for Hick is very similar to the three-point problem outlined in Chapter 1. He does not believe that the existence of an eternal hell is compatible with a God of love. Thus Hick believes that a Christian account of God, which he takes to be a God of love excludes belief in an eternal hell. However Hick also wants to avoid suggesting that we are not free to make our own choices or that there is no value in our soul-making existence in this life. Thus Hick constructs a theory of eventual universal salvation, where all people will through a progression of lives, eventually, of their own free choice, arrive at their ultimate resting place with God.

John Hick

John Hick is one of the most prominent philosophers of religion of the late twentieth century. His work has had considerable influence in his field and he has encouraged many to tackle the challenges which he has identified as significant in contemporary theology. This has not always made him popular amongst the adherents and authorities of his own religious tradition.[1] Hick has responded to the challenges of the world in which he lives. This has not been an easy task and Hick's work has gained him what approaches notoriety in certain sections of the church. Indeed Keith W. Clements names Hick as one of five of 'this generation's discomforters'.[2]

As a young man at University in Hull studying law, Hick had a conversion experience. He reports that over a few days he became very aware of the presence

---

[1] Indeed in 1961 -1962 Hick's suitability to serve as a United Presbyterian minister in the USA was challenged by: 'A very conservative minority [who] sought to exclude me from the ministry of the United Presbyterian Church for declining to affirm one of the more manifestly mythological aspects of Christian tradition'. John Hick *God and the Universe of Faiths* (1973) London: Macmillan p.183.

[2] Keith W. Clements *Lovers of Discord: Twentieth Century Theological Controversies in England* (1988) London: SPCK p.219.

of God.[3] He joined the Christian Union and although he enjoyed it, he recalls that he was 'already beginning to sense in it a certain narrowness and a lack of sympathy with questioning thought'.[4] This kind of environment soon became too stifling for Hick and after the war, during which he was a conscientious objector, he could no longer accept this sort of dogmatic thought. Hick writes that anyone in:

> The conservative evangelical thought world, and who has a questioning mind, will find that he has to face challenges to the belief system within which his Christian faith was first available to him, and will almost certainly be led by rational or moral considerations to modify or discard many of its elements.[5]

Hick read philosophy at Edinburgh, and then went to Oxford to read for a doctorate in philosophy, entitled *The Relationship Between Faith and Belief,* before entering ministerial training at Cambridge. After serving as a Presbyterian Minister in Northumberland for three years, Hick was Stuart Professor of Christian Philosophy at Cornell University from 1959 - 1964.[6] He then returned to England to take up the post of Lecturer in the Philosophy of Religion at Cambridge University. In 1966, what is arguably Hick's *magnum opus, Evil and the God of Love* was published.

Hick's move to Birmingham in 1967 had a significant and lasting influence on his theology. Living in a multi-cultural and multi-religious city, Hick found plenty of new challenges to his faith. It was here that his preoccupation with religious pluralism began, and it is that which has dominated his later career. Hick recalls in several of his writings, the effect it had upon him to encounter holy people from other religious traditions. He was no longer able to ignore the existence of the other great world religions, or indeed to dismiss them as misguided. This challenged Hick to consider the relationship between Christianity and other religions and this is a challenge which he still confronts. In 'Living in a multi-cultural society' Hick writes: 'This has always been the way in which the divine Spirit teaches new truths - not by issuing verbally inspired formulations but by leading men and women into new and challenging historical situations'.[7] It is this approach which characterises Hick's work: his response to those issues in society and the world which challenge theology and philosophy.

Hick's first major work *Faith and Knowledge* was concerned with the epistemology of religion and much of Hick's early work was concerned with religious language. Hick's inaugural lecture at the University of Birmingham in 1968, was a discussion of what was for him, at that time, 'Theology's Central

---

[3] John Hick, *God Has Many Names* (1980) London: Macmillan pp.2-3.

[4] Hick, 1980 p.3.

[5] Hick, 1980 p.3.

[6] These biographical details are from Paul Badham, *A John Hick Reader* (1993) Basingstoke: Macmillan p.3.

[7] John Hick, 'Living in a Multi-cultural Society: Practical Reflections of a Theologian' *Expository Times* vol. 89 no.4 (1978) p.101.

Problem'. This address explains: 'In a sentence the issue is whether distinctively religious utterances are instances of the cognitive or the non-cognitive uses of language'.[8] For Hick it was important to show that religious language was meaningful and he claims that religious language is meaningful because it can ultimately be verified in the afterlife.

God and the Universe of Faiths was published in 1973 and is concerned with what was to be the new 'central problem' of theology for Hick - developing a theology of religions. Hick visited Sri Lanka and India in 1974 and returned to India in 1975 - 1976. This experience of eastern life contributed significantly to his next publication. *Death and Eternal Life* reflected not just Hick's interest in the serious study of eastern religions but also his continued interest in the after-life. As he had previously done in *Evil and the God of Love*, Hick discusses his objections to hell and his inclination towards universalism. Another area of theology which has concerned Hick is the uniqueness of Christ. *The Myth of God Incarnate* was perhaps perceived to be one of the most controversial books with which Hick has been involved. Its publication in 1977 was followed by something of a storm in the world of British theology. The book suggested that the idea that in Jesus, God had become man should be taken mythically. Hick contributed to a follow up to this book *Incarnation and Myth: The Debate Continued*, published in 1979.

Hick began the 1980s with the publication of *God Has Many Names*, which reflected his growing interest in the relationship of Christianity to other faiths. In 1982 Hick moved to the Claremont Graduate School, California to take up the full-time post as Danforth Professor of the Philosophy of Religion. In 1986 Hick was invited to give the Gifford Lectures in Edinburgh and these were later published as a comprehensive account of Hick's understanding of religion, *An Interpretation of Religion: Human Responses to the Transcendent* in 1989. Hick followed up *The Myth of God Incarnate,* with a work of his own entitled *The Metaphor of God Incarnate*, published in 1993. In this book, Hick suggests that the idea that God in person, founded the Christian religion is understood to be figurative language, and Hick believes that this change in focus enables both the Church and individual Christians to participate in the 'global theology' which he advocates. *The Rainbow of Faiths* published in 1995 is written as a dialogue and concentrates on the relationship between the major faiths. Hick's most recent book *The Fifth Dimension - An Exploration into the Spiritual Realm*, published in 1999 is really Hick's description of the 'big picture' and draws on his earlier material to produce an account of his understanding of the universe and the place of religions and humans within it.

Although the topic of eschatology has not been given much explicit coverage by Hick since *Evil and the God of Love* and *Death and Eternal Life*, his rejection of hell and affirmation of universal salvation are integral to other areas of his work. The areas in which he has shown particular interest throughout his career in many ways overlap. The sense in which Jesus can be said to be unique, of course

---

[8] This address is published as the first chapter of *God and the Universe of Faiths* Hick, 1973 p.1.

has great significance on Christian attitudes to other religions. Hick, despite his claim that he remains a Christian, has been variously criticised for his unorthodox theology. Stafford Betty writes of him that, 'Hick is like a kite–flyer who, in order to allow his kite maximum height and freedom, cuts the string'.[9] and D'Costa accuses him of advocating a 'covert agnosticism'.[10] However, our concern in this work is not with Hick's later shifts to try to accommodate all religions in his revolution, but to evaluate his arguments against hell and his reason for accepting universal salvation, within the context of the Christian tradition.

The God of Love

Since the mid 1980s, Hick has been dogged by the criticism that his thought is no longer within the boundaries of a Christian framework. The purpose of this work is to discuss the viability of a Christian theory of universalism and thus it seems necessary to determine a minimum criteria of what will be classed as 'Christian' thought. It is of course, a highly subjective exercise to determine what is within and what is beyond the boundaries of a Christian framework. Indeed the various Churches constantly struggle with this question, and it could undoubtedly be the subject of a book in itself. The definition decided upon here will perhaps be unsatisfactory as a general account of Christian belief, but will be helpful for the purposes of this study.

In his earliest works, Hick held to an orthodox view of the Incarnation. Indeed one of his earliest published articles was a criticism of the unorthodox Christology of D.M. Baille.[11] In *Faith and Knowledge,* Hick writes: 'Only God himself knows his infinite nature: and our human belief about that nature is based upon his self-revelation in Christ to men'.[12] Thus we see in this work, a very Christocentric view of God. Hick holds that the content of that revelation was essentially love. In *Christianity at the Centre* he writes: 'The love for men and women that we see in Jesus of Nazareth is *God's* love for them embodied in a particular time and place in the attitudes and action of a human being'.[13] Gillis writes that in this volume: 'There is no doubt that Hick holds to the doctrine of the Incarnation in this presentation of a contemporary theological view of Christianity'.[14] And it is clear that his thought at this stage is firmly rooted in a God of love.

[9] L.S. Betty, 'The Glitch in *An Interpretation of Religion'* in Harold Hewitt (ed.), *Problems in the Philosophy of Religion: Critical Studies of the Work of John Hick* (1991) Basingstoke: Macmillan p.101.

[10] Gavin D'Costa, 'John Hick and Religious Pluralism' in Hewitt (ed.), 1991 p.6.

[11] John Hick, 'The Christology of D. M. Baille' *Scottish Journal of Theology* vol.11 (1958) pp.1- 12.

[12] John Hick, *Faith and Knowledge* 2nd Edition (1966) Ithaca: Cornell University Press, referred to as 1966(b), p.190.

[13] John Hick, *Christianity at the Centre* (1968) London: Macmillan p.28.

[14] Chester Gillis, *A Question of Final Belief: John Hick's Pluralistic Theory of Salvation*

However, in later works, Hick reassess his understanding of the Incarnation, and claims that it is not actually a coherent doctrine. Most notably in *The Myth of God Incarnate* Hick asserts: 'That Jesus was God the Son incarnate is not literally true, since it has no literal meaning'.[15] For many, this takes Hick's work beyond a Christian framework. Molly Truman Marshall writes: 'The effect of Hick's reductionist Christology is to leave no viable basis for a continuing devotion to the Lordship of Jesus Christ which seems to jettison the core of Christian faith'.[16] The follow-up book to *The Myth of God Incarnate*, contains a section entitled 'Are the Authors of the Myth still Christian?' Brian Hebblethwaite writes that although the authors are:

> Christians in the sense of churchmen and followers of Christ ... they are not, to my mind, Christian views, in the sense of views which the church could ever endorse as permissible variants within the broad spectrum of its official doctrine.[17]

Hick, and the other authors of *The Myth of God Incarnate* hold that this reinterpretation of the concept of Incarnation was, rather than being damaging to the Christian faith, helpful for many believers. Although he denies the deity of Christ, Hick is still a follower of Christ. In *The Centre of Christianity* Hick writes:

> The humanist should be willing to join the Christian in looking again at the Centre of Christianity, which is the person of Jesus, and at the beliefs about God and about the living of life and facing of death which have grown out of the impact of this person.[18]

Christ has not been removed from the centre of Christianity, Hick claims that it is not necessary to affirm the Incarnation to be able to respond to Christ. He continues:

> We do not have to go beyond his [Jesus'] humanity to find the Christian starting point. The original response was made by his disciples to Jesus as a man, though it was a response which soon deepened into a religious faith; and if we today come to share their faith we are likely to do so by first being stirred either by the qualities of the human figure or the meaning of his teaching.[19]

(1989) Basingstoke: Macmillan p.74.

[15] Hick, 1977 (c) p.178.

[16] Molly Truman Marshall, *No Salvation Outside the Church? A Critical Inquiry* (1993) Lewiston, New York: Edwin Mellen Press.

[17] Brian Hebblethwaite, '*The Myth* and Christian Faith' in Goulder (ed.) 1979 p.16.

[18] John Hick, *The Centre of Christianity* (1977) London: SCM Press, referred to as 1977(b) p.13.

[19] Hick, 1977 (b) p.19.

Thus it seems possible that Hick's 'reduced' christology need not take him outside of a Christian framework as it still allows Hick to be a follower of the God of love revealed in Christ.

This Christology allows Hick to develop his theory that the great world religions are responses to the one God who inhabits the centre of our universe of faiths. Hick's belief in the God of love revealed in the person of Jesus, leads him to affirm:

> That God is the Creator of all mankind, that he has limitless love towards all men, and that he is seeking to save all men and women, and not only Christians and their Old Testament spiritual ancestors ... Given a faith in the universal saving activity of God, it is impossible to hold that salvation is only for those living within one particular strand of history, namely the Judaic-Christian strand.[20]

It is this understanding of God which is the basis for Hick's Copernican Revolution.[21] Hick describes the old Ptolemaic understanding of the universe, with the earth at the centre and the sun, moon and stars moving around the earth. As astronomers realised that the planets did not move around the earth, they did not abandon this theory but rather added epicycles to chart the movement of the planets. The Copernican revolution proved that in fact the earth and the planets moved around the sun. Hick suggests that similarly, the old way of thinking of Christianity as being at the centre should be replaced with a God-centered universe with each of the different great world religions revolving around God.

Hick's Copernican revolution has been widely criticised, as it is based on an understanding of God revealed by Christ, but requires that this revelation be accepted as one amongst many and not viewed as the normative revelation of God. D'Costa asks: 'Can Hick's God of love be divorced from the events which disclose such a God - that is Christ? If not, then Hick's move away from Christocentrism is untenable'.[22] Similarly, Chester Gillis observes: 'We only know that God is love and that there is salvation because of Christ'.[23] Clark H. Pinnock writes: 'God loses decisive meaning when the Incarnation is reduced to myth, and loses all content once God is required to be the centre of religions, including those without any clear belief in God'.[24] However at this stage Hick retains his belief in the God who was revealed by Christ, despite his denial of the divinity of Christ.

[20] Hick, 1968 p.74.

[21] See chapter 9 of John Hick, *The Second Christianity* (1983) London: SCM Press.

[22] Gavin D'Costa, *John Hick's Theology of Religions* (1987) Lanham: University Press of America p.102.

[23] Gillis, 1989 p.170. See also Julius Lipner, 'Does Copernicus Help?' *Religious Studies* vol.13 no.2 (1977) p.253 and Marshall, 1993 p.192.

[24] Pinnock, 1992 p.46.

There are undoubtedly many aspects of Christianity as it has developed through the centuries that we can leave aside. But it seems to me that we cannot, if we are to respond realistically to Jesus of Nazareth, leave aside that God in whom he believed.[25]

Hebblethwaite writes that the authors of *The Myth of God Incarnate* although ascribing to a belief only in the historical person of Jesus, hold fast to a belief in the personal God revealed by Christ. He writes: 'The authors of *The Myth* and their critics are agreed that faith in God is a necessary condition of genuinely Christian faith'.[26] Indeed Hick asserts that Christianity 'has always steadfastly adhered to the pure monotheism of its Judaic source in attributing both omnipotence and infinite goodness to God'.[27] Hick writes that one of the most fundamental items of Christian belief is:

> Belief in the reality of the infinite and eternal God, who is the sole creator of heaven and earth and of all things visible and invisible. This belief is so deeply rooted in the Bible, in Christian worship, and in Christian theology of all schools that it cannot be abandoned without vitally affecting the nature of Christianity itself. The absolute monotheism of the Judaic-Christian faith is not, so to say, negotiable.[28]

When Hick later begins to negotiate the idea of God in the hope of developing a concept of the Real, which would not exclude religions who do not believe in a personal God, he steps beyond his own liberal boundaries of Christian thought. Although Hick abandons the idea of the self-revelation of God, he still seems to believe in the universal salvific will of God.[29] However Hick cannot attribute love manifested in a universal salvific will to 'the Real' and remain agnostic about the nature of the Real. Chris Sinkinson observes that:

> Hick's case for universalism depends upon the truth of the Christian conception of God as personal, all powerful and all loving. The position to which his universalism leads him requires that he remain uncertain about the ultimate validity of universalism.[30]

Thus Hick has moved away from his starting point for universalism.

The 1985 publication *Problems of Religious Pluralism* is a collection of articles written between 1977 and 1984, and clearly shows the shift in Hick's

---

[25] Hick, 1968 p.23.

[26] Hebblethwaite, 1979 p.16.

[27] Hick, 1966 p.4.

[28] Hick, 1966 p.35.

[29] John Hick, *A Rainbow of Faiths* (1995) London: SCM Press p.19.

[30] Chris Sinkinson, *John Hick: An Introduction to his Theology* (1995) Leicester: RTSF p.28.

thought over this time. In the 1977 article 'Present and Future Life' he writes: 'All schools of thought are agreed that, whatever we may mean by "God", we at least mean unlimited personal consciousness'.[31] However in a later article, 'On Grading Religions' Hick writes:

> The ultimately real is also the ultimately valuable. It is a limitlessly loving or merciful God; or it is the infinite being-consciousness-bliss of Brahman; or the ineffable 'further shore' of *nirvana* or *sunyata*, in whose emptiness of ego the world of time and change is found again as wondrous being.[32]

The title of the 1989 book *An Interpretation of Religion: Human Responses to the Transcendent* further demonstrates Hick's move away from affirming theism.[33] Hick is no longer concerned with his original apologetic task of proving the validity of religious claims, but seems concerned to defend religions themselves rather than their object. D'Costa writes: 'Over the years Hick has therefore moved from *Christocentrism* to *Theocentrism* to *Realocentrism*' and he continues that Hick 'perpetuates a vague form of agnosticism'.[34] Similarly, Peter Byrne writes: 'I have argued that Hick's views contain an agnosticism which entails that unreliability of religious conceptions and posits too great a gulf between belief and its object'.[35] Hick himself had previously written that in practical terms, agnosticism amounts to the same as atheism:

> As a ground of action - whether the intellectual activity of forming a view of our human situation or the concrete activity of our living our human life - agnosticism comes to the same thing as atheism. That is to say, the agnostic and the atheist both have to proceed for all practical purposes on the basis that there is no God and on the assumption that a humanistic understanding of the universe is valid.[36]

Thus beyond Hick's shift from theocentrism his work will not aid this inquiry into a Christian theory of universalism. When Hick no longer affirms belief in a personal God, he goes beyond our Christian framework, which for the purposes of this book I will define as a God of love as revealed in Jesus. It is often difficult to isolate the

---

[31] This article was first published as John Hick, 'Present and Future Life' *Harvard Theological Review* vol.71 no.1-2 (1977), referred to as 1977(d), p.132.

[32] John Hick, 'On Grading Religions' *Religious Studies* vol.17 no.4 (1981) p.459.

[33] Indeed in this work he writes: 'This [belief in the transcendent] is not of the essence of religion - for, as I have just suggested, there is no such essence - nevertheless most forms of religion have affirmed a salvific reality that transcends ... human beings and the world'. John Hick, *An Interpretation of Religion: Human Responses to the Transcendent* (1989) Basingstoke: Macmillan p.6.

[34] D'Costa, 1991 pp.5-6.

[35] Peter Byrne, 'John Hick's Philosophy of World Religions' *Scottish Journal of Theology* vol.35 no.4 (1982) p.299.

[36] Hick, 1968 p.12.

exact point in a person's work and thought where a shift in their position occurs. Generally this happens gradually, over a period of time and this is true of Hick's move away from theocentrism. However, it is necessary to decide a cut-off point. As we have seen from the book *Problems of Religious Pluralism*,[37] Hick's thought moved away from theism in the early 1980s. In the 1983 publications *The Second Christianity*[38] and *Why Believe in God?*[39] Hick is still concerned to defend (a much modified) Christian theism. In *The Second Christianity* Hick writes: 'The idea of God is the idea of an eternal at-least-personal Being who has created everything that exists other than himself'.[40] In *Why believe in God?* Hick repeatedly affirms that he, unlike his co-authors of *The Myth of God Incarnate* Michael Goulder and Don Cupitt, does still believe in God. This chapter will then focus on Hick's work up until 1983. However later works may occasionally be referred to if they contain Hick's direct responses to criticisms of his earlier work.

The objection may be raised that Hick's later work and his shift to Realocentrism and even beyond that to soteriocentrism[41] are simply the logical outworkings of his earlier position. However this work is not concerned directly with Hick's Copernican Revolution and global theology *per se*, only in as much as they affect his theory of universalism. And further, I believe that it is a valid aim to see if Hick's universalism can stand as a coherent theory within the broad Christian framework which has been defined, and in which it was developed. Indeed Hick's universalism, as we have seen, is based on a God of love. When he moves beyond affirming a God of love his universalism is ungrounded, as he no longer affirms the major premise of his argument. Thus we can only examine Hick's universalism, as primarily presented in *Evil and the God of Love* and *Death and Eternal Life*, effectively from the works in which he still held to the premises on which it is based.

The Moment of Decision

Traditional theories have claimed that on the point of death, one's eternal destiny will be decided. Hick argues that one's eternal resting place should not be decided on the state of one's soul at death.

> The sentence pronounced upon the individual as he passed out of this life became the real crisis upon which men's hopes and fears were fixed, and the popular Christian view came to be that each man as he died went to heaven (directly or via purgatory) or to hell.[42]

---

[37] John Hick, *Problems of Religious Pluralism* (1985) London: Macmillan.

[38] Hick, 1983.

[39] Hick and Goulder, 1983.

[40] Hick, 1983 p.11.

[41] See D'Costa, 1991.

[42] Hick, 1976 p.194.

Hick comments: 'This scheme is unrealistic both as regards what is to happen before death and as regards what is to happen after death'.[43] It is integral to Hick's philosophy that 'salvation in its fullness involves the actual transformation of human character'[44] and as we can observe that this does not take place in this life, Hick surmises: 'There must, then, be further time beyond death in which the process of perfecting can continue'.[45] Death is not the end of the process of human development.

Purgatory

Hick readily admits that there are many people who, by the time of their death are not prepared for their eternal resting place with God. In *Faith and Knowledge* he writes:

> It may then be a condition of post-mortem verification that we be already in some degree conscious of God by an uncompelled response to his modes of revelation in this world. It may be that such a voluntary consciousness of God is an essential element in the fulfillment of the divine purpose for human nature, so that the verification of theism ... can only be experienced by those who have already entered upon an awareness of God by the religious mode of apperception which we call faith.[46]

Thus those who in this life have not come to faith in any degree are not ready to experience the fulfillment of the divine purpose. Hick proposes that after death there is some sort of continued existence, for those who are not yet ready to join the company of heaven. Either these people must be transformed after death into perfect people ready for the company of heaven, or there must be some further time in which they can continue to develop into 'children of God'.

> The difficulty attaching to the first alternative is that it is far from clear that an individual who had been instantaneously perfected would be in any morally significant sense the same person as the frail, erring mortal who had lived and died ... if we are thus to be transmuted in the twinkling of an eye into perfect creatures, the whole earthly travail of faith and moral effort is rendered needless.[47]

---

[43] Hick, 1976 p.455. Hick is particularly interested in the work of Laudislaus Boros. See Ladislaus Boros, *The Moment of Truth: Mysterium Mortis* (1962) London: Burns & Oates discussed in Hick, 1976 pp. 235 - 240.

[44] Hick, 1976 p.455.

[45] Hick, 1976 p.455.

[46] Hick, 1966 (b) p.192.

[47] Hick, 1966 p.347.

Hick accounts for the sufferings one must undergo in this world by saying that they are necessary for our moral development. Virtues automatically built into our nature would be Hick claims, valueless. Therefore if God initially intends us to develop during this life, it would be contradictory for him to bring that development to perfection instantaneously at death. Rather, Hick suggests, God desires us to develop, of our own free will into 'children of God'. Thus in order for God's purpose for us to be fully worked out, we must have opportunity after this life to continue our development.

Hick appeals to the Roman Catholic concept of purgatory. He observes that within this tradition the concept of purgatory was developed because:

> The great majority of those destined by grace for heaven (whether this be all men or only some) are too imperfect to enter it immediately; and purgatory comprehends the range of further experiences through which they face the consequences of their own sins and become purified in character and prepared for the beatific vision.[48]

Hick suggests that this idea of purgatory is along the right lines and redevelops the doctrine to create his theory of a progressive after-life.

Hick divides life after death into the ultimate state, and further stages of life which are still leading to the ultimate state. He is influenced by the insights of other, particularly eastern, religions.

> When we listen to what the great religious traditions say about man's future beyond the grave it becomes important to distinguish between eschatologies, or 'pictures' of the ultimate state ... and pareschatologies or 'pictures' of what happens between death and that ultimate state.[49]

Thus Hick proposes a series of progressive afterlives which will, sooner or later, lead to the ultimate state.

The Progressive Afterlives

According to Hick then, this present life is not our only opportunity for development into children of God. He believes that the purpose of our creation is for fellowship with God, and asks: 'Would it not contradict God's love for the creatures made in His image if He caused them to pass out of existence while His purpose for them was still largely unfulfilled?'.[50] His answer to that is, of course,

---

[48] Hick, 1976 p.201.

[49] Hick, 1976 p.12.

[50] Hick, 1966 p.338.

'yes' and his solution is to suggest that one experiences any number of different lives after this one. As many as are required to complete the process of fulfilling the potential one was given when made in the image of God. Hick believes that this is the only way in which this present life can have sufficient purpose.

> If in the end the human individual is brought, through a process of soul-making continued in other spheres beyond this world, to the perfection intended for him by God, then the meaning of this present life is transformed for those who suffer and is enhanced for those for whom it is already good.[51]

These further lives then, like this one, offer the opportunity for soul making and development. Hick explains of the after-lives that: 'At every stage regress is possible as well as progress and that the total journey of the self from human animal to child of God is no smooth and automatic ascent but a hard and adventurous journey'.[52]

Our lives after death will then continue until we become children of God. These lives after death will offer further opportunity for moral development.[53] Hick writes: 'The further lives are not mere quantative continuations of the present life, but part of a spiritual progress towards the ultimate state which lies beyond the series of finite lives'.[54] Each individual will have as many lives as are required for God to bring them to himself. Hick affirms:

> God will eventually succeed in His purpose of winning all men to Himself in faith and love. That this is indeed God's purpose in relation to man is surely evident from the living revelation of that purpose in Jesus Christ.[55]

For Hick then, a Christian view of life after death must include further lives in which to continue our moral and spiritual development.

Hick explores the teaching of certain eastern religions, which posit more than one existence after death. The Buddhist and Hindu religions both advocate theories of reincarnation. Hick claims that some forms of reincarnation theory are not unlike the series of after-lives he postulates.

---

[51] John Hick, 'The Purpose of Evil' *The Listener* August 12 (1965) p.232.

[52] Hick, 1977 (d) p.16.

[53] The objection could be made that there is no point dying if after death we continue living in similar environments. Hick believes that death is a necessary part of our journey, which enables us to live, knowing that it is for a limited time. He claims: 'It is the prospect of its termination that gives urgency and meaning to our life in time'. Hick, 1976 p.456. Thus he concludes: 'The function of death is to give us, at the present stage of our spiritual growth, a portion of life that we can cope with', Hick, 1977 (b) p.113.

[54] John Hick, 'An Irenaean Theodicy' in Stephen T. Davies (ed.), *Encountering Evil* (1981) Edinburgh: T & T Clarke p.66.

[55] Hick, 1966 p.342.

The Irenaean type of theology rejects the thought that men are at death distributed to an eternal heaven or hell. It thinks instead in terms of continued responsible life in which the soul-making process continues in other environments beyond this world.[56]

The differences between Hindu reincarnation and the 'Irenaean' type progressive after life are:

Not very great. For they agree concerning the basic principle of continued responsible life in which the individual may still learn and grow by interacting with other human beings in a common environment or environments. They differ only as to *where* this continued life takes place.[57]

Thus Hick finds the paraeschatology of Hinduism comparable to his own theory. From the Buddhist religion, Hick looks in some detail at the *Bardo Thödol,* or the *Tibetan Book of the Dead.*[58] This book from the tantric branch of Mahayana Buddhism describes the state between death and rebirth. Individuals go through three distinct stages after death. The first is an encounter with an intense light, which is actually an encounter with the ultimate reality. If the self is ready to abandon their ego-existence they will at this point enter Nirvana and never return to earth. However, most do not even recognise the ultimate reality during their encounter and they continue to exist as individuals. The second stage in the bardo world consists of a series of 'karmic illusions' which are formed by one's own past thoughts and deeds. Reality is again encountered, but this time it is seen as angry and frightening. There follows an 'experience of inexorable judgement before the Lord of the Dead and of ensuing punishments in various hells'.[59] The third stage in the *bardo* world is when the soul is drawn towards its next birth.

Hick comments:

A striking feature of this account of the soul's experiences between physical death and the next phase of its existence is the *Bardo Thödol's* insistence that the mind created its own post-mortem world in accordance with its beliefs ... after death, released from the pressures and threats which sustain our self-image in this life, the mind realistically appraises itself in a kind of psychoanalytic

---

[56] Hick, 1976 p.370.

[57] Hick, 1976 p.371.

[58] Padma Sambhua, *The Tibetan Book of the Dead* discovered by Karma Lingpa, translated by Robert A.F. Thurman (1994) London: Aquarian.

[59] Hick, 1976 p.403.

experience and the outcome reaches consciousness in the imagery provided by one's religious faith.[60]

The suggestion that each person will create their own post-mortem world, which: 'According to the indication both of the *Bardo Thödol* and of western mediumistic communication, is subjective or dream-like',[61] means that the various after-life scenarios, expected by adherents of different traditions, may each be fulfilled. The mind of an individual fully expecting the form of divine judgement described in the New Testament, would indeed project such a scenario. Hick explains that for such an individual:

> His coming to self awareness would have taken the form of a divine judgement ... a great assize in the presence of throngs of angels, saints and martyrs, presided over either by the towering figure of God the Father seated on a great white throne and shining in unapproachable light ... And from this divine judgement he would proceed towards something which he would anticipate under the imagery of heaven or purgatory or hell. His expectations might then create for him a period of blissful or painful experiences according to the pattern of his beliefs.[62]

In a sense the different expectations of each religion and the different expectations within those religions of individuals could all prove to be correct. For whatever one believes will happen after death, will perhaps be the situation created by one's own mind. Thus Hick writes:

> An inhabitant of our present secularized culture would - we may surmise - be more likely in the absence of any vivid and compelling religious or other expectations, to find that this next world is in many ways very like our present world. Since he would not know what else to expect.[63]

The continuation of existence until one is able to recognise the 'Real' described in the *Bardo Thödol*, is similar to Hick's own paraeschatology, and indeed his eschatology. However Hick concludes that these continued existences do not take place in this world, but in other realms. In this strain of Buddhism, the self eventually becomes part of the 'ultimate reality' however in Theravada Buddhism, the many reincarnations of the self are ultimately concluded in extinction. Hick finds this teaching highly objectionable. He writes: 'If there is any philosophy which is even more pessimistic [than the materialist and humanist philosophies], it

---

[60] Hick, 1976 p.403.

[61] Hick, 1976 p.414.

[62] Hick, 1976 p.415.

[63] Hick, 1976 p.416.

is the minimal and ultimately annihilationist version of Therevada Buddhism'.[64] It is intrinsic for Hick that continued existence after death should have an ultimate purpose, namely to allow individuals to: 'Grow as free beings towards that fullness of personal life, in conscious relationship to God'.[65]

Hick however, does not provide details of what will take place in these further existences which individuals will experience after the initial stage of subjective, dreamlike existence. He claims that ultimately we can only speculate concerning these various after-lives.

> We cannot know how many such worlds or series of worlds there are; and indeed the number and nature of the individual's successive embodiments will presumably depend upon what is needed for him to reach the point at which he transcends ego-hood and attains the ultimate unitive state.[66]

Thus the nature of one's stages after death will be dependent upon the progress one has made in this world toward reality-centredness. However Hick does state that existence beyond the *bardo* state:

> Will be a real spatio-temporal environment, functioning in accordance with its own laws, within which there will be a real personal life - a world with its own concrete character, its own history, its own absorbing and urgent concerns, its own perils, achievements, sacrifices.[67]

Each individual will have different experiences and it will not be until the 'ultimate unitive state' is reached that there is a common eschatology.

Hick is certain that whatever the nature of the final state it is not a reward or compensation for previous lives. He writes: 'The "good eschaton" will not be a reward or a compensation proportioned to each individual's trials, but an infinite good that would render worthwhile *any* finite suffering endured in the course of attaining to it'.[68] Rather than reward, for Hick, the point of the afterlife is fulfillment. Just as he objects to the idea of hell as retribution for sins, so Hick rejects the notion of heaven as reward for good deeds.

> There has always been something morally unattractive about the idea of the compensatory joys of heaven. It suggests a comparatively low

---

[64] Hick, 1976 p.437.
[65] Hick, 1976 p.49.
[66] Hick, 1976 p.419.
[67] Hick, 1976 p.418.
[68] Hick, 1966 p.341.

level of ethical insight centred upon the notion of justice as exact reciprocity.[69]

However Hick does not enter into much discussion about the nature of the final state. In *Death and Eternal Life* he does give some description of the nature the 'ultimate unitive state' may take.

> The individual's series of live culminates eventually in a last life beyond which there is no further embodiment but instead entry into the common Vision of God, or nirvana, or eternal consciousness of the atman in its relation to Ultimate Reality.[70]

Hick then concludes:

> Our eschatological speculation terminates in the idea of the unity of mankind in a state in which the ego-aspect of individual consciousness has been left behind and the relational aspect has developed into a total community which is one-in-many and many-in-one, existing in a state which is probably not embodied and probably not in time.[71]

Thus Hick is positive about the outcome of these lives and describes an ultimate state in which all will not only take part, but will be part.

Conclusion

Hick expands the traditional idea of purgatory and proposes a series of further lives in which there is opportunity to develop. The idea of a progressive after-life is crucial to Hick's theology in order to allow humans sufficient opportunity to fully develop into the 'children of God' which Hick thinks we are not only able, but are meant to become. Thus Hick rejects the teaching: 'At death a person's relationship to God is irrevocably fixed'.[72] Indeed for Hick, this relationship is not fixed until the individual reaches the ultimate state. The process of reaching that state may be a lengthy one or it may be relatively short depending on the progress of the individual. As Hick writes:

---

[69] Hick, 1976 p.160

[70] Hick, 1976 p.464

[71] Hick, 1976 p.464. Hick later reviews these conclusions, and points out that in *Death and Eternal Life* he had sided with 'Ramanuja against Shankara in speculating about the ultimate eschatological state. But in *An Interpretation of Religion* I had come to think that we are not justified in making any descriptive assertions about that ultimate state', Hick, 1995 p.72.

[72] This is one of the ten 'aspects of traditional theology which are, in the opinion of many theologians today (including myself) either quite untenable or open to serious doubt,' which he cites in 'The Reconstruction of Christian Belief for Today and Tomorrow: I' *Theology* vol.LXIII no.602 (1970) p.339.

> When we look at the best human lives, we can conceive of humanity reaching its perfection in them within one more life, and in others within a very few more. But when we look at the worst human lives we are more inclined to think in terms of our hundreds of lives.[73]

Hick turns to Buddhist and Hindu thought on life after death to develop his understanding of a series of progressive lives. He rejects the idea of further reincarnations in this world but suggests that they are in different worlds. He is very much influenced by the *Bardo Thödol*, the *Tibetan Book of the Dead*, and postulates a stage of dreamlike existence immediately after death, very similar to that described in the *Bardo Thödol*. Through these different lives Hick is certain that there will eventually be universal salvation as these progressive after-lives will lead each individual to the ultimate state.

Hell Versus Universalism

For Hick, the problem of hell is that an eternal hell is incompatible with a good and sovereign God.

> The doctrine of hell has as its implied premise either that God does not desire to save all His human creatures, in which case He is only limitedly good, or that His purpose has finally failed in the case of some - and indeed, according to theological tradition, most - of them, in which case He is only limitedly sovereign.[74]

Hick assumes that for the Christian view of God to remain intact, neither of these limitations are acceptable. Thus Hick believes that a Christian view requires the rejection of an eternal hell. One of Hick's major objections to separation in the afterlife is to the claim that God will send to hell all those who have not confessed Jesus as their Lord and Saviour. Hick quotes this statement from the Congress on World Mission at Chicago in 1960 in many of his publications:

> In the years since the war, more than one billion souls have passed into eternity and more than half of these went to the torment of hell fire without even hearing of Jesus Christ, who He was or why He died on the cross of Calvary.[75]

---

[73] Hick, 1976 p.419.

[74] Hick, 1966 p.342.

[75] J. O. Percy, *Facing The Unfinished Task* (1961) Grand Rapids, Michigan: Eerdmans p.9 quoted in Hick, 1973 p.121; Hick, 1980 p.49 and Hick, 1983 p.77 amongst others.

The half-billion people mentioned had never even heard of Jesus and so could not have rejected him, but according to the Congress on World Mission, they would be damned anyway. Indeed the majority of people who have ever lived have never heard the Gospel, and yet traditional Christian thought teaches that they will consequently be subjected to an eternal punishment. Hick cannot accept this is compatible with a God of love. He writes:

> We say as Christians that God is the God of universal love, that he is the creator and Father of all mankind, that he wills the ultimate good and salvation of all men ... Can we then accept the conclusion that the God of love who seeks to save all mankind has nevertheless ordained that men must be saved in such a way that only a small minority can in fact receive this salvation?[76]

Hick's response is of course not. Thus there are several factors which draw Hick towards a theory of universal salvation. Universal salvation, he believes, will not only fulfill the potential of every individual and their experiences in previous lives, it will also fulfill the purpose of creation as a whole. Hick believes that there are very good grounds to assert the reality of ultimate universal salvation, not only because it would be the logical outcome of creation as he sees it, but crucially because it will be the result of the activity of a God of love. In this section I will look at Hick's grounds for rejecting hell and advocating universalism.

The Origins of Hell

In *Death and Eternal Life* Hick looks at the development of beliefs about hell. Originally, he observes, thought concerning both Hades and Sheol was: 'The belief in an undesired because pointless survival, but as yet [there was] no thought of a valuable immortality'.[77] Indeed as the concept of Hades and Sheol developed it was believed that all indiscriminately went there.[78] It was not until later that the afterlife took on connotations of reward and punishment. Hick notes that significant developments in thought about the afterlife took place in ancient Egypt.

> In a period perhaps a thousand years before the time of Moses, a developed moral consciousness [was] being applied to the already existing belief in an after-life ... in the religion of ancient Egypt we

---

[76] Hick, 1973 p.122.

[77] Hick, 1976 p.60.

[78] Alan Bernstein agrees with Hick's account. He writes: 'The notion of distinction of fates in the Greek afterlife arose later than the concept of neutral death ... it suggests that the division of the dead occurs in part as an objection to the older view'. Alan Bernstein, *The Formation of Hell* (1993) Ithaca: Cornell University Press p.50.

see ethical considerations prompting the thought of a blessed future for the righteous and a contrasting punishment for the wicked.[79]

However Hick believes that specific events really brought about the very distinct fates that have been predominant in Christian thought. This was brought about, he suggests, by the lessening of a corporate identity which led to the question of how God would treat individuals.

> With the crushing Babylonian conquest of Judah in the sixth century and the exile of so many of Jerusalem's leading citizens, faith in continuing national existence was shaken and the individual became more conscious of his own personal status and destiny ... with this dawning individual self-consciousness there came the agonizing question of God's justice to the individual, so powerfully and poignantly expressed in the book of Job. Possibly the question of the fate of the martyrs in the Maccabean period made the issue especially urgent.[80]

Hick believes that this development of the doctrine strengthens the case for life after death as it seems less likely to have been developed simply to satisfy a desire for some ultimate purpose. He points out that because of the nature of the earliest beliefs in life after death, the doctrine was not, as is often suggested, merely a result of wish-fulfilment of religious people. Hick notes: 'Such wishful thinking can hardly lie at the origin of early men's belief in their survival; for the post-mortem states in which they believed were not such as to hold any attraction, or to offer any worthwhile compensation, for the vast majority of people'.[81]

Our current doctrines about life after death were not fully established by the New Testament period, and indeed much development has taken place since then. Hick claims:

> It was above all Augustine, in the fifth century, who first wove the dark themes of guilt, remorse and punishment into the tremendous drama of creation, fall, incarnation, heaven and hell which has dominated the Christian imagination in the west until within the last hundred years or so.[82]

Thus Hick argues that the origins of hell consist of a gradual development of ideas concerning the afterlife. The most significant changes from the earliest view of a shadowy underworld are the beliefs that every individual is responsible for their own end and that in the afterlife God will justly punish and reward individuals

---

[79] Hick, 1976 p.68.
[80] Hick, 1976 p.70.
[81] Hick, 1976 p.62.
[82] Hick, 1976 p.207.

according to their behavior in this life. It was however the Church Fathers and particularly Augustine who gave hell the significance it has had for much of Christian history.

Hell in the New Testament

Hick is not primarily concerned to develop a Biblical exposition of hell, but as a Christian is concerned with the teaching of Scripture and particularly of the Gospels.

> There are ... certain well–known objections to belief in ultimate universal salvation, and these must ... be faced. The most serious objection is that the New Testament, and in particular the teaching of our Lord, seems to proclaim an eternal punishment for sinners.[83]

However Hick is hesitant to set too much store by the teaching of Jesus. He writes: 'We cannot now be sure that any of the sayings are precise verbatim reports of Jesus' own words, or that any of the narratives are in detail accurate descriptions of what happened'.[84] However Hick discusses several of these passages. There are several references to hell in the New Testament, but Hick points out that the majority of them do not mention an eternal damnation.

In Mark's Gospel, Hick is most interested in the phrase: 'But whosoever blasphemes against the Holy Spirit never has forgiveness, but is guilty of an eternal sin'.[85] This occurs in all three synoptic gospels, and Hick notes that it is one of only two passages which contains the word 'eternal'. However he does not discuss this saying but simply describes it as 'puzzling'.[86] In Matthew's Gospel Hick comments on the passage, 'Woe to you scribes and Pharisees, hypocrites! For you devour widow's houses and for a pretence you make long prayers; therefore you will receive the greater condemnation'.[87] He writes:

> We have no warrant for assuming that it will be a sentence of *eternal* punishment. Indeed, the very notion of a greater condemnation suggests a range of punishments and not a simple dichotomy between infinite penalty and infinite reward.[88]

The other passage in Matthew which is of interest to Hick is the Sheep and the Goats (25:31 - 46). This passage is notable as it describes an 'eternal' torment. Hick writes: 'It is the only passage in the recorded teachings of Jesus in the

---

[83] Hick, 1966 pp.345 -346.

[84] Hick, 1983 pp.58-59.

[85] Mk 3:29, Mt 12:32, Lk 12:10.

[86] Hick, 1976 p.245.

[87] Mt 23:14. This verse is actually omitted from the main text of Matthew's Gospel in the RSV, but it is noted that some authorities include it.

[88] Hick, 1976 pp.243-244.

synoptic gospels in which eternal punishment is threatened and a final and permanent division is asserted between the saved and the damned'.[89] Hick observes that the Greek word αιονιος is somewhat ambiguous and could mean 'eternal' or could mean 'age-long'.[90] Hick also cites: 'Intrusions of Jewish apocalyptic themes into the developing gospel traditions'[91] as reason to doubt the authenticity of this and other such passages. In reference to the parable of the sheep and the goats, Hick concludes:

> On the generally accepted theory of Marcan priority the evidence of source criticism thus points away from the originality of the judgement sayings as we have them in the later gospel of Matthew, and towards their emergence within the life of the church during the post – apostolic age of persecution, when the Christian community might only too naturally have been receptive to the thought that its persecutors will face a fearful doom in the future.[92]

Thus Hick is doubtful about the authenticity of the passage and consequently does not consider it to be an obstacle to accepting universal salvation.

In Luke's Gospel Hick looks at 6:24, 'But woe to you that are rich, for you have received your consolation'. Hick writes: 'We have no warrant to treat this as asserting an eternal felicity and torment in heaven and hell'.[93] The other significant passage peculiar to this Gospel is the story of Dives and Lazarus. Hick claims from this only that:

> The self which faces judgement after death is the same self that has lived on earth in the body. Dives and Lazarus remember their former lives and are aware of the moral appropriateness of the consequences which they encounter after death.[94]

Again he does not believe that this passage offers a substantive argument against universal salvation.

Hick goes on to look at the Fourth Gospel which: 'Sets itself apart from the Synoptics on this matter'.[95] Indeed the teaching of John's Gospel on this subject does take a different form.

---

[89] Hick, 1976 p.245

[90] Hick, 1966 p. 346

[91] Hick, 1966 p.346

[92] Hick, 1976 pp.245 - 6

[93] Hick, 1976 p.243

[94] Hick, 1976 p.38

[95] Hick, 1976 p.246 He quotes John 3:36, 5:29, 8:47 and 10:25 which demonstrate the 'parallelism of eternal life and eternal death'.

> The notion of a free human response to Christ upon which men's
> eternal destinies depend is obscured and indeed undermined by the
> disconcerting idea that mankind is already irrevocably divided into
> two races, children of God and children of the devil, the former of
> whom, are to enjoy eternal life and the latter to undergo eternal
> death.[96]

Hick comments: 'This quite explicit two-races conception is no more acceptable to the modern non-universalist than it is to the modern universalist'.[97] He suggests that this idea arose during periods of Christian persecution and thus concludes: 'The Fourth Gospel cannot be used in evidence on either side of our contemporary debate'.[98] Hick briefly notes that different writings of St Paul could similarly be used on either side of the debate. He writes that such passages as 1 Corinthians 15:22, 'For as in Adam all die, so also in Christ all shall be made alive'; and Romans 11:32 'For God has consigned all men to disobedience, that he may have mercy upon all', could be used to show that Paul was a universalist.[99] Although he does not claim Paul as a universalist, he writes: 'I suggest that sometimes as he wrote about the saving activity of God the inner logic of that about which he was writing inevitably unfolded itself into the thought of universal salvation'.[100] However there are equally passages in the writing of Paul, which could be used to argue against universalism, so Hick feels that Paul cannot be used on either side of the debate.[101]

    The teaching of St Paul then does not further the argument, and Hick's primary concern is with the gospel evidence. He writes: 'The Gospels are secondary and tertiary portraits dependent on oral and written traditions which had developed over a number of decades'.[102] Consequently: 'No statements about what Jesus did or did not say or think can be made with certainty'.[103] Yet Hick is concerned not simply to dismiss the Biblical evidence. 'These sayings and others in the same category are,' he writes, 'to be taken with the utmost seriousness. An eschatology that merely ignored them, or ruled them out *a priori* as inauthentic, would not be dealing responsibly with the Bible'.[104] However the historical-critical method which Hick employs to evaluate the Biblical evidence, means that he is concerned only with an over-view of the whole New Testament and not with specific passages, which may or may not be the teaching of Jesus.

---

[96] Hick, 1976 p.246 .

[97] Hick, 1976 p.246.

[98] Hick, 1976 p.246.

[99] Hick, 1976 pp.247-248, he also cites Romans 5:18, Ephesians 1:10 and 1 Timothy 2:4.

[100] Hick, 1976 p.248.

[101] Hick, 1976 p.248. He notes the discussion of predestination in Romans 9 and 2 Thessalonians 1:8-9 as passages against universalism.

[102] Hick, 1993 p.16.

[103] Hick, 1993 p.27.

[104] Hick, 1966 p.346.

Hick claims: 'It is possible, however, to give the fullest weight and urgency to Jesus' sayings about suffering beyond this life without being led thereby to the dualistic notion of eternal hell'.[105] Rather for Hick, Jesus is simply using the language of his time to speak to his hearer. With regard to the passages concerning the suffering of the wicked after death, Hick suggests: 'The context of this teaching is ethical rather than theological – "hell" is a result of lovelessness towards the neighbour in his life'.[106] The warnings found on the lips of Jesus are not after all related to existence beyond this life. Indeed they are teachings concerned only with this existence and one's attitude to one's neighbours. Jesus, Hick claims, 'was not concerned with systematic theology but with the vital "existential" impart of his convictions about God and about the future'.[107]

From his reading of the Gospels, Hick deduces: 'That our Lord taught that such misery is to continue through endless time in a perpetual torture inflicted by God cannot be affirmed'.[108] According to Hick: 'About all that we can say with full assurance is that, in agreement with the contemporary Judaism of the time, with the notable exception of the Sadducees, Jesus affirmed the future resurrection and judgement of the dead'.[109] Hick claims that the Gospel passages about hell are not as clear as many might think. He notes that most of the passages which refer to retribution and punishment do not state that it is eternal. According to Hick, this often leads to a distortion in the representation of Jesus' teaching on the subject. Indeed he believes that of the passages in the New Testament which support an eternal hell and those which support universalism, disproportional importance is placed on the 'hell passages'.

> Exegetically, the mistake consists in lumping together two different classes of sayings, one fairly numerous and the other extremely sparse, and then interpreting the larger by means of the smaller.[110]

Hick suggests that when evaluating the sayings of Jesus on this subject, it should be remembered that he: 'Was concerned for and was dealing with concrete individuals, not formulating general theological truths'.[111] He further warns: 'The textual evidence must accordingly be interpreted in the light of wider considerations drawn from Jesus' teaching as a whole'.[112] He is concerned to show that the New Testament is not as clear on the subject as many may think and that the teaching of Jesus must be read with an awareness of its original context. Hick does not look in great detail at the Biblical evidence, but his ultimate evaluation is:

---

[105] Hick, 1966 p.346.
[106] Hick, 1968 (b) pp.600 - 601.
[107] Hick, 1976 p.183.
[108] Hick, 1966 p.346.
[109] Hick, 1976 pp.181 -182.
[110] Hick, 1976 p.244.
[111] Hick, 1976 p.250.
[112] Hick, 1966 p.346.

'The logic of the New Testament as a whole, though admittedly not always its explicit content, leads to a belief in universal salvation'.[113] Thus the evidence of the New Testament is not a stumbling block for Hick's universalism, but indeed he claims that when understood rightly, it supports his rejection of an eternal hell.

Hell and Theodicy

One of Hick's major objections to the doctrine of hell is that it adds to the problem of evil and makes harder, if not impossible, the task of theodicy. Hick's work on theodicy leads him to conclude: 'An eschatological theodicy pointing to the ultimate fulfilment of God's good purpose for his creatures, is only intelligible if it affirms the eventual salvation of all men'.[114] In *Evil and the God of Love* Hick distinguishes between two types of theodicy, the Augustinian and the Irenaean. The Augustinian type of theodicy, which has dominated Western Christianity for centuries, does not affirm the eventual salvation of all, and therefore does not, Hick claims, succeed as a theodicy. Hick rejects much of Augustine's belief system, and instead favours that of Eastern Church Father, Irenaeas. Augustine and Irenaeas begin their theologies from opposite poles. Whilst Augustinian thought takes seriously the doctrine of the fall and blames man for the existence of evil, the Irenaean theodicy: 'Accepts God's ultimate omni-responsibility and seeks to show for what good and justifying reason He has created a universe in which evil was inevitable'.[115]

Hick develops his own Irenaean type theodicy. Rather than humanity having been made perfect he believes humans were made imperfect and thus must strive to become more like 'children of God'. Hick argues that this understanding is more compatible with 'modern anthropological knowledge'[116] which shows that humans have evolved from a less sophisticated life form, not regressed from a perfect one. The idea of the gradual development of people inherent in this type of theodicy, requires that it be eschatological in nature. Hick reports that this is another factor which: 'Compels us to question the validity of belief in hell, in the traditional sense of eternal suffering inflicted by God upon those of His creatures who have sinfully rejected him'.[117]

The nature of his Irenaean theodicy requires that there will be a final resolution to life, which is good for all people. 'In wrestling with the problem of evil I had concluded that any viable Christian theodicy must affirm the ultimate salvation of all God's creatures'.[118] Hick claims that there can be no purpose to an eternal hell and therefore God can have no good reason for allowing it. He writes: 'The sufferings of the damned in hell, since they are interminable, can never lead to

---

[113] Hick, 1966(b) p.193.
[114] Hick, 1965 p.232.
[115] Hick, 1966 p.236.
[116] Hick, 1966 p.255.
[117] Hick, 1966 p.341.
[118] Hick, 1980 p.4.

any constructive end beyond themselves and are thus the very type of ultimately wasted and pointless anguish'.[119] Theodicy is reliant on an explanation or justification for the evil present in this world and for Hick, the best response is that it gives us the opportunity to form our characters and develop and grow into the children of God which he believes we have the potential to become. Any suffering that lasted eternally could not be justified in this way and thus, Hick believes is indefensible and would invalidate his defense of evil in this world.

Hell Exists But Is Empty

Despite his emphatic denial of the possibility of an eternal hell, Hick does not abandon the doctrine altogether. There is a perceived danger in abandoning the doctrine of hell that this will be a license for all kinds of behaviour. This has indeed been one of the most popular objections to rejecting the doctrine of hell. In the seventeenth century, it was felt that if there were to be any serious doubts put forward about the existence of such a punishment and judgement, society would immediately become wanton and depraved.[120] Although it is doubtful whether Hick would share this specific concern, he is adamant that our behaviour and choices in this life are valuable and significant. Thus Hick does not want to say that this life is inconsequential as the outcome will be the same for all. Hick attempts to give the doctrine of hell a reduced role as a mythological concept.

The suggestion that we have many chances to perfect ourselves as children of God, does not, according to Hick, mean that they should be taken lightly. He writes: 'The idea of hell may be de-literalized and valued as a *mythos*, as a powerful and pregnant symbol of the grave responsibility inherent in man's freedom in relation to his maker'.[121] Although we are free to accept or reject God in this life it should not be assumed that this choice is of no consequence. It may not cause our eternal death but Hick is keen to show that is of consequence. Universalism:

> Does not entail that human choices are unreal and not of eternal significance, or that hell does not stand before all men as a terrible possibility. It means that this terrible possibility will not in fact be realised. In mythological language, hell exists, but is empty.[122]

Thus Hick attempts to hold in tandem the threat of hell and the assurance of universalism.

Elsewhere, Hick describes hell as one (or more) of the stages in the afterlife. Thus making it real, but not eternal and therefore purposeful.

---

[119] Hick, 1966 p.341.

[120] See Walker, 1964 p.90ff.

[121] John Hick, *Philosophy of Religion* (1963) Englewood Cliffs, New Jersey: Prentice-Hall p.53.

[122] Hick, 1968 (b), p.599.

> Although 'hell' - using this term now as a name for the fact of
> purgatorial experiences made necessary by our imperfections and
> sins in this life - is not eternal, it is nevertheless real and dreadful and
> rationally to be feared.[123]

Again Hick is postulating a hell which we still need to be afraid of, but which will
not ultimately prevent all people from being with God. He believes that this threat
may be a useful one. Hick writes:

> There is thus still a place in Christian preaching for the theme of
> living righteously as a way of 'fleeing form the wrath to come' -
> though surely only as a shock tactic to cause grossly selfish minds to
> look beyond their immediate gratifications.[124]

Hick does not want to advocate the use of hell to hold power over people or to
threaten them into accepting Christianity, however neither is he quite ready to say
that it has no role at all in Christian doctrine.

Thus the warnings about hell in the New Testament and throughout
Christian history, are relevant and real. Hick in *Evil and the God of Love* claims
that hell is relevant as a myth *and* as a temporary state that one may pass through
during a succession of stages in the afterlife. Hick tries here to assimilate two very
modified concepts of hell into his work. In *Death and Eternal Life* Hick seems to
have abandoned the idea of hell as myth, but maintains its importance as a stage or
stages in his theory of progressive after lives.

Conditional Immortality

It is clear that Hick has various grounds for rejecting the doctrine of an eternal hell.
One response to this, as we have seen, is the doctrine of conditional immortality or
annihilation. In *Evil and the God of Love* Hick writes that at least with annihilation:

> There would not be eternally useless and unredeemed suffering such
> as is entailed by the notion of hell as unending torment; and in
> working out a theodicy it would perhaps be possible to stop at this
> point.[125]

---

[123] Hick, 1966 p.349.

[124] Hick, 1966 p.349. This is similar to Swinburne's claim that the threat of hell will be a
'useful spur to virtue' Swinburne, 1989 p.168. However Hick does not place the same
degree of emphasis as does Swinburne on this use of hell, and of course Swinburne believes
that the threat could be realised whereas Hick assumes that it will not be, and certainly not
eternally.

[125] Hick, 1966 p.342.

However Hick does not believe that this theory can adequately answer the problems of hell. He continues that even on this view: 'God's good purpose would have failed in the case of all those souls whose fate is extinction. To this extent evil would have prevailed over good and would have permanently marred God's creation'.[126] Thus Hick concludes that the doctrine of conditional immortality is: 'A very dubious doctrine for Christian theism to sponsor'.[127] Although the doctrine of conditional immortality may be a softer option than physical torment in an eternal hell, for Hick it does not overcome the objections to an eternal hell. His main objection is that God's purpose is still unfulfilled and thus conditional immortality is open to many of the criticisms made against an eternal hell.

As Hick dismisses conditional immortality as unable to avoid the objections to an eternal hell it will not be necessary to look at this subject separately in the following chapter. It has already been discussed in chapter 3 as it forms part of Swinburne's defence of hell, but as we have seen it is a peripheral issue to Hick's argument.

God's Universal Salvific Will

We have seen that Hick believes the Christian God to be a God of love, and further that he believes that a God of love will seek the salvation of all people. For Hick, God cannot be truly loving without a universal salvific will. Hick believes that God's love entails God wanting the best for individuals, which he defines as fulfilling the purpose for which God made us, namely to be in communion with God. Hick asserts that God's love for us implies that there will be existence following this life. Indeed he claims: 'the life everlasting has always been recognized as a central implicate of the Christian doctrine of the love of God for his human creatures'.[128] However Hick does not just suppose an afterlife, but he is certain that there must be an afterlife that will be finally good for all people. For Hick, this can be assumed from the economics of creation. He asks: 'Would it not contradict God's love for the creatures made in His image if He caused them to pass out of existence whilst His purpose for them was still largely unfulfilled?'.[129] And again he writes: 'A God of infinite love would not create finite persons and then drop them out of existence when the potentialities of their nature, including their awareness of himself, have only just begun to be realized'.[130] God's love for us not only means that God desires the best for us but, Hick supposes, that God has created the universe in such a way that these desires will finally be realised. He writes:

---

[126] Hick, 1966 p.342.

[127] Hick, 1966 p.342.

[128] John Hick, 'Remarks on the Problem of Evil' in Stuart C. Brown (ed.), *Reason and Religion* (1977) New York: Ithaca, referred to as 1977(e), p.128.

[129] Hick, 1966 p.338.

[130] Hick, 1983 p.118.

Augustinian and Calvinist theology never doubted that whatever God willed in relation to mankind would finally be brought about. And in this way they were surely right; their grave mistake was to suppose that God did not want to save all men.[131]

Unlike Swinburne, Hick believes that God's universal salvific will is ultimately efficacious and that divine love will not forever be frustrated.

What Type of Universalism Is Hick Proposing?

It is clear that Hick looks to an ultimate universal salvation. However he is claiming something more than a hopeful universalism. Hick does talk of universal salvation as being 'the Christian hope' however it is evident that he thinks we have grounds for more than hope in the belief that this will be the outcome. He writes: 'Within faith and hope we may confidently affirm the ultimate salvation of all God's children'.[132] For Hick universal salvation is the basis of the Christian hope and not a result of it, and this hope stems from the nature of God. Hick writes: 'It is because God is real and because God is gracious and opens to us the richness of his eternal life, that there is a basis of hope, not only for the elite few but for all humanity'.[133] Thus whilst Hick is a hopeful universalist, he is prepared to go further and state that we can be confident of the outcome of universalism.

Neither, however, is Hick advocating a contingent universalism, which only makes the claim that in this particular world it so happens that all people will finally be brought to God. Whilst Hick claims that all will be brought to God, he suggests that this is because of the forces at work and because of a loving God. Although Hick is not explicit on this point, the implication is that God would not have created any world in which universal salvation was not the final outcome, thus Hick is advocating more than a merely contingent universalism. However Hick denies that universalism is necessary in the sense of being strictly determined. In *Evil and the God of Love*, he writes:

There would be a logical contradiction in its being, in the strict sense, *predetermined* that creatures endowed with free will shall come to love and obey God ... It would infringe the nature of personal order if we could assert as a matter of assured knowledge that all men *will* respond to God.[134]

Hick continues:

---

[131] Hick, 1966 p.343.

[132] Hick, 1966 p.345.

[133] Hick and Goulder, 1983 p.111.

[134] Hick, 1966 p.343.

> Having insisted that some, or even all, men will in their freedom
> eternally reject God and eternally exclude themselves from His
> presence, we may go on to note the actual forces at work and to
> consider what outcome is to be expected ... [Can we] affirm that
> somehow, sooner or later, God will succeed in His loving purpose? It
> seems to me that we can.[135]

Thus whilst Hick does not want to say that it is determined that all will ultimately
be saved, he wishes to affirm that we can expect this outcome. Thus Hick is not
intending to advocate a necessary universalism. Many, however, have argued that
he does exactly that and I will continue this discussion in the following chapter.
Although Hick maintains that he avoids a necessary universalism he is not
advocating only a soft universalism so it may be necessary to define another
category for Hick's universalism, again I will return to this in the next chapter.

Christian Universalism

Hick postulates an ultimate life, where all will finally be joined with God and
discusses what will be the nature of this life. In the first edition of *Faith and
Knowledge*, Hick discusses the two traditional Christian strands of thought
regarding heaven: The Roman Catholic teaching of the beatific vision and the more
Protestant understanding of the kingdom of God. Hick rejects the beatific vision, as
he does not believe that God is a physical being and therefore cannot be seen.[136]
Instead he opts for the following understanding of the kingdom of God. 'We are
supposing redeemed and perfected human personalities to be embodies (their
embodiment being, of course not physical but in the σῶμα πνευματικον of which
Paul speaks) and to dwell with one another in an unclouded communion with
God'.[137] Similarly in the second edition, discussing what would be required to
verify his eschatological claims he writes:

> Surely our participation in an eschatological situation in which the
> reality of God's loving purpose for us is confirmed by its fullness in a
> heavenly world, and in which the authority of Jesus, and thus of his
> teaching, is confirmed by his exalted place in that world, would
> properly count as confirmatory.[138]

These accounts of the ultimate state are specifically Christ-centred accounts of the
kingdom, in keeping with Hick's theology at the time. However, with the shifts in
his thought towards a global theology, Hick's picture of the ultimate state also
changes.

---

[135] Hick, 1966 pp.343 –344.
[136] Hick, 1957 pp.157 -158.
[137] Hick, 1957 p.160.
[138] Hick, 1966 (b) p.199.

In *Evil and the God of Love* he writes: 'We cannot of course, concretely picture to ourselves the nature of this [ultimate] fulfillment; we can only say that it represents the best gift of God's infinite love for his children'.[139] There is no mention here of the place of Christ in the final state, but for Hick it is important only to note that it will be the ultimate outworking of God's love for His creation. Hick writes: 'In the teachings of Jesus the heavenly Father is seen as loving His human children individually and as seeking their salvation as a human father might seek his lost son'.[140] Thus Hick implies here that salvation is being drawn to God.

> A theology based upon the Incarnation will point above all to the great redemptive reality that is known in Christian experience and to which the New Testament documents are the primary witness - the active agape of God at work in human life.[141]

The experience of Christianity in itself, is then redemptive in nature. Indeed this is the focus of the religion. In *Christianity at the Centre* Hick writes:

> The teaching of Jesus includes as an essential element the affirmation of life after death. That our life is renewed beyond death because God's graciousness to us has an absolute and therefore eternal quality was form him one of the basic facts in terms of which we have to live.[142]

Although he appeals to the teaching of Jesus to support his account of life after death, Hick does not put Christ at the centre of this afterlife and claims that the New Testament description of the kingdom is symbolic. He writes: 'The symbol of the kingdom points to a future in which God's rule will be directly evident and in which all things will reflect the divine goodness'.[143]

In *Death and Eternal Life* Hick discusses the physical form that humans will have in the ultimate state, which he here describes as an: 'Eschatological community of perfected human persons'. He continues:

> Their corporate unity as a single personal life will be as real as the internal complexities of that life. There will be many persons, in the sense of many centres of personal relationship, not however existing over against one another as separate atomic individuals but rather within one another in the mutual coinherence or interpermeation which has been predicated of the Persons of the Trinity.[144]

---

[139] Hick, 1966 p.340
[140] Hick, 1966 p.106
[141] Hick, 1966 p.198
[142] Hick, 1968 p.108
[143] Hick, 1968 p104
[144] Hick, 1976 p.461.

Thus he seems to have abandoned the notion of final existence in separate, spirit-like bodies that he accepts in *Faith and Knowledge* in favour of a corporate existence, perhaps influenced by the vishisht-advaitic form of Hinduism which describes individuals ultimately merging into the infinite consciousness of Brahman, illustrated by the picture of a drop of water falling into the sea.

In these early works, Hick's understanding of salvation and Christ's role in it are fairly traditional, even though his move from a Christ-centred to a God-centred kingdom is clear. In *Death and Eternal Life* he writes: 'Western outlook has radically changed and now centres more upon the tension between egoity and personality, with the way from ego to atman lying through personal life, i.e. through the individual's relationships to others'.[145] This is an idea that Hick later develops much further. However in *God Has Many Names,* Hick describes Christ as a: 'Saviour from alienation from God'.[146] This description, would seem acceptable to most who hold a more traditional Christian view, namely that salvation is through Christ.

For Hick the process of getting to heaven entails coming to know God. He believes that each person at some point on their journey will come to know God and thus accept God's gracious offer of salvation.

> There can ...be no atheists in heaven ... the reason why there are no atheists in heaven will be that in the end there are no atheists: every former atheist will in the course of his or her personal history ...have become a theist. If on the other hand this universalist opinion is mistaken, then the reason why there are no atheists in heaven will be that so long as one remains an atheist one is not in heaven.[147]

Hick does not believe that for any individual it is ever too late to be with God. The offer of salvation is not taken away at death, or after a certain number of afterlife experiences. God's offer of salvation is eternal and will never be retracted. Whatever the nature of the realm in which it will be realised, or the nature of the continued existence of individuals, Hick is assured that ultimate universal salvation will eventually be realised.

Conclusion

Hick's rejection of hell initially stems from his objections to the strong view and the teaching that there is no salvation outside the church. However Hick also rejects any modified version of hell other than the view that it is one of several stages on the way to the final state. Hick does not find that the teaching of the New Testament compels him to believe in an eternal hell and further claims that the message of the

---

[145] Hick, 1976 pp.451-452.
[146] Hick, 1980 p.3.
[147] Hick, 1985 pp.119 -120.

New Testament as a whole is ultimate universal salvation. Conditional Immortality does not overcome Hick's objections to an eternal hell and thus he advocates a universalist position.

Hick believes that every person was created with the capacity to become a child of God and further that everyone will be given the opportunities necessary for them to fulfill that potential. It is God's desire, and indeed Hick supposes, God's purpose in creation, that all people will ultimately be saved. Thus Hick proposes a certain universalist outcome. In his earlier works this universal salvation is within the Christian framework established at the beginning of his chapter. So during the number of lives required by each individual, every person will freely accept God.

Human Freedom

The question of human freedom is integral to the success of Hick's theory. As we shall see in the next chapter one of the major criticisms made against his universalist theory is that it overrides human freedom. Thus it is essential to understand Hick's account of human freedom. Hick is particularly concerned with our freedom in relation to God and consequently engages in a significant amount of discussion about the Fall.

Predestination

The idea of an eternal hell is even more repellent to Hick when it is combined with a doctrine of predestination. The suggestion that a good and all-powerful God would create some people in the knowledge that they would be damned is not, Hick argues, in anyway defensible. The most well known advocate of a theology of predestination is Calvin. According to Hick: 'Calvin's is almost as extreme and uncompromising as a doctrine of predestination can be'.[148] Calvin does not just claim that God foresees what will happen to each individual and therefore knows their final fate, rather he believes that God makes 'men that they will, out of their own nature, freely follow the path for which He has predestined them, some to heaven and others to hell'.[149] This situation has resulted from the fall. Calvin believes that humanity is now inherently sinful and it is only the few who receive God's grace as part of the elect who can hope to be saved.

Hick does not accept as literally true the account in Genesis 1:26ff. of the fall of Adam and Eve. Indeed he cannot accept the description of God, which he finds in this story. Hick writes: 'the idea that God would punish the whole subsequent human race for the disobedience of its first two members, attributes to God what to our human understanding can only be called a monstrous injustice'.[150]

---

[148] Hick, 1966 p.121.
[149] Hick, 1966 p.119. Hick is referring to John Calvin, *The Institutes of the Christian Religion* John T. McNeill (ed.) Ford Lewis Battles (trans.) (1961) London: SCM Press.
[150] Hick, 1965 p.231.

Neither, Hick thinks, can God truly love all of his creation if this doctrine is true. Hick is:

> Compelled to infer that if God had a greater love for His creatures He *would* desire the salvation of each, and therefore all, of them. For he cannot be said in any intelligible sense to love those whom He has predestined to eternal guilt and misery.[151]

Calvin does not believe that God does love those who have been predestined to eternal guilt and misery, but this would be totally unacceptable to Hick and would contradict his primary premise of a God of love. Indeed, in *The Centre of Christianity* Hick writes:

> Through the centuries Christian theology has produced a number of doctrines which are unchristian in that they conflict with Jesus' revelation of God's love (for example, the doctrine that God 'from before all ages' predestined some men to be saved and others to be damned).[152]

Thus Hick has several grounds for rejecting the traditional doctrine of predestination. Firstly he objects to it on moral grounds and claims that a God of love would not create some people who never had a chance of salvation. Further he objects that our free choices are of some value.

Hick discusses the work of Schleiermacher who advocates an Irenaean type theology and concludes that there will be universal salvation. Schleiermacher objects to the double predestination of Augustine and Calvin. He writes

> No divine foreordination can be admitted as a result of which the individual would be lost to fellowship with Christ. Thus we may reasonably persist in holding this single divine fore-ordination to blessedness.[153]

Hick thus concludes:

> At the end of a long and complex discussion of the notion of a double destiny he rejects the Augustinian and Calvinist doctrine of eternal damnation and concludes, undogmatically, in favour of the eventual universal efficacy of Christ's redeeming work.[154]

This seems to be a somewhat understated conclusion from Hick. Schleiermacher is adamant that a single destiny has been ordained by God. He goes on to state: 'If we

---

[151] Hick, 1966 p.126.

[152] Hick, 1977 (b), p.16.

[153] Schleiermacher, 1960 pp.548 - 549 quoted in Hick, 1966 pp.234-235.

[154] Hick, 1966 p.235.

proceed on the definite assumption that all belonging to the human race are eventually taken up into living fellowship with Christ, there is nothing for it but this single divine foreordination'.[155] Thus Schleiermacher proclaims predestination as dogmatically as Augustine and Calvin, but claims that there is a single and not a double predestination. Hick aligns himself with Schleiermacher in the Irenaean camp and thus attempts to make his theology credible. However it is clear that Schleiermacher is talking of a single predestination and Hick does not challenge this element of Schleiermacher's thought, thus leaving himself open to the charge that he too is advocating a single predestination.

Epistemic Distance

In *Faith and Knowledge*, Hick explains how, in his view: 'The infinite nature of the Deity requires him to veil himself from us if we are to exist as autonomous persons in his presence'.[156] Thus he believes that in order to give humans true freedom in relation to God, we were created without full knowledge or awareness of God, indeed we were created at a distance from God. This is of course contradictory to the traditional Christian belief that man was created in the company of God, and then fell from that perfect state. In *Evil and the God of Love* he writes:

> Men (or angels) cannot meaningfully be thought of as finitely perfect creatures who fall out of the glory and blessedness of God's Kingdom. Sin - self-centredness rather than God-centredness - can only have come about in creatures placed in an environment other than the direct divine presence. Only in such an environment could they have the freedom in relation to God that is presupposed by the state of *posse pecarre* (able to sin) that is evidenced by their actual fall. [157]

Hick thus claims that Adam and Eve could not have fallen if they had been brought into this 'God-filled' environment. Rather Hick suggests: 'The creation of man in his own relatively autonomous world, in which the awareness of God is not forced upon him, but in which he is cognitively free in relation to his maker, is what mythological language calls the fall of man'.[158]

Hick maintains that if our freedom is to be meaningful, we cannot initially have been created at this sort of closeness to God.

> For only if man is a free being existing in his own sphere at a distance from his Creator can he make a free response of faith and worship to that Creator. The 'distance' from himself at which God

[155] Schleiermacher, 1960 p.549.

[156] Hick, 1966 (b) p.133.

[157] Hick, 1966 p.280.

[158] Hick, 1966 p.283.

has created man is not, however a spatial distance; spatially the infinite Being cannot be at a distance from anything or anyone. It is an epistemic distance, a distance in the dimension of knowledge, consisting in the fact that we do not automatically know God.[159]

Hick writes that God: 'Has not merely given us the freedom to obey or disobey him once we are aware of him, but the more fundamental freedom to be or fail to be conscious of him in the first place'.[160]

Given this epistemic distance, it may be unclear how Hick can assert a final universal salvation. However he balances this distance from God with the belief that we are made with a deep longing for God. Epistemic distance works in conjunction with our inherent desire for God to bring about the freely chosen salvation of every person. It is Hick's belief that humans are made with a disposition for communion with God. In *Evil and the God of Love* he explains: 'God has made us for Himself, and our whole being seeks its fulfilment in relation to Him'.[161] And again in *Death and Eternal Life* he writes: 'God has so made us that the inherent gravitation of our being is towards him'.[162]

The realisation of this, Hick contends will eventually be reached by each person as he/she goes through the progressive lives which follow this one. It is this predilection which means that God will eventually be able to draw all people to himself without infringing their individual freedom. Rather it will be their own nature, which makes individuals seek their Creator.

God has formed the free human person with a nature that can find its perfect fulfilment and happiness only in active enjoyment of the infinite goodness of the Creator ... For He has made them for Himself, and their hearts are restless until they find their rest in Him.[163]

Epistemic distance then allows us freely to fulfil the longing of our hearts in seeking God, rather than God enforcing God's presence on us from the start. Thus Hick sees no contradiction in the thesis that God does not need to impinge upon the freedom of individuals, to bring about universal salvation because we have already been created with the capacity for fellowship with God. As Hick succinctly puts it: 'The notion of divine coercion is set aside by the fact of divine creation'.[164]

---

[159] Hick, 1977 (b) p.93.

[160] Hick, 1983 p.56.

[161] Hick, 1966 p.344.

[162] Hick, 1976 p.251. Hick appeals to Augustine's claim '*quia fecisti nos ad te, domine, et inquietum est cor nostrum donec requiescat in te.*' Augustine, *Confessions* trans. Henry Chadwick (1991) Oxford: Oxford University Press book 1 chapter 1. Hick explains that Augustine means 'thou hast made us towards thyself'.

[163] Hick, 1966 pp.344 - 345.

[164] Hick, 1976 p.252.

Good World

The question is often raised as to whether God could have made humans free, and yet so that they never choose to sin. Hick's response to the question whether God could 'have so made a free and peccable creature that he would nevertheless always choose to be good'? is that: 'What is here proposed is self-contradictory'.[165] However Hick observes that Charles Journet[166] formulates this question in a slightly different way. Journet would say:

> That God knew with regard to each possible free being whose creation He contemplated that he would or would not voluntarily cleave to the good; with the implication that God could, if he wished, have given existence only to those whom He knew would, if He created them persist in good.[167]

Journet's answer to this, is the Augustinian idea of *felix culpa,* it is a fortunate sin which brings about the advent of Jesus Christ and his redemption of the world. Journet is assuming that God has foreknowledge in order to know what the outcome of creation would be, and also middle knowledge to enable God to know the free choices of potential beings. Journet concludes that even with these benefits, God would not choose to create a world in which all freely refrain from sinning. Journet suggests that the benefits of the actual world, with all the sin and suffering it entails, still outweigh the benefits of such a good world.

J.L. Mackie[168] has raised the issue of whether or not God could have created humans so that they would freely act rightly towards one another. Although Hick is able to agree that this would be possible, he concludes:

> Having granted that it would be logically possible for God so to make men that they will always freely act rightly towards each other, we must go on to ask the question: is it logically possible for God so to make men that they will freely respond to Himself in love and trust and faith? I believe that the answer is no.[169]

Hick goes on to explain why he does not think this would have been possible.

---

[165] Hick, 1966 p.108.

[166] Charles Journet, *Le Mal* (1961) Paris: Desclee de Brouwer, Hick refers to the English translation by Michael Barry *The Meaning of Evil* (1963) London: Geoffrey Chapman.

[167] Hick, 1966 p.108.

[168] Hick cites J.L. Mackie, 'Theism and Utopia' *Philosophy* vol.37 no.148 (1962) pp.153-158.

[169] Hick, 1966 p.272.

If trust, love, admiration, respect, affection, are produced by some kind of psychological manipulation which by-passes the conscious responsible centre of personality, then they are not real trust and love etc., but something else of an entirely different nature and quality which does not have at all the same value in the contexts of personal life and personal relationship.[170]

Hick cannot accept that God-given virtues would be of any value. In 'An Irenaean Theodicy' he explains:

Virtues which have been formed within the agent as a hard won deposit of his own right decisions in situations of challenge and temptation, are intrinsically more valuable than virtues created within him ready made and without any effort on his part.[171]

Indeed for Hick, the purpose of this existence is to develop such virtues. Thus for Hick, it is essential for the purposes of this world that human freedom to choose good or bad, and particularly to accept or reject God remains.

Compatibilist Freedom

Hick discusses Augustine's view of freedom. He notes that free will being the cause of evil doing: 'Is the heart of Augustine's theodicy'.[172] Augustine's understanding of free will is an act which is willed by the individual and not forced upon him/her by an external agent. Hick writes: 'Thus to say that man has free will is, essentially, simply to say that he wills'.[173] He continues that on this account: 'Man's freedom, so conceived, is not equivalent to randomness, indeterminacy, and unpredictability. On the contrary, a man's actions are determined by his own inner nature'.[174] Hick agrees that an adequate account of freedom must include the rejection of external determinism and acts must not be detached from the agent. He writes: 'It is not sufficient to say that a free action is undetermined even by the nature of the agent. For to divorce the action from the agent would be to equate freedom with randomness of behaviour'.[175]

Morally responsible action is not normally regarded as being free in the sense that it is random and undetermined, but on the contrary as being determined by ethical principles or the demands of values ... It is very difficult to see how such concepts as responsibility and

---

[170] Hick, 1966 p.273.
[171] Hick, 1981 p.44.
[172] Hick, 1966 p.59.
[173] Hick, 1966 p.68.
[174] Hick, 1966 p.68.
[175] Hick, 1966 p.275.

obligation could have any application if human volitions occurred at random instead of flowing from the nature of the agent.[176]

Although Hick recognizes that an act must be related to the nature of the agent, he does not want to say that a free act is nothing more than a result of the nature of the agent. He asks: 'Is there a third concept of freedom such that a free act is neither, on the one hand, the inevitable outworking of a man's character nor, on the other hand, a merely random occurrence?'.[177] Hick believes that there is a third option, which he describes as 'the notion of freedom as a limited creativity'.[178] He explains:

> Whilst a free action arises out of the agent's character it does not arise in a fully determined and predictable way ... For the character is itself partially formed and sometimes partially re-formed in the very moment of free decision.[179]

Keith Ward understands Hick to be saying that freedom must mean that man's choices are 'inexplicable and incomprehensible'.[180] Hick responds:

> An 'Irenaean' theology at least as I understand it, does not claim that 'man must be totally free' with a freedom which is 'inexplicable and unpredictable choice' so that 'the ultimate moral choices of man must be 'inexplicable and incomprehensible'. On the contrary, a man cannot be totally free ... our freedom can only operate within the basic situation of our being the kind of creatures that we are in the kind of world in which we are.[181]

Rather Hick is suggesting that freedom is not totally determined by one's character, which is liable to change during the process of decision making. Neither does freedom entail entirely random actions totally dissociated from the individual, but it is: 'The actual self alive in the moment of the decision'.[182] Thus choice may sometimes be 'unpredictable' but is not 'inexplicable' or 'incomprehensible'. Hick claims: 'The concept of freedom as creativity would make it possible to speak of God as endowing His creatures with a genuine though limited autonomy'.[183] This freedom of humans in relation to God is essential to Hick's theodicy.

---

[176] Hick, 1966 p.276.

[177] Hick, 1966 p.276.

[178] Hick, 1966 p.276.

[179] Hick, 1966 p.276.

[180] Keith Ward ,'Freedom and the Irenaean Theodicy' *Journal Of Theological Studies* vol.XX (1969) p.250.

[181] Hick, 1970 (c), p.420.

[182] Charles Hartshorne, *The Logic of Perfection* (1962) Illinois: Open Court p.20, quoted in Hick, 1966 p.276.

[183] Hick, 1966 p.277.

However, that freedom is not a total freedom, it is limited initially.

That we are free beings cannot mean that we are unconditioned, but that within the limits set by all the conditioning circumstances of our pedigree and environment we are nevertheless able self-creatively to exercise a certain energy of our own.[184]

Our freedom is thus of a distinct kind. It is the freedom of created beings. Indeed Hick claims: 'That the basic conditions of our existence are thus set by forces beyond ourselves must be presupposed in any viable concept of human freedom'.[185] We are limited and restricted by the nature of our beings and by our environments. Hick gives the example of our gender and the time and place in which we are born. We do not normally object that these factors encroach on our freedom as humans. Thus although our freedom is genuine, it is limited by the fact that we are created. Although our actions are not externally caused, they may be internally caused although Hick maintains that internal influences are not fully sufficient causes because character itself can be transformed by the process of decision. Hick is not proclaiming a strong libertarian freedom. It is clearly different to Swinburne's account of human freedom. Hick's account of freedom as limited creativity is best categorized as a type of compatibilist freedom as it recognizes internal influences even though Hick allows for a third influence on action which seems to be the process of action or decision itself.

Conclusion

The question of freedom is crucial to Hick's theodicy and indeed it is on this question that many argue Hick's universal salvation fails. Hick claims that we are made at an epistemic distance from God in order to allow us to freely choose for or against God. Hick maintains that we are genuinely free, although not in the strong libertarian way that Swinburne supposes, but with the restricted freedom of created beings. Hick rejects double predestination but it is not clear that he also rejects single predestination, such as that advocated by Schleiermacher. Although Hick believes that it would have been possible for God to create a Good World, he concludes that the actual world is actually better suited to God' purposes in creation. Thus our freedom and the opportunity to grow and develop through experiencing soul-making environments are essential to Hick's account of universal salvation.

---

[184] Hick, 1970 (c) pp.420-421.
[185] Hick, 1976 p.255.

God's Knowledge

Hick does not discuss the sort of knowledge he believes God to have. However it is apparent that Hick is assuming at least simple foreknowledge. It would seem that Hick is also assuming God has middle knowledge. If God did not have the benefit of these two types of knowledge, how would God know that humans had been created: 'With a nature that can find its perfect fulfillment and happiness only in active enjoyment of the infinite goodness of the Creator'?[186]. If God did not have foreknowledge and middle knowledge it could turn out that the nature of humans could find equal or even greater happiness in an alternative end. Or it could be that this happiness is only to be found in God but that because of the epistemic distance, nobody ever came to know God and thus everyone remained unfulfilled. Hick is sure that this will not be the case and thus he is dependent on God having both foreknowledge and middle knowledge.

In *Evil and the God of Love* Hick notes that Augustine claims that God has foreknowledge. Although he does not comment in any detail on this, he writes: 'it follows, as Augustine points out, that the fact that an action is willed and is thus a free act is compatible with it being an object of divine foreknowledge'.[187] Thus Hick does not deny, as Swinburne does, that God's foreknowledge would destroy human freedom but claims that they are compatible.

Despite the fact that Hick does not explicitly discuss the topic of God's knowledge, it is crucial for the success of his theory. If God has middle knowledge then Hick can legitimately claim that God knows that all will ultimately be saved through their own free choice.

Conclusion

Hick rejects outright any idea of an eternal hell, the concept of which he believes is 'morally intolerable'.[188] He suggests that the idea of hell might be useful as a myth, but then seems to exclude that in favour of a belief that various temporary hells may be entered in the progressive after-lives which he suggests. Hick initially claims that the outcome of this salvation will be participation in the kingdom of God, where the authenticity of Jesus' ministry will be verified. He later modifies this to the idea of a kingdom in which God will show love for all of creation.

In response to the question: 'Are we free to reject God?' Hick would claim that although we are free none in the end will want to. According to Hick, the epistemic distance between humanity and God allows us to be drawn to God without God tampering with our freedom. Although Hick acknowledges:

---

[186] Hick, 1966 p.344.
[187] Hick, 1966 p.68.
[188] Hick, 1976 p.456.

The individual's own free receptivity or responsiveness plays a part in his dawning consciousness of God, even though once he *has* become conscious of God that consciousness may possess a coercive and indubitable quality.[189]

Indeed it is because of this quality that Hick maintains that humans can only be free when created at an epistemic distance from God. This freedom, at least in principle, allows us to reject God and damn ourselves. Hick claims: 'The doctrine of ultimate universal salvation does not deny that men can damn themselves; but it affirms that although they can, yet in the end none will'.[190] The vast number of after-lives, which Hick supposes, means that there is an abundance of opportunity for individuals to develop their relationship with God. Though an individual may, at a certain stage or stages, choose to reject God, there will be further scope to alter this decision. It is, Hick maintains, a real option that people could damn themselves and yet, he asserts: 'The God-given bias of our nature will not forever be frustrated'.[191] Neither will God's salvific will cease trying to bring all people to him. In 'An Irenaean Theodicy' Hick writes:

> We can conceive that God, in the infinite resourcefulness of infinite love, acts in many ways, through many worlds, to bring his creatures to himself by their own free insights and choices, thereby fulfilling their own deepest nature as beings made in his image.[192]

Thus although one could choose to reject God, the inclination of one's own nature, Hick supposes, will eventually lead each individual to accept God. Many objections have been raised to Hick's understanding of freedom and these will be discussed in the next chapter.

---

[189] John Hick, *Faith and the Philosophers* (1964) London: Macmillan, referred to as 1964(b), p.246.
[190] Hick, 1968 (b) p.600.
[191] Hick, 1968 (b) p.600 .
[192] Hick, 1981 p.25.

Chapter 5

Evaluation of Hick's Universalism

Introduction

The published works of Hick have invariably aroused controversy, and his belief in universal salvation and understanding of the different areas relevant to that theory have received a great deal of criticism. Any scholar, but perhaps especially one seen to be on the fringes of the Christian religion is open to such criticism. The aim of this chapter is to evaluate Hick's work and the work of his critics. The topics related to Hick's rejection of a doctrine of eternal hell will be discussed in the same order as in the previous chapter. However, here I will outline the criticisms of other scholars relating to each area and Hick's response to the critics where appropriate, before concluding if Hick's position is tenable, or whether he is unable adequately to respond to his critics. Finally, I will attempt to determine whether in the light of criticism, Hick's theory of ultimate universal salvation is an acceptable and coherent doctrine.

Hick's God of Love

It is evident that the God of love is at the very heart of Hick's belief in universal salvation. It is further crucial that the loving God's purpose is ultimately to draw all people to Godself. However, there are two major criticisms of Hick's God of love; first that a God of love would not have created a world such as ours with all the suffering it contains and second that a God of love does not necessarily desire the salvation of all people.

Hick's theodicy attempts to demonstrate that our world with all its injustice and suffering could be the creation of a loving God, and indeed that this would be the best possible world for such a God to have created. It is generally supposed that a loving parent would intervene in order to try and prevent its child suffering, yet there is much suffering in our world which God seemingly does not attempt to prevent. Pucetti writes:

> The humane veterinarian need not give his pets LSD or heroin, but he should at least shorten their suffering. The model of the Loving Parent is similarly misleading. True, we often sacrifice our children's pleasure for their moral gain; but we also try to spare them pain when

it is not necessary for that purpose, and it is just this which Hick's postulated 'Father of us all' does not seem concerned to do.[1]

Whilst it may be accepted that the purpose of soul-making may be important, it equally may be argued that this could still take place effectively in a world where there is less suffering. Mesle writes: 'Even if some kind of soul-making process is really necessary to create truly valuable people, God could have created both us and the world in ways much better suited to success'.[2] He suggests that persons would more effectively learn to be loving, if they occupied a more loving environment. A loving God could have created a soul-making world in which there did not exist the proportion of evil that exists in this world. Further: 'One may legitimately question whether a loving God would really prefer soul-making to happiness as the goal of his creation and whether he might not perhaps have simultaneously aimed at both'.[3] Thus whilst the purpose of soul-making is seen to be of value, it may be objected that a loving God could and should have achieved this in an environment more conducive to human happiness. It is clear that the question of what is to be of greatest value, happiness or soul-making is at the heart of this topic. Hick clearly believes that it is soul-making, and that the amount of suffering that exists in the actual world is necessary for a good and loving God's purposes for the world.

Hick is adamant that a God of love will at least desire the salvation of all people and will seek to bring it about, but not all agree that this follows. Chester Gillis comments that 'Hick's argument for universal salvation is strongest when starting from the stance of a loving creator'.[4] And it is the idea of the loving creator which leads Hick to reject that any of God's Creation will be lost. Gillis continues, 'It is reasonable to think that such a Creator would wish to bring all creatures to fulfillment'.[5] However not all agree that a God of love will desire the salvation of all people.

Joseph Bettis in 'A Critique of the Doctrine of Salvation' writes, 'universalism appears to provide the fullest description of God's love for men. At issue is whether or not it is actually the best description'.[6] He goes on to ask:

> Can the final victory of God's love be identified with the salvation of all men? Is God's love better and greater if it reaches all men? Or does this assertion involve a prideful assumption that God's love is

---

[1] Roland Pucetti, 'The Loving God - Some observations on John Hick's *Evil and the God of Love' Religious Studies* vol.2 no.2 (1969) p.260.

[2] Robert C. Mesle, *John Hick's Theodicy: A Process Humanist Critique* (1991) London: Macmilllan p.33.

[3] E.H. Madden, R. Handy and M. Faber (eds.), *The Idea of God* (1968) Springfield, Illinois: Charles C. Thomas pp.58 - 59.

[4] Gillis, 1987 p.109.

[5] Gillis, 1987 p.109.

[6] Bettis, 1970 p.336.

love because of what it does for man, and that men are necessary as objects for God to love? Does the universalist argument really presuppose that men are the basic reality and that God's love is a secondary reality dependent on its relationship to them?[7]

Bettis objects to the argument that God's love must result in universalism. He believes that this argument is based on a humanistic premise. He claims that 'the universalist assumes that men exist autonomously and the measure of God's love is the sweep it makes through this mass of men. The more it includes the better'.[8] Bettis thinks that this is an invalid assumption because humans are not autonomous. He writes:

> Contrary to the humanistic premise, traditional Christianity has insisted that men have no existence whatsoever on their own apart from God's love. Men are not pre-existing objects for God to love. They are the results of his creative, sustaining and redeeming love.[9]

Indeed Bettis' objection goes further than this. He claims that measuring God's love in relation to men makes God an idol. He explains:

> When the Old Testament rejects idols because they are man-made that does not mean that they are rejected because they are formed out of wood or metal by a craftsman. An idol is defined by its relationship to men and not by its substance.[10]

Thus if God's love is measured by the number of people it reaches, God is being defined in relationship to people. Bettis continues that 'idolatry makes God a means to an end. The end, eternal salvation is the real goal. God is a means for attaining the goal'.[11] Bettis concludes that this leads the universalist to a position where 'the Good News tends to become information about God or about what God has done for men rather than the presence of the Christ himself who enables men to participate in God's own love and life'.[12] Thus Bettis claims that belief in universal salvation actually distorts the message of the gospel and leads to an inappropriate view of God. Although he believes God to be a God of love, Bettis does not accept that God's love in any way implies universal salvation.

However it is not apparent that Bettis creates a convincing case. Marilyn McCord Adams in 'Universal Salvation: A Reply to Mr Bettis' writes, 'Bettis is

---

[7] Bettis, 1970 p.336. Tony Gray also raises this objection. He writes, 'God's love would be neither better nor richer if it reaches all individuals'. Gray, 1996 p.113.

[8] Bettis, 1970 p.337.

[9] Bettis, 1970 p.337.

[10] Bettis, 1970 p.338.

[11] Bettis, 1970 p.339.

[12] Bettis, 1970 p.340.

doubtless unfair to many universalists when he suggests that they think the best news is the doctrine of universal future salvation or that this exhausts the content of the Gospel message'.[13] Indeed it seems that Bettis' charge against universalists is unfair. Although universalists may well claim that universal salvation is part of the good news and even that it is implied by it, Bettis does not support his claim that universalists think of God only in relation to what God has done for them at the expense of Christ and participation in God's own love and life. Indeed for Hick it is the example of Christ and his own participation in God's love and life which led him to conclude that there must be an universalist outcome. Bettis makes the further claim that eternal salvation becomes the goal for the universalist and that God is simply a means for attaining that goal. He claims that the universalist is engaging in a form of idolatry. Bettis explains:

> An idol is a god which is worshipped for the benefit he brings to the worshippers, but when reprobation remains as a possibility in the relationship between God and man, idolatry is minimized.[14]

This is a curious claim from Bettis. It would seem that when reprobation remains as a possibility there is a greater reason for idolatry to exist in the relationship between humans and God. For whilst there is the same to be gained, when reprobation is still in the picture, there is a great deal more to be lost. With the assurance of universal salvation, there is no need to treat God as a means to an end, for the end is guaranteed. On the contrary with the possibility of reprobation there would surely be a greater temptation to treat God as a means of avoiding hell and gaining heaven. Thus there is no reason to suppose that the universalist is more likely to treat God as a means to an end than the separatist, indeed the reverse may be the case.

Adams writes: 'Bettis assumes that since men are the effects of God's activity, the extent of God's love cannot be measured by how many of the men that he creates are men that he loves'.[15] She comments that 'unless Bettis is using "love" in some extraordinary sense ... [this] claim is blatantly false'.[16] Paul Gooch and David L. Mosher in their article 'Divine Love and the Limits of Language' write that Bettis:

> Seems to think that God's love is so free that it can take whatever expression God happens to choose. Any limitation on what constitutes a loving action on God's part is automatically a limitation on God's sovereignty, and is therefore to be rejected, on theological grounds as idolatry.[17]

---

[13] Adams, 1971 p.248.

[14] Bettis, 1970 p.342.

[15] Adams, 1971 p.245.

[16] Adams, 1971 pp.245 - 246.

[17] Paul Gooch and David L. Mosher, 'Divine Love and the Limits of Language' *Journal of*

Thus the notion of love, on this account, has no definition other than that which God cares to give to it. They continue that without evidence of recognizably loving behaviour, the claim that God is loving becomes meaningless.

> Were God to profess that he loves us, yet do or promise nothing at all which would count as evidence for this as we understand it, we would be forced to conclude (as a matter of logic and not sinful autonomy or idolatry) that God just did not know the meaning of the word 'love'.[18]

Gooch and Mosher note that Bettis refers to the 'goodness of God's love' and ask the question, 'good for who?'[19] They write:

> If the answer is that it is good for God that he is loving, but not necessarily for any other creature, then we approach Bettis' novel position on divine love. Unfortunately we also approach and can never leave, the realm of unintelligibility.[20]

Thus Gooch and Mosher, like Adams, conclude that Bettis is not using 'love' in its usual sense. They comment that although Bettis claims to give meaning to the idea of a God of love he actually ends up using a term which, according to his theory, can have no actual meaning.

> While Bettis appears to be concerned for the prerogatives of God's love, he is in fact concerned for no such thing. His real concern is for the sovereignty and freedom attributed to that love. Therefore, in order to protect the meaning of the terms 'sovereign' and 'free' as applied to God, he empties the term 'love' of all content ... on Bettis's account, the expression 'to act in free and sovereign love' is equivalent to the expression 'to act freely and sovereignly'! The term 'love' adds no additional content to the first expression. Hence it is quite possible for God in his freedom, to 'express his love' by not giving a damn for anybody or anything.[21]

Thus Gooch and Mosher claim that Bettis sacrifices any meaningful sense of 'love' in order to protect God's sovereignty and freedom.

Adams suggests the analogy of the parents of twins. If they were kind and good and loving to one, yet cruel and mean and uncaring to the other one, they

---

Theological Studies vol. 23 (1972) p.423.

[18] Gooch and Mosher, 1972 p.423.

[19] Gooch and Mosher, 1972 p.424. They are referring to Bettis, 1970 p.339.

[20] Gooch and Mosher, 1972 p.424.

[21] Gooch and Mosher pp.428 - 429.

would according to Bettis, be as loving as they could be.[22] Clearly we would not think this the case. Adams claims that the universalist argument does not necessarily entail that God's love is dependent on it being received by creation. She writes: 'Suppose God's love would be complete in his loving himself, if no creation existed. That would not show that his failure to love some existing men would place no limits on his love'.[23] Bettis fails to show that God can still be regarded as loving regardless of how God treats those already created. Indeed the description of love offered by Bettis is nothing we would recognise as constituting love but an empty term which can be given whatever meaning God chooses to apply.

Bettis fails convincingly to demonstrate that a loving God would not desire the salvation of all people. He claims that 'God is good in himself and not because he does nice things (even giving eternal life) for men. God's love does not imply the salvation of any man'. Bettis continues, 'God would still be God and would still be self-giving love even without men at all'.[24] Whilst this may be true, it is not the issue here. The point is that there are men and women who have been created by God and if God's love and goodness are to have any objective meaning, then they certainly are related to what God does for men and women. Adams comments that:

> Since permanent reprobation is not compatible with the ultimate interests of men (especially given the doctrine alluded to by Bettis, that men can become fully human only when nourished by the grace of God) an omniscient, all-loving God would not willingly condemn some men to permanent reprobation.[25]

Thus God's love surely implies the salvation of some people and at least the desire for the salvation of all.

It is incomprehensible to Adams, and indeed to Hick, that the love of God would be limited to only some of humanity. For Hick, God's love would not be perfect if it failed to reach all people. It would not just be greater and better if God's love reached every person, but would also, for Hick, demonstrate one of the profound insights of the Christian religion. In response to the idea of God's love only being for some people, Hick writes:

> In such a doctrine, the supreme insight and faith of New Testament monotheism, that God loves all His human children with an infinite and irrevocable love, is lost and there is a relapse to the conception of God as the Lord of a chosen in-group whom He loves, who are surrounded by an alien out-group, whom he hates.[26]

[22] Adams, 1971 p.246.
[23] Adams, 1971 p.247.
[24] Bettis, 1970 p.339.
[25] Adams, 1971 p.247.
[26] Hick, 1966 p.125.

Thus for Hick, it is central to Christian belief that God's love does reach all people. To ask whether it would be better or greater if it reached all people is to misunderstand the very nature of God's love. The love of God, by definition, is a universal love.

Despite the various objections to Hick's God of love, belief in an all-powerful and all-loving God is in complete accordance with the Christian tradition based on the New Testament. That some do not believe in such a God, Hick would ascribe to the ambiguous nature of the universe and the freedom we have in relation to God. Further it is reasonable to suppose that a God of love will at least desire the salvation of all people. For Hick, it is necessary that God's love be manifested in a universal salvific will and it would seem that this purpose is in accordance with the Christian view of God and is an acceptable premise for a Christian theory of universalism. The question remains whether God's desire for universal salvation will be efficacious and I will return to this discussion below.

The Moment of Decision

Hick's position on the moment of decision is very different to traditional Christian accounts. He is certain that there are as many chances as are required for individuals to accept God, and until they choose in favour of God, the decision is not finally made. Hick's theory is not without difficulties and several objections have been made to his theory of a progressive after-life. As we have seen, Hick reworks the traditional idea of purgatory into the progressive afterlives. They may have a purgatorial function but really are very different to the traditional doctrine. Although Hick suggests that he is developing this traditional doctrine, as we have seen in the previous chapter, the result is so far removed from the traditional doctrine that it is unhelpful to think of it as a form of purgatory.

Hick's Progressive Afterlife

Hick's progressive afterlife has been quite controversial and there are several objections to it. It is not clear that a decision must ever be made for or against God and this creates a difficulty for his affirmation of ultimate universal salvation. Further, many challenge Hick's belief that continued existence will result in more, and eventually all, coming to know and accept God. In this section I will inspect these difficulties with Hick's account.

Delaying the Decision

Hick argues that one's relationship with God cannot be irrevocably fixed at death. However, under the system of progressive after-lives that he postulates, it seems possible that it may not be fixed at all. The only cut off point in this system comes when individuals are sufficiently transformed into children of God and so are released from the continual progression of soul-making lives and go to their ultimate end with God. There is then no universal or distinct point when one is required to make a decision. Even the end of each life does not seem automatically to provide one with an opportunity to decide for or against God.[27] Thus the point need never come when one *has* to make a decision for or against God. One would never be in a situation of being forced or even encouraged to decide. Hick's theory lacks that element of decision making.

These elements of Hick's theory could be seen as a strength. Walls, writes: 'Talk of failure [of God to save] would only be appropriate if at some point the sinner was irreversibly damned ... this point never comes according to Hick'.[28] Thus God has never failed to bring any individual to Godself but rather could be infinitely in the process of bringing about their salvation. No person's ultimate state is other than with God, but there is no guarantee that individuals will ever reach that ultimate state. So, although Hick avoids the necessity of any eternal hell, it seems that he cannot as such, ensure universal salvation. Hick's particular account of the progressive after-life could, in principle, only result in verification of his universal salvation, it could not result in falsification. His early parable of the two travelers on their way to the Celestial City is in many ways an appropriate analogy for his understanding of progressive afterlives and ultimate universal salvation.[29] It is surely a strength of any theory that it could be proved right but never proved wrong!

Hick's progressive afterlives seem to be something like sitting a test that you must get right. However you are not actually allowed to finish taking the test and hand the paper in, until all of the answers on the sheet are right. You will never fail the test, even if at any given times you have the wrong answers on the paper, rather you will continually be in the process of taking the test, until the time comes, if it ever does, when you have got all the answers right. Thus it is not clear that the test will ever end. This possible indeterminate outcome is clearly at odds with the universalist outcome which Hick asserts.

A further issue with these continuing lives is that it denies that there is any urgency about accepting God. This is not the picture given in the New Testament. Geivett writes:

> The means said to be at God's disposal often work only on the presupposition that time is running out. The prophet's plea and the saint's example, strong incentives that they are, are generally interpreted in the context of a sense of urgency and finality.[30]

---

[27] See Hick, 1976 p.400ff.

[28] Walls, 1992 p.77.

[29] Hick, 1966 (b) pp.177-178.

[30] Rupert D. Geivett, *Evil and the Evidence for God* (1993) Philadelphia: Temple University Press p.222.

The lack of focus on any immediate situation could mean that there was never sufficient incentive to heed the prophet's plea or the saint's example. However Robinson writes:

> A matter is not really made morally more urgent by the fact that one has only a short while in which to make up one's mind about it. Such urgency is derived from the intrinsic nature of the moral situation and cannot be increased or decreased by time, any more than it can be by space.[31]

Robinson suggests that the urgency expressed by the idea of time is an illustration of the importance of the decision. He refers to Romans 13:9-12, he writes of this passage, 'the moral urgency is expressed in the temporal, not derived from it'.[32] Robinson explains:

> There is not necessarily a simple correspondence between temporal and moral finality ... it is to reverse the eschatological equation: to say that the final in time is the ultimate in significance, rather than that the ultimate in significance is the final in time.[33]

Thus Robinson rejects the idea that the moment of decision benefits from having a time pressure. He claims that the decision is still an urgent one even without it being temporally immediate. For Hick the process of accepting God will happen differently for different people, however he does not believe that it is made more significant if it must be made within a certain amount of time. Rather Hick thinks that this will prevent a significant amount of people from being able to make a decision in favour of God.

Will the Progressive Afterlives Work?

A further objection to Hick's progressive afterlives is that if individuals have rejected God in this life, there does not seem to be any reason to suppose that they will be particularly open to God in another life. It is possible that these further worlds which we encounter, will only be effective at drawing people nearer to God, if they are less ambiguous than this one. That is, if there is less epistemic distance and a clearer revelation of God. Davies comments:

> If people are as morally and spiritually free after death as they are now - as Hick claims - then the evidence of how people behave here and now does not give me much hope that the human race will

---

[31] Robinson, 1950 pp.52 - 53.

[32] Robinson, 1950 p.53.

[33] Robinson, 1950 p.54.

gradually improve till all are the God conscious persons God
intended. [34]

Similarly, Holten writes that he is 'inclined to be less certain than Hick that in the
end all will come to see that the ultimate good and happiness for human beings
consists in a relationship with God'.[35] Indeed many claim that Hick's view is
unduly hopeful. Karl Schmitt writes: 'Hick displays a very optimistic view of man's
inevitable progress... The mere extension of existence in time could be viewed like
life on a treadmill which goes nowhere and would therefore be accursed'. [36] Thus
Schmitt warns that if these lives do not lead all people to God they will be a never-
ending cycle of existences which are leading nowhere. If they fail to reach the end
which Hick proposes, his continued afterlives would be bad and not the good that
he suggests.

If there is a clearer revelation of God in further lives in order that
individuals can be made aware of God's presence and love, then perhaps these lives
would succeed ultimately in bringing all people to God. If God does not do this,
those who doubt would have no reason to begin to believe. There would be nothing
in the further lives to start their process of transformation. However if there were to
be a clearer revelation of God, it would of course raise the question, why could
God have not made this world less ambiguous?

Hick would respond that the soul-making value of the world lies in its
ambiguity. However, the purpose of these subsequent lives is also soul-making.
Hick is clear that their purpose is to provide further opportunity for growth and
development into children of God. If then, a less ambiguous environment would
invalidate that process in this life, it would similarly invalidate it in further lives.
Thus the further lives cannot be realms with clearer revelations of God. Hick would
claim that there is no need of further revelation of God, because the desire for
communion with God is inherent in human nature. Consequently, all people will, of
their own free choice, eventually accept God. Therefore it is reasonable to hold that
given more time and opportunity all people will come to love God. Thus Hick's
theory of progressive after-lives are dependent on it truly being the nature of every
person to desire to be with God. If, as Hick believes, everyone is created in the
image of God, and with the capacity, and even the deep–rooted desire, to be in
communion with God, then it is seems reasonable to assume that he/she will
eventually accept God.

In the first edition of *Faith and Knowledge* Hick postulates a continued life
in which:

The world to come turns out to be essentially a continuation of the
life of this world, and to be religiously no less ambiguous ... If the
proportion of theistic and non-theistic evidences continued to be

---

[34] Davies, 1981 p.59.
[35] Holten, 1999 p.47.
[36] Schmitt, 1985 p.198.

much the same as in the present life, we should, I think, expect as a psychological prediction that the Christian believer would, at least for a while, retain his faith in a loving God dealing with him through the phenomena of life, and would continue to anticipate a state in which God is manifestly 'all in all'. But whether he would continue in this hope forever is more doubtful. From the fact that we can live in faith for some three score years and ten it does not follow that we can live thus for a period equivalent to thousands of millions of years, still less during an unending existence.[37]

Although it would not be fair to point this out as being an inconsistency in Hick's work, it raises a valid objection to the sort of theory of progressive afterlife which he later develops. The faithful Christian surely believes that at death he/she is going to have some sort of encounter with God, indeed Hick relies on this to give meaning to religious claims. If at death this does not happen but one instead begins another life of soul-making, it is possible that sooner or later one would come to the conclusion that one had been mistaken in believing that one would encounter God, and consequently may come to disbelieve God's existence at all.

In the 1976 article 'Eschatological Falsification' Kavka claims that 'certain possible resurrection world experiences would, given Hick's assumptions, constitute a falsification of the existence of the Christian God for the individuals having those experiences'.[38] Kavka postulates an after-life in which Satan rules and rewards those who have been evil in this life and punishes those who have been good. He tells them that Christianity was simply a joke on his part to give them false hope. He comments that 'the only rational conclusion for the person undergoing such experiences then, is that the Christian God does not exist'.[39] Kavka recognises that Hick might respond that this realm of Satan is not the ultimate state and that individuals will go on to a further state where belief in God may be verified. However Kavka writes that 'verifying a proposition consists merely of removing grounds for rationally doubting'[40] and surely this criteria should also apply to falsification. Thus a kind of after-life can be imagined which could reasonably destroy the faith of those who do believe in a good God. Although Hick acknowledges that lives can consist of regress as well as progress it would surely be an undesirable outcome for further existences to result in a loss of faith. Hick would presumably argue that this would be a temporary setback and that faith would be re-found in a further life and perhaps that it would be stronger for going through this process.

A further problem with Hick's account of the progressive afterlives could be that the only criteria needed for reaching the ultimate state would be the

---

[37] Hick, 1957 p.155.
[38] George S. Kavka, 'Eschatological Falsification' *Religious Studies* vol.12 no.2 (1976) p.202.
[39] Kavka, 1976 p.202.
[40] Kavka, 1976 p.203.

expectation of encountering God or the Ultimate Reality. Hick adopts the idea influenced by the *Bardo Thödol* that what happens at death will be an experience of whatever one was anticipating. Thus the Christian who is expecting to encounter God at death would experience such an encounter.[41] Hick notes that the *Bardo Thödol* claims that only those who recognise the Ultimate Reality will, at that stage, reach the eschaton. However, if individuals die firmly believing that their next experience will be meeting God or the Ultimate Reality, will they not assume that whatever they encounter is this? Thus they may recognise the Ultimate Reality immediately after death, not because they have achieved Hick's process of complete transformation, but because they were expecting an encounter of this nature. Thus it could be that the only criteria actually needed for individuals to reach Nirvana or the eschaton, is the expectation that at death they will see the Ultimate Reality or God.

Conclusion

There are several difficulties with Hick's account of the progressive afterlife. There is no Biblical support for the idea of a series of further lives after death, and this concept is alien to the Christian tradition. The major difficulty in terms of Hick's own theory is whether or not these progressive lives will ever actually lead to universal salvation. However if we accept Hick's account of human nature then it seems reasonable to assume that finally, they will. Indeed if they can be relied upon to produce the desired outcome then there is a sense in which this theory maximizes the purpose of creation. Most of us today will not just live in an earthly environment for our average eighty years, but will continue to develop and experience in a number of further lives before finally reaching the eschaton, where we will live in communion with God. On this account each individual's life consists of a lot more than our present life and thus it could be argued that on this account there is a great deal more purpose to our life.

For the progressive afterlives to be effective, Hick's understanding of human nature and his optimism about the progress individuals will make is essential. However, it does seem reasonable to believe, as Hick does, that God would have created humans with an inherent desire for communion with God. If Hick's understanding of human nature is accepted, his theory of progressive after lives may also be accepted as a reasonable suggestion. Indeed this is all that Hick requires. He writes, 'the suggestion I have made that further-person-making beyond this life may well occur in a series of infinite lives ... is offered as a reasonable suggestion not theological dogma'.[42] Thus whilst Hick may be right about the eventual result and that the series of progressive afterlives are one way this could be achieved it is not clear that this is the only way or indeed the most likely way, as it is one far removed from traditional Christian teaching.

---

[41] Hick, 1976 pp.415 - 416.
[42] Hick, 1993 p.237.

Universalism versus Hell

In this section I will look at criticisms of Hick's understanding and consequent rejection of hell as well as some objections to his own theory of universalism and some difficulties with general universalism. In order to defend his universalism against the traditional teaching of hell, Hick must be able to respond to the objections made against his theory.

Hell in the New Testament

Hick's use of the Bible has been widely criticised and I will discuss some of the objections to his use of Scripture before looking at an example of one passage which is important to the discussion about hell.

Hick believes that the New Testament does not unequivocally teach an eternal hell and further that the overall message of the New Testament can be used to support a universalist position. As we have seen Hick is not concerned to provide a systematic exposition of the Biblical material. However he is concerned to take the teaching of the Bible seriously. Many scholars claim that Hick's Biblical approach is far from satisfactory. Ajith Fernando comments that 'reverent Bible students should arrive at their conclusions only after studying the Scriptures and they should revise their biases if Scripture contradicts them'.[43] David Pawson advocates a thorough, systematic examination of the Bible and concludes from his own engagement with Scripture: 'The New Testament consistently divides the human race into two categories. People are blessed or cursed, they are saved or lost, they go to heaven or hell'.[44]

Hick does not claim to be a 'reverent Bible student' and only wishes to demonstrate that the teaching of the Bible can support his position. However many still object to Hick's use of the Bible. D'Costa writes of Hick's work that there is a 'lack of attention to tradition, ecclesiology and biblical theology'[45] and that 'Hick's use of biblical criticism is something of an afterthought'.[46] Gillis comments: 'the argument on scriptural grounds is the weakest'. [47] Norman Anderson claims that Hick's use of the Bible is 'a singularly arbitrary selection of evidence'.[48] Whilst this is perhaps a fair comment, it is not a failing unique to Hick, but a criticism which many scholars would be open to. Indeed it is very difficult to use the Bible to support an argument or justify a position, *without* it being a somewhat arbitrary

---

[43] Fernando, 1991 p.123.

[44] David Pawson, *The Road to Hell: Everlasting Torment or Annihilation* (1992) London: Hodder and Stoughton p.23.

[45] D'Costa, 1987 p.7.

[46] D'Costa, 1987 p.57.

[47] Gillis, 1987 p.109.

[48] Norman Anderson, *The Mystery of the Incarnation* (1978) London: Hodder and Stoughton p.69.

selection of evidence. It is probably impossible with a book such as the Bible, not to select arbitrarily from it, as it is such a mixture of materials and sometimes, seemingly, of messages.

Hick's use of the Bible in his work is not particularly exemplary. However, I think Anderson is wrong, that his is a '*singularly* arbitrary selection of evidence'. Rather I think Hick's attitude towards using Biblical material is typical of a liberal scholar. He does use it, but in the full recognition that there are few arguments which cannot appeal, however dubiously to some passage of Scripture for support. As Schmitt writes, 'it is apparent that Hick does not wish to eliminate the possibility of universalism's being present in the Bible'.[49] Neither does he claim that this is the only viewpoint sustainable from the evidence of the New Testament. Hick might strengthen his position by making more of the passages in the New Testament which support universalism, however he would also then need to give more weight to the passages which support the separation of the saved and the lost.

Ultimately, for Hick, it is not reliance on the Bible, which will give credibility or merit to his theory. Whilst the criticism that Hick's use of the Bible is perhaps weaker than many other areas of his work may be a valid one, there is a sense in which this is an unfair objection to Hick's work. Hick does not aim to provide a detailed Biblical exposition of his position and is often more concerned with the philosophical coherence of his theory. It is clear from his writing, and Hick himself acknowledges, that he is not a Biblical scholar. Julius Lipner observes that while more fundamentalist, exclusivist Christian theology 'claims to have a primarily Biblical basis, Professor Hick's position lays greater store by the role of reason in the matter (though he does think that contemporary New Testament exegesis supports his views)'.[50] It could be argued that Hick has recognized a need amongst the Christian community not just for Biblical evidence but also for logical thought. Dilley writes: 'When exclusivism fell, along with it went the notion that the biblical view was true in any absolute sense and Hick has spent the rest of his career working out the details of that realization in a rather brilliant way'.[51] The merits of Hick's work to individuals, does at least in part, depend on the view they take of the Bible. For those who adopt the view that the Bible is true in an absolute sense, Hick's work will, on the whole, be unacceptable. Davies observes: 'It is clear that for most universalists exegetical considerations are outweighed by philosophical ones'.[52]

Therefore the criticism that his Biblical work is weak criticizes Hick's work for not being something that it does not set out to be. However the other side of this is that Christianity cannot be separated from the Bible and any Christian theory must take this into account. Although Hick does not set out to provide a

---

[49] Schmitt, 1985 p.131.

[50] Lipner, 1977 p.249.

[51] Frank B. Dilley, 'John Hick on the Self and Resurrection' (1991) in Harold Hewitt (ed.) *Problems in the Philosophy of Religion: Critical Studies of the Work of John Hick* (1991) Basingstoke: Macmillan p.138.

[52] Davies, 1990 p.177 .

Biblical exposition, the fact that he is developing a Christian theory means that he cannot ignore Biblical teaching and must defend his account in the light of Scripture. Thus the objection that Hick's Biblical work is weak is a valid objection to a Christian theory, however given Hick's aims this objection is not sufficient to invalidate his work.

One of the Biblical passages with which Hick is particularly concerned is the parable of the Sheep and the Goats from Matthew's Gospel. John Robinson supports Hick's assessment of this passage. Robinson does not believe that the story originally existed in the form in which it is found in Matthew 25. He claims that it is a mixture of two distinct pieces, combined by the editor to create a powerful parable about the final judgement. 'The original core is', he claims, 'a parable about a shepherd separating his flock and a set of antithetical sayings concerning the eschatological consequences of accepting or rejecting Jesus in the outcast and helpless'.[53] He extracts parts he considers to be reasonably proved to be merely editorial, and suggests that the parable that is left, is comparable to the earlier one about weeds and could aptly be called the Parable of the Flock. Robinson accepts that the teaching on looking after the hungry, thirsty, strangers and prisoners is probably authentic, but that the interjected sayings about the final judgement are the work of the author of Matthew.

> Matthew's artistry consists in having fused the parable with an allegory of the Last Judgement, and then with great skill introduced the sayings of Jesus as the ground upon which the judgement is given.[54]

Of course, many others would disagree with Robinson's account and the teaching of this passage, reputedly teaching of Jesus, would be a serious barrier to accepting universal salvation. Indeed Weiss classes this passage as one which shows that Jesus taught that there would be eternal torment.[55] Nigel Wright writes:

> The real significance here belongs to the word 'eternal' which is primarily a qualitative rather than a quantitative adjective: the life and punishment to be accorded at the last judgement have an eschatological character. This is not temporal life or punishment, which is meted out and which could be reversed, but that which belongs to the coming age, signifying inclusion in or exclusion from God's eternal kingdom, final gain and final loss.[56]

---

[53] John A. T. Robinson, *Twelve New Testament Studies* (1962) London: SCM Press p.90.

[54] Robinson, 1962 p.91.

[55] Johannes Weiss, *Jesus' Proclamation of the Kingdom of God* (1971) London: SCM Press p.99.

[56] Wright, 1996 p.93.

The discussion about the meaning of the Greek αιονιος is not resolvable. A.H. McNeile writes that the word 'connoted perpetuity, permanence, inviolability'.[57] David Hill however, claims that 'the word eternal with reference to punishment and life means "that which is characteristic of the Age to come;" the emphasis on temporal lastingness is secondary'.[58] Strawson writes:

> 'Eternal punishment' is probably used as a well known phrase descriptive of the fate of the wicked, without any attempt to face the question of the suitability of punishment which goes on forever ... Jesus (or, more certainly the author of the gospel) only repeated the current popular notion to indicate divine disapproval without entering into any discussion of the matter.[59]

Hick concludes that there is insufficient evidence to proclaim that Jesus taught an eternal punishment and this is a reasonable conclusion given the discussion surrounding the passages and Hick's Biblical approach.

It is clear that Hick's use of the Bible is a sticking point for many. It has generally been assumed that the Bible does teach an eternal separation and thus the suggestion that this is not conclusive contradicts much traditional teaching. However Hick demonstrates that the Bible teaching concerning the afterlife is not unequivocal and there is at least grounds for a universalist hope. So his use of the Bible, whilst it may be weak and is certainly not exemplary, is adequate for what Hick aims to show, namely that the New Testament does not uncontestably proclaim an eternal separation of fates and that there is support for the universalist position.

Hell Exists But is Empty

If God's justice demands the existence of hell, the question must be raised as to whether morally there can be said to be any difference between threatening to do something and actually doing it. An analogous argument would be the ongoing discussion concerning nuclear weapons and whether not using them makes them morally acceptable. Bruce Kent, a leader of the Christian Campaign for Nuclear Disarmament, claims that simply owning nuclear weapons is in itself an evil. He writes that the basis of the argument that having nuclear weapons would deter anyone else from using them against you, is an 'ever present threat to do something quite wicked'. Kent asks the question: 'How can I love people while I threaten to burn them and their families and to turn their cities into ashes?'. [60] God could then

---

[57] A. H. McNeile, *The Gospel According to Matthew* (1938) London: Macmillan p.263.

[58] David Hill, *The Gospel of Matthew* (1972) London: Marshall, Morgan and Scott p.331.

[59] William Strawson, *Jesus and the Future Life* (1959) London: Epworth Press p.135.

[60] Bruce Kent, *A Christian Response to Nuclear Weapons* (1984) London: Christian Campaign for Nuclear Disarmament p.5.

ask a similar question - 'How can I love people while I threaten to send them and their families into eternal damnation?'.

If hell is empty because none in the end choose to send themselves there, then God is still responsible for creating a world where hell is a possible outcome of human existence, that is if there is only a contingent universalism. It does not make any difference whether this is merely a threat or a reality. If there is a hell, empty or not, God, the Creator of all must be responsible for it. And the challenge to show how this would be the action of an all-loving and powerful God remains. Further if there is a world in which this is a possible outcome God is taking the risk that some people will end up in hell. If however the claim is that God knows that the outcome will be an empty hell, why would God have created hell in the first place knowing that none would end up there? The only justification for this would be that the existence of hell somehow contributes to the outcome that none will finally go there, but as we do not know whether or not hell exists it is difficult to see how this could be the case.

Christian ethics rooted in the New Testament do not distinguish, morally between committing a sin and thinking of committing a sin. To think of doing something is, according to the Gospel, as bad as actually doing it. Matthew's Gospel puts a new emphasis on the teaching 'Do not commit adultery'. Jesus says 'What I tell you is this: if a man looks at a woman with a lustful eye, he has already committed adultery with her in his heart' (Mt. 5:27,28). The existence or possibility of hell cannot be excused on the grounds that no-one will ever go there. For God is as morally responsible for hell if it is empty, as if it is full. If the eternal suffering of some in hell is deemed incompatible with an all-powerful God of love, then the existence of an empty hell must also be incompatible with such a God. Thus the defence that hell is empty, is no defence at all.

Hick, does not depend on the line of defence that hell exists although it is empty, and seems only to suggest this possibility in order to show that he does not take the threat of hell lightly. It does not do much to advance his argument. If taken literally, God would still be responsible for creating a place of eternal torment. If, as Hick suggests, it is taken mythically, then it does not actually seem to be a very meaningful idea. Hick later abandons this line of thought and suggests that hell is a temporary state or one of the stages in the continued lives after death.[61] However, the sort of hell that he suggests here, is so far removed from the traditional understandings of hell that it seems inappropriate to use the term. Hick is not referring to a permanent or irreversible state, it is not a place of torture or separation from God. Indeed what he describes is more like the traditional concept of purgatory. Thus Hick's reduced accounts of hell add little to his rejection of hell.

God's Universal Salvific Will

Like Swinburne, Hick believes that God has a universal salvific will. Swinburne claims that this will not necessarily result in the salvation of all people. Hick,

---

[61] Hick, 1976 p.403ff.

however claims that God's desire for ultimate universal salvation must be efficacious. It is Hick's contention that if an all-good, all-powerful God does not succeed in winning all people to himself, He will have failed. Walls comments that Hick: 'speaks of God as trying to save men, as being frustrated if he cannot, and even goes so far as to say it would be a failure on his part if all are not saved. This is anthropomorphism gone absurd'.[62] Walls argues that this language is inappropriate to God, as being frustrated and failing are not attributes we associate with God. However Hick could argue that this depends on one's understanding of God's knowledge, a God with only present knowledge may well be frustrated and ultimately fail to achieve the salvation of all. However if God has foreknowledge and middle knowledge, it would perhaps not be appropriate to describe God as being frustrated. As we have seen Hick does not clearly define his position on God's knowledge and this would allow him further to defend his universalist theory and show that God can ensure that God's plans will not ultimately be frustrated.

In *Ethics and Christianity* Keith Ward argues that God is not sovereign now as there are many who do not accept God and the world is not as God intends. But Hick does not accept this as an argument against God's omnipotence. For Ward, the rejection of God by individuals now, should also, on Hick's theory, be classed as God's failure. He writes: 'God's omnipotence is therefore undermined equally much - or equally little - by one small disobedience as by the final disobedience of all men'.[63] Hick's response would be that God, like a loving parent, allows us the freedom to make mistakes and develop from our own experiences. Linda Zagzebski writes in defence of Hick: 'loving persons is something good persons do and loving persons in such a radical way that any evil is permitted for the sake of their personhood is something a perfectly good person would do'.[64] That all persons do not presently love God, is not then due to his lack of omnipotence, but is a result of God's loving nature and desire that each individual will follow a process of growth and development until they become children of God.

The further argument is made that although God may desire the salvation of all people, God cannot ensure that this will be the outcome given that those people are free. This of course, is Swinburne's argument against affirming universal salvation. However, Peter Geach writes:

> We shall see that some propositions of the form 'God cannot do so-and-so' have to be accepted as true, but what God cannot be said to be able to do he likewise cannot will to do, one cannot drive a logical wedge between his power and his will, which are, as the Scholastics

---

[62] Jerry L. Walls, 'Can God Save Anyone He Will?' *Scottish Journal of Theology* vol.38 (1985) p.160.

[63] Keith Ward, *Ethics and Christianity* (1970) London: George Allen & Unwin p.262.

[64] Linda Zagzebski, 'A Critical Response' in Hewitt (ed.) 1991 Basingstoke: Macmillan p.128.

said, really identical, and there is no application to God of the concept of trying but failing.[65]

Thus, according to Geach, if God wills the ultimate salvation of all people then this will be realised. However, the desire for ultimate universal salvation and allowing genuine human freedom, may be a proposition that falls into the category of things God cannot do. Walls writes:

> If we are free to either accept or reject God's offer of salvation, then perhaps God, even though omnipotent, *cannot* save everyone. Some may decisively choose to reject salvation, and if they do, God cannot save them without revoking their freedom. Thus Hick's argument for universalism fails.[66]

Hick believes that no individual will reject God. There will be so many opportunities to become aware of God and accept salvation that ultimately each individual will freely choose to do so. Again a discussion of God's knowledge could strengthen Hick's argument at this point. By claiming that God has foreknowledge and middle knowledge, Hick may be able to respond to Walls that God could save everyone without revoking freedom. I will develop this argument in the following chapter.

Thus Hick's belief in the efficaciousness of God's universal salvific will is challenged on the grounds that God fails to be sovereign now, as not all people accept God, and that human freedom means that even if God desires to save all people, God cannot be sure of this outcome. Hick believes that no person will ultimately have any reason to reject God as we are made with an inherent desire for God. This premise and an appeal to God's middle knowledge would help Hick out of this difficulty and give him grounds to affirm ultimate universal salvation. In chapter six I will look at the benefit of middle knowledge for Hick's position and show that with the addition of this type of God's knowledge to his argument, Hick could indeed be in a position to justify the claims he makes.

Contingent versus Necessary Universalism

It is not immediately apparent what sort of universalism Hick advocates. Many scholars have objected that Hick advocates a necessary universalism. Walls writes that Hick:

> Implicitly denies omnipotence to a God who cannot save everyone. Thus he never really admits that it is logically possible that a good,

---

[65] Geach, 1977 p.5.
[66] Walls, 1992 p.73.

omnipotent God might not be able to save everyone, despite his numerous claims to the contrary.[67]

Walls further comments that Hick cannot be certain of ultimate universal salvation, and maintain a 'complete' human freedom. If universal salvation has not been predetermined, there is a real chance that some will not accept it and thus neither God nor Hick can be certain of it. Walls writes:

> [Hick's] initial argument is that universalism is a certainty. It follows, as a matter of logical necessity that if God is perfectly good and sovereign, then all will be saved. But on the other hand, Hick affirms a conception of freedom from which it follows that universalism is at best contingently true.[68]

At best Hick, according to Walls, can say that it is *probable* that all will be saved but, because of human freedom, he cannot be certain. Hick does make this point himself. He writes: 'it would infringe the nature of personal order if we could assert as a matter of assured knowledge that all men will respond to God'.[69] However he does not stop at this point and affirms that this will be the outcome. As Geivett writes, for Hick: 'the power of God and the love of God ensure that what must happen will happen. It is therefore a matter of fact'.[70] Thus although Hick intends to allow for human freedom, he is certain that the outcome will be universal salvation. Thus Hick's position seems to be necessary universalism. However Hick is concerned to show that this outcome is compatible with his definition of human freedom. I will look at some difficulties with Hick's account of freedom in the following section, but it seems that even if his account of freedom is compatible with ultimate universal salvation, it also needs to be supported by a discussion of God's knowledge.

Hick wavers between contingent and necessary universalism but does not want his theory to fall into either category. Hick wants to proclaim more than a contingent universalism but still retain human freedom. Again Hick cannot fully defend his account without appealing to God's knowledge. Unless he claims that God has foreknowledge, the outcome is not certain and some people may never accept God but continue with the progressive afterlives eternally. Thus the position Hick finds himself in is not that of a universalist, as he cannot affirm that some will not live perpetually in a purgatorial state. It would seem then, that a further category must be added to our definitions of hell and universalism to accommodate this perpetual purgatory.[71]

---

[67] Walls, 1985 p.161.

[68] Walls, 1992 p.74.

[69] Hick, 1966 p.343.

[70] Geivett, 1993 p.196.

[71] It is worth noting that although Hick does not intend a perpetual purgatory, some argue that this outcome may be the result of libertarian freedom and a rejection of

General Objections to Universalism

The universalist position is a controversial one and many objections have been made to this theory. Hick, as a universalist, must not only defend criticisms of his own position but also generic criticisms of universalism. The weight of Christian tradition, as we have seen, has been in favour of an eternal separation of fates and thus it is left to the advocate of a universal reconciliation to defend the coherence of universal salvation and respond to the objections raised. In this section I will look at Hick's response to three well known criticisms of universalism.

Superfluousness of Religion

A major criticism of any universalist theory is that it seems to make religious belief superfluous. Hick's theory is, of course, open to this objection. Hick believes that religion is of great importance to the way we live. It should not be assumed that it is only because it will lead to an after life that religion is of value. The Christian message is also about transformation of people now. This is reflected in Hick's theory of salvation as transformation to Reality-centredness. The Kingdom of God or Heaven described in the New Testament is not just about a future state, but it is also about the here and now. The Kingdom is 'at hand' (Mk 1:15); it is 'in the midst of you' (Lk 17:21). Its importance is not merely to be found in the afterlife. Jesus told his disciples 'I came that they may have life, and have it abundantly' (Jn 10:10). Indeed in John's Gospel eternal life is not something to be looked forward to after death, but it begins straight away. Jesus says: 'Truly, truly, I say to you, he who hears my word and believes him who sent me, has eternal life' (Jn 5:24). Hick writes: 'Christians believe that we human beings are living a double life - a mortal life and, overlapping and interpenetrating it, an eternal life'.[72] The idea that Christianity is primarily concerned with the after-life is misleading. The importance of religion for this life is clear.

Hick believes that ultimate universal salvation gives purpose to this life. As far as he is concerned, if at death any were to be annihilated or lost, their earthly life would have been futile. However, it may be argued that the opposite is true. The promise of ultimate universal salvation makes our actions and choices in this life meaningless. It is not significant what we do or achieve during our earthly life, and it does not matter whether we have lived with faith in God or not, as we will all finally have the same end. It is not important whether we have hurt and exploited people for our own ends and abused the resources we have or whether we tried to value people and work for justice. Indeed the anomaly between the way people use their earthly lives is surely a powerful motivation for belief in separate after-lives according to what one has contributed during one's earthly life.

---

hell. Some will stay in purgatory because no-one is sent to hell but God will not override individual's freedom to ensure that all end up in heaven.
[72] Hick, 1968 p.107.

The Injustice of Universalism

There are two ways in which it is objected that universalism creates an unjust situation. First it cannot compensate those who have encountered difficult circumstances in this life as everyone will have the same end. And second those who have committed sins in this life will not be punished for them in the afterlife.

Pucetti observes: 'In the total reckoning they [individuals who have suffered different degrees of pain and hardship] have been treated differently by God and no talk of an ultimate infinite reward can gloss over that'.[73] Hick's theory then cannot explain why individuals have such different fortunes in this life. Neither can it compensate for them or equal them out. Finally, everybody is in the same position and so the differences we experience in this world remain unfair. For Hick, the after-life is not about reward or compensation but about completion. Every person finally reaches individual completion as a child of God. Thus Hick does not, as Pucetti suggests, talk of infinite reward.

Hick might suggest that when individuals have reached their saintly status, they will look back with gratitude, or at least acceptance, on the trials of their lives which have enabled them to develop fully. Each person will see their pain and hardship as part of their development and thus it will not be relevant to compare it to anybody else's. Their fortunes will be seen as part of their personal journey, and it is possible that those whom we consider to be fortunate in this life, will not have such easy existences in subsequent lives. Hick further claims that our ultimate ends cannot be seen as merely individual matters, but are interrelated. The important thing is our final salvation and the situations we experience on the way are ultimately irrelevant. Hick explains:

> We have to learn as an aspect of our spiritual growth, not to see ourselves as separate units, each with our own inalienable rights, but rather as parts of the one organic bundle of life in which 'no man is an island unto himself' but each is 'a part of the main'. This aspect of our existence in its relationship to God's creative purpose, is captured in Jesus' parable of the vineyard owner who at the end of the day rewards equally those who have borne the heat and burden of the day and those who have had a relatively light and easy task (Mt 20:1-6). In the presence of the Eternal Love none will complain but all will rejoice together in a common fullness of life.[74]

Hick then would maintain that Pucetti's objections are ultimately irrelevant to the purpose of the after-life and the way in which it fulfils earthly lives.

---

[73] Pucetti, 1967 p.264.

[74] John Hick, 'A Response to Mesle' in Robert C. Mesle, *John Hick's Theodicy: A Process Humanist Critique* (1991) London: Macmilllan, referred to as Hick, 1991(b), p.129.

Another common objection to universalism is to point to humans who have committed atrocious evils and claim that it is not possible to believe that they, with all other people, including their victims, finally rest with God. Hitler, as the individual seen to have brought about the most evil in the twentieth century, is held up as a classic example of why *all* cannot ultimately be saved. Pinnock asks 'How could one imagine that Hitler would change his mind, forsake evil, and love goodness in the afterlife?'.[75] Surely the Gospel teaches us that even the most hardened sinner can change and anyone who acknowledges the transforming power of God could believe that it would be possible for Hitler or anyone else to undergo such an alteration.

Similarly, Graham writes: 'We will fail to take seriously the holocaust, the Stalinist purges and so on, if our conception of God's goodness attributes to him a desire or tendency to treat equally the victims and the perpetrators'.[76] Surely God's goodness does require that God loves these individuals. Jesus teaches his disciples 'Love your enemies and pray for those who persecute you' (Mt 5:44). If we are required to do this, surely God will do at least as much! Robinson describes the idea that some must be damned to fulfil God's justice, 'If they will not be drawn by His love, they shall bow to His justice. In each case He is omnipotent; He has not failed'.[77] He does not accept that God's love and justice are conflicting attributes, he writes 'it is most important to hold to the fact that justice is in no sense a substitute for love, which comes into operation when the other has failed to be effective'.[78]

Many Christians would be happy to affirm God's salvific will and claim that he does indeed desire to bring all people to himself. However, they may not necessarily affirm from this, that God will ultimately succeed. Davies writes:

> To affirm that God is ultimately victorious over all enemies and that God's authority will one day be universally recognized is one thing and will be agreed on by all Christians. But to say that every person will eventually be reconciled to God is quite another.[79]

Perhaps then given God's salvific will the best one can say is that there may be ultimate universal salvation. However Hick is convinced that God's desire is to bring all people to Godself and the resources of God's nature mean that we can confidently believe that all will finally be drawn to God.

---

[75] Pinnock, 1992 p.173.

[76] Graham, 1988 p.487.

[77] Robinson, 1950 p.104.

[78] Robinson, 1950 pp.104 - 105.

[79] Davies, 1990, p.176.

No Heaven Without Hell

A further objection that is raised to the idea of universal salvation is that if there is no hell there can be no heaven. Davies suggests that based on Biblical evidence and the Christian tradition, this objection is justified. He writes:

> It seems methodologically odd for a person both to deny the reality of eternal hell and (because of biblical teaching and Christian tradition) affirm the reality of heaven. For both seem to stand on an equally firm exegetical and traditional foundation.[80]

The issue for Davies, is then how one can be accepted and the other dismissed. Others have argued that heaven and hell are dependent opposites: there cannot be one and not the other. Hick would not accept this criticism at all, but would be in agreement with Küng's statement:

> What is absolutely indefensible is that stupid dualistic systematization which thoughtlessly assumes that, because there is a personal God, there must also be a personal devil; because there is a heaven, there must be a hell; because there is an eternal life there must be an eternal suffering.[81]

Similarly, Gray observes that for Rahner, 'Heaven and hell are not mere alternatives, they are not equal paths to be chosen'.[82] There does not seem to be any sound basis for assuming that the existence of heaven requires the existence of hell. They are not dependent on each other. There is no reason to assume that the existence of one necessarily requires the existence of the other.

It seems clear that universal salvation does not render a religious life pointless, as Christian faith is not only concerned with the afterlife but with existence now. Hick claims that the afterlife does not provide compensation dependent on one's experiences in this life, but rather allows each person fulfilment. Rather than God judging individuals on what they have done in this life, Hick suggests that they themselves fulfil their own potential and eventually become children of God. If God created humanity with the intention that all would finally be drawn to Godself, then the existence of heaven is in no way dependent on the existence of hell. Thus it would seem that Hick's premise of an all-powerful God of Love results in a strong argument for universal salvation.

---

[80] Davies, 1990 p.177.

[81] Hans Küng, *Eternal Life?* (1984) London: Collins p.135.

[82] Gray, 1996 p.154. He is quoting Karl Rahner, 'The Human Question of Meaning in Face of the Absolute Mystery of God' in *Theological Investigations Vol. 18 - God and Revelation* (1983) Darton, Longmann and Todd pp.89-104.

Conclusion

One of the major difficulties with Hick's universalism is the weight of Scripture, which is often supposed to teach an eternal separation of fates. Although Hick does not attend to the evidence of Scripture as much as he might, he does show that the teaching about hell is not unequivocal and that there is significant support for the universalist position. It is probable that a more thorough examination of the New Testament would not have further helped Hick's case as he would still interpret the separatist passages in the light of the universalist passages and thus would have reached the same conclusion. Hick only aimed to show that there is support for the universalist position in the New Testament and I believe he succeeds in this aim. However I will look further at the use of the New Testament in this debate in the following chapter. Hick holds on to a much reduced idea of hell. However this does not aid his argument in any way and he ends up with a 'hell' so far removed from the traditional doctrine that it is in fact a different concept. Hick's argument for the efficaciousness of God's salvific will is convincing but he cannot adequately support it without appeal to God's foreknowledge and middle knowledge. The lack of discussion of God's knowledge is a serious weakness in Hick's theory and I will look at the benefit of middle knowledge for a universalist position in the following chapter. Despite these difficulties, Hick's rejection of hell is adequately defended from criticism and with some further development his universalist position could be a strong one.

Human Freedom

One of the major criticisms of Hick's universal salvation is that he cannot affirm this eventual outcome and also retain genuine human freedom. It is intrinsic to Hick's thought that he does retain the genuine free will of each individual, and thus it is important to establish whether Hick offers a coherent definition of human freedom. There are four main areas within Hick's view of freedom that will be critiqued below.

Predestination

Hick is open to the charge that his theory amounts to a single predestination that must result in the salvation of all people. Hick discusses the work of Schleiermacher whom he notes as a nineteenth century advocate of an Irenaean type theology. Schleiermacher advocated a single predestination and Hick, although theoretically denying single predestination aligns himself with Schleiermacher and his school of thought. However it is not clear that if it must be conceded that Hick advocates a single predestination that this is detrimental to his theory.

Chester Gillis writes, that Hick's universalism 'could easily be interpreted to mean that there is a predeterminism from the beginning towards salvation'.[83] He claims that this makes Hick's universal salvation incompatible with human freedom. 'Such a position', he writes, 'diminishes the genuine freedom of the individual'.[84] It is possible that predestination diminishes human freedom as it would change human freedom from being of the strong libertarian kind which Swinburne proposes, to being a compatibilst freedom. However it is not clear that this is not a genuine human freedom and thus predestination only causes a difficulty for Hick if it destroys human freedom. Although the outcome of our lives is predestined, this does not mean that we are determined and without genuine human freedom. The attainment of salvation by each person will not happen in a way specifically prescribed by God, but will happen differently and over different periods of time for each individual as a result of his/her own choices. Thus Hick believes that predestination does not override the limited freedom which we have as created beings.

Although Hick strongly objects to Calvin's double predestination he does state that Calvin's claim that there can be predestination and moral responsibility is 'intelligible'. Calvin argues that 'the sinner whose fallen nature is such that he necessarily wills wrongly and who cannot, with his perverted nature, will rightly, remains nevertheless a free and responsible agent; for he is acting voluntarily and not from external compulsion'.[85] Hick concludes that this account of freedom serves 'to render intelligible Calvin's assertion that a sinner sins necessarily, out of a fallen nature, and yet that he is morally responsible for his sins and is justly punished by his Maker'.[86] Thus Hick accepts that predestination does not annihilate human freedom and therefore moral accountability. Thus Hick's objection is not that one's destiny is prearranged because he claims that one can still be free to reach it of one's own decision. In Calvin's case, Hick, of course, objects to the idea that God should predestine any to eternal hell but it would seem that Hick is amenable to a predestination which would result in the salvation of all.

Thus it would be fair to say that Hick does propose a single predetestination. However this does not mean that Hick has sacrificed genuine human freedom in order to arrive at this outcome. If an alternative account of freedom, namely compatibilist freedom, can be shown to allow genuine human freedom then Hick can justifiably propose both a single predestination and free human choices. I will be looking further at compatibilist freedom below.

---

[83] Gillis, 1987 p.107.

[84] Gillis, 1987 p.109.

[85] Hick, 1966 p.121. He is referring to John Calvin *Institutes of the Christian Religion* II. iii. 5 John T. McNeilie (ed.) Ford Lewis battles (trans.) (1961) London: SCM Press.

[86] Hick, 1966 p.121.

Epistemic Distance

Epistemic distance is essential to Hick's theodicy and to his theory of universal salvation. Without epistemic distance Hick does not believe that we would have a free choice in relation to God. However not all agree that creating us at an epistemic distance is the action of a good God, as Hick claims. Indeed, as we saw in the objections to Swinburne's account of epistemic distance, it has been protested that this epistemic distance is detrimental to human development and our relationship with God. There are several difficulties with Hick's account of epistemic distance which I shall discuss in this section.

Does being able freely to recognise God's existence outweigh the value of being ignorant about God? Both Ward and Mesle would say that it does not, and that our choices would be more valuable if they were based on knowledge rather than ignorance. They argue that the creation of humans at an epistemic distance simply means that they are created in ignorance and thus at a disadvantage for coming to know God. Ward writes:

> Hick supposes that all men really would desire God as the fulfillment
> of their own lives if only they could see him as he is. But in that case,
> why can they not see him as he is? Because, says Hick, it is important
> that they should be free to reject him. But all that can mean is that it
> is important that they should act mistakenly through ignorance.[87]

However this summation is unfair to Hick. It does not mean that individuals act mistakenly through ignorance but rather means that everyone will eventually freely arrive at the right choice. In agreement with Ward, Mesle writes:

> I cannot accept Hick's solution that a loving God has intentionally
> made the world look as if there is no God so that we will be free to
> choose faith. I do not believe that ignorance is the ground of freedom
> or faith.[88]

Again this is to exaggerate Hick's position. He does not claim that it looks as if there is no God, only that we are not fully aware of God and thus choose whether or not we believe there to be a God. So Ward and Mesle claim that rather than allowing a free relationship between humans and God, epistemic distance only serves to make humans ignorant about God. Mesle writes:

> [Hick's] theodicy forces us into the religiously, ethically and
> philosophically offensive position of saying that God considers it a
> virtue for us to believe without sufficient evidence and has
> intentionally created the world so that such blind belief is the only

---

[87] Ward, 1970 p.227.
[88] Mesle, 1991 p.19.

way we can come to believe in God.[89]

Hick does not actually suggest that there is *no* evidence of God or even that the evidence is insufficient. Rather he believes it is necessary that the world can rationally be interpreted either way. Mesle's objection goes further, he argues that there is an awful irony in a good God choosing to make the world ambiguous and, in effect hide from us. He writes:

> God has gone through the entire charade of creating the world through an evolutionary process to make it look as if there were no God. But much more than this, God has created a world of intense suffering, a world in which people are raped and murdered, in which children starve, in which cancer and AIDS torture and dehumanize millions - all created by God to conceal from us how truly loving God really is.[90]

This is a powerful objection from Mesle. Hick responds to it:

> The metaphors of hiding, divine concealment, *deus absconditus*, can indeed be used, with due caution, and have often been so used in the literature; but they must not be taken with anthropomorphic literalness and twisted into moral absurdities.[91]

The purpose of the nature of the world, does according to Hick show how truly loving God is, but it also has other purposes, namely human soul-making. God does not desire to 'conceal' God's loving nature. Rather, according to Hick, God wants to allow individuals to find God for themselves and thus we are not made with full awareness of God. However this is not the same as God hiding from us or concealing the fact that God is loving. As Hick suggests, Mesle twists Hick's account of epistemic distance and paints an unacceptable picture of God.

William Rowe concedes that full awareness of God would compel a response from us in terms of recognizing that God exists. However he claims that Hick carries the argument too far.

> If God is directly present to me in all his power, glory and love, my intellect compels my assent to the proposition that he exists, there is no room for free assent. The problem is that Hick does not stop with this point. He sometimes says that, in order to be a *person*, in order to be *morally free*, in order to be free with respect to *loving God*, we must exist at an epistemic distance from God.[92]

---

[89] Mesle, 1991 p.77.
[90] Mesle, 1991 p.29.
[91] Hick, 1991 (b) p.122.
[92] William Rowe, 'Paradox and Promise - Hick's Solution to the Problem of Evil' in Hewitt (ed.), 1991 p.115.

It is these claims to which Rowe objects. He comments that he:

> Can find no good reasons in Hick's writings to support his further claims that epistemic distance from God is necessary for the very existence of human persons, for their being free to develop morally, and for their being free with respect to coming to love God.[93]

Rowe quotes three passages of Hick's in which he claims Hick implies that epistemic distance is not necessary merely for the freedom to know God, but also in order to be a person, to love God and in order to be morally free.[94] Rowe argues that full knowledge of God would provide humans with a very good reason to love God, but it would not compel them to do so. He writes, 'it is, alas, part of the very nature of freedom to have the power not to do what one has a very good reason to do'. And he concludes 'if I am right about this, one must wonder about what good is served by our state of epistemic distance from God'.[95]

Hick responds to the challenge made by Rowe. He acknowledges that the passages cited by Rowe need revising. 'I think', he writes, 'Rowe is right that this [epistemic distance] cannot be a necessary condition of our being persons'.[96] However Hick maintains that his primary point holds.

> Being compelled to be conscious of God would not leave us … free to adopt any attitude to God. To be inescapably aware that we are in the presence of the ultimate power of the universe … would be a situation in which we could only respond by worship and an answering love. This is, of course, not a matter of logical necessity but one of strong psychological inclination, given the (God-given) structure of our human nature.[97]

For Hick, knowledge of God would compel a response of love and worship. Although God does not force that upon us, even humans who are quite liable to do what they have good reason not to do would recognise the presence of God and find the fulfilment of their desires in God. Thus they would respond to God with love and worship.

Thus Hick accepts Rowe's challenge that epistemic distance cannot be a condition of us being a person. However he maintains that we need epistemic distance in order to be morally free and have a genuine relationship with God. The criticisms made by Ward and Mesle are serious ones, however they misrepresent

---

[93] Rowe, 1991 p.116.

[94] Rowe quotes from John Hick, *The Philosophy of Religion* 3rd Edition (1983) New Jersey: Prentice Hall, referred to as Hick, 1983 (c), pp.45 - 46; and Hick, 1981 pp. 42 - 43.

[95] Rowe, 1991 p.116.

[96] John Hick, 'Reply' in Hewitt (ed.), 1991 p.134.

[97] Hick, 1991 p.134.

Hick's position. Hick does not claim that God goes to great lengths to conceal God from us, but that God has created us so that we do not have full knowledge of God and the world can be interpreted with or without God.

Ward agrees with Hick that being aware of the presence of the Creator would also make us aware that a response was required.

> One may certainly wish to say that one could not apprehend God without at the same time acknowledging that he made a total moral demand on one's life; but the acknowledgement that a moral demand exists is not the same as the acknowledgement of that demand, in the sense of submission of one's will to it.[98]

Thus Ward does not agree that 'epistemic distance' is required in order for us to be able to make free responses to God. He writes: 'There is, I conclude, no absurdity in the notion of a creature existing in full consciousness of its Creator and yet free to reject the Creator's love for and demand upon its existence'.[99] Ward is right that awareness that a moral demand exists is not the same as fulfilling that moral demand. However Hick's argument is that the nature of God and the fact that we are all made with an inherent desire for God means that no human could be fully aware of God without wanting to submit his/her will to God's. For Hick it is clear that a full awareness of God could not leave us neutral with regards to our creator, but would prompt every person to fulfil his/her desire for God.

A further objection is that we are fully aware of the physical world without this annihilating our freedom or compelling a certain sort of response from us. D.R. Duff-Forbes argues: 'If human freedom is *not* vitiated by the coerciveness of the physical world, then God, supposing he exists, *could* "force" himself upon men in the way the physical world does *without* destroying their freedom'.[100] He argues that full awareness of God would not compel us to respond in a certain way to God.

> Hick nowhere demonstrates or attempts to demonstrate that it is logically impossible for God to disclose himself 'coercively' in the way the physical world does, and hence provide adequate evidence for his existence, without thereby depriving men of the option of faith.[101]

Hick does not show this, as he thinks it is apparent that knowledge of God would compel a response. Miller responds that sense experience unlike God cannot 'draw

---

[98] Ward, 1970 p.225.

[99] Ward, 1970 p.231.

[100] D.R. Duff-Forbes, 'Faith, Evidence, Coercion' *Australasian Journal of Philosophy* vol.47 no.2 (1969) p.212.

[101] Duff-Forbes, 1969 p.214.

us irresistibly to itself'[102] and thus the same argument cannot apply to God and the physical world.

Hick's argument for epistemic distance relies on two premises. The claim that we are all made with an inherent desire for God, and Hick's belief that full awareness of God's loving nature would be irresistible. If these two premises are true than it seems reasonable to conclude that full knowledge of God would mean that we could not be free in relation to God. That is, if we were fully aware of God we would immediately choose to submit our wills to God's. Miller writes in defence of Hick that if the Christian God exists: 'He is infinitely good, and therefore infinitely attractive and infallibly elicits commitment to himself once he is experienced as such'.[103] Miller's point is that the nature of God is so appealing that we could not fail to respond to it. Miller further claims:

> An infinitely good being (experienced as such) would be irresistible: that is analytic. To deny that it would be irresistible would be to say that it would be in some way unattractive and that is to deny that it is infinitely good.[104]

Again Miller assumes that we have some bias towards God, and thus God is irresistible to us. Given that Hick makes the point that we are made for communion with God, his conclusion that we could not be free in the face of God is a reasonable one. That is to say that we could not resist an infinitely good being and thus we would not be free to live in this world, developing our own character through soul-making and coming to know God as a result of our free choices.

Both Ward and Mesle raise the further issue that Hick cannot object to the state of humans being in the direct presence of God *per se*. Mesle explains: 'Ultimately, according to the Irenaean theodicy, we *shall* find ourselves in the immediate presence of God. So it cannot be *that* which Hick finds objectionable'.[105] Ward writes that, in Hick's theory, all will eventually be more directly in the presence of God, and so then will have no freedom in relation to God. Thus, 'on his view freedom becomes only a transitional stage on the way to necessity'.[106] When we are finally in the presence of God we will have no freedom. However Hick may respond that this would not matter as we would already have made our choice in favour of God and effectively fulfilled our potential as children of God.

For Swinburne to be able to respond adequately to the challenges against his epistemic distance, I concluded that he needed to show that a meeting with God would be compelling. Hick goes much further towards making this point. Given his

---

[102] Barry Miller, 'The No - Evidence Defence' *International Journal for Philosophy of Religion* vol.3 no.1 (1972) p.3.

[103] Miller, 1972 p.3.

[104] Miller, 1972 p.3.

[105] Mesle, 1991 p.27.

[106] Ward, 1970 p.226.

claims that we are made with an inherent desire for God and that full awareness of God would be irresistible, it is reasonable to conclude that epistemic distance is necessary to preserve our freedom. Although the objections, particularly as made by Mesle are powerful ones, they misrepresent Hick's position and do not recognise Hick's reasons for claiming that full awareness of God would not allow us freedom. In conclusion it seems that Hick and Swinburne are right that a full awareness of God would inhibit human freedom because we would be not be able to avoid responding to God in love and worship. However it is also clear that this epistemic distance will not last eternally and in the following chapter I will discuss the purpose of epistemic distance in this life and why it is abandoned in the eschaton.

Compatibilist Freedom

Hick is insistent that humans are free, so in order to defend his account of universal salvation and particularly his claim that we can be made with an inherent desire for God but still be free, Hick must demonstrate the coherence of compatibilist human freedom. Many scholars have criticised compatibilism, the main objection being that it is not genuine human freedom, but a sort of determinism. If it can be shown that compatibilist freedom is genuine human freedom, and not determinism, then Hick's account of ultimate universal salvation is defensible. Thus Hick must show that our preconditioning towards God, in the shape of our desire for God, does not override our freedom.

Jerry Walls writes: 'If freedom and determinism are compatible, then I would agree with Hick that universalism is entailed by God's perfect goodness and sovereignty'.[107] Thus the universalist position has great strength if it can combine a certain outcome with human freedom. Compatabilists hold that there is no logical contradiction in affirming both freedom and determinism, or soft determinism. Soft determinists simply assert that there is a reason why we make particular decisions. Our decisions are, in a weak sense, caused by our natures. As Dennett writes:

> 'Compatabilists' or 'soft determinists' - those who believe that free will and responsibility are compatible with determinism - typically claim in one way or another that one acts freely and responsibly just so long as one does what one decides, based on what one believes and desires.[108]

Thus if we have been given natures which actually yearn for communion with God, as Hick suggests, this will be the reason for our eventual acceptance of God, but it is compatible with our human freedom.

---

[107] Walls, 1992 p.79.
[108] Dennett, 1984 p.83.

Many object to even a soft determinism on the grounds that it erodes our responsibility for our own actions. However, Dennett suggests that this is based on a mistaken view of determinism. He writes that if we take the line that determinism means that everything is inevitable, then 'no agent can do anything about anything. But this is just fatalism, and we must not confuse determinism with fatalism'.[109] Determinism does not suggest that there can be no freedom of decision, rather it acknowledges that there is an explanation for decision. Double explains that:

> Traditional compatabilism's solution to the free-will question was that freedom is the ability to act as one wishes. Since acting as one wishes is clearly compatible with determinism, freedom was seen as possible within a determined universe.[110]

Lucas writes that confusion often arises in discussing determinism, as at some point the definition of it is changed, and the acceptance of soft determinism, becomes confused with strong determinism, or, what Dennett would describe as fatalism. Lucas writes:

> It is easy to accept 'determinism' in some dilute sense, in which all that is being claimed is that there is some reason for every action, and then believe that one is committed to determinism in a strong sense, in which all our actions are causally determined by conditions outside our control because occurring before our birth ... Our starting point was the principle that every event has an explanation; which is not the same as, and does not imply, the contention that every event has a regularity explanation.[111]

It could be argued that Ward is guilty of making this leap. He writes: 'If we admit freedom at all then we cannot hope to understand it or explain it in terms of anything other than itself; for if it was explicable by reference to causes or reasons then it would no longer be freedom'.[112] And again: 'One cannot say why the choice that was made, was made - for that would be to suggest reasons or causes for it. Therefore freedom must, by its essential nature, be inexplicable'.[113] Thus Ward makes no distinction between soft determinism which acknowledges that actions have an explanation and strong determinism which claims that every event is determined by its explanation.

Ward understands Hick to be saying that all people will eventually accept God because they will have no reason not to. Ward claims that Hick, rather than allowing individual freedom, is actually advocating a kind of determinism which insists that people will ultimately accept God because that is the reasonable thing to

---

[109] Dennett, 1984 p.123.

[110] Double, 1991 p.27.

[111] Lucas, 1970 p.54.

[112] Ward, 1970 p.223.

[113] Ward, 1970 p.224.

do and their natures are such that they are made to do what is reasonable. Ward argues that freedom cannot be confined to what it is reasonable to do.

> To give an account of moral choice in terms of reasonableness, is a
> very understandable one; for it seems to protect human freedom from
> the charge of being a merely arbitrary choice ... if one tries to
> suggest that one choice is explicable because it is or seems more
> reasonable than the other to the agent one must be rejecting belief in
> freedom, in favour of some kind of determinism.[114]

However Hick responds that Ward has misinterpreted his explanation of human freedom as reasonable choice. Hick is not concerned by Ward's accusation of determinism. Hick explains that 'any theology must, surely, reckon with the fact that to be created is to be subject to an ultimate arbitrariness and determination'.[115] However any freedom humans have is the freedom of created beings. Our freedom only involves choices about how to respond to the environment that we are given with the abilities we have. It does not involve us choosing our own environment and abilities. We can only be free within the confines of our species and our nature. Hick writes:

> That we are free beings cannot mean that we are unconditional, but
> that within the limits set by all the conditioning circumstances of our
> pedigree and environment we are nevertheless able self-creatively to
> exercise a certain energy of our own.[116]

Indeed it seems that compatibilist freedom in fact provides the most realistic account of our freedom as created beings.

Arguably, this still involves God controlling our choices on some level. Holten writes: 'Although God in Hick's model would not in a strict sense override human freedom, he would at least be patronizing human beings, treating them "for their own good", rather than granting them choices'.[117] However Hick's response would be that because we were created with a desire for God, this is not the case. It is an essential aspect of Hick's whole theory that we were initially created with natures that yearn for God.[118] Ward objects to this premise.

> Man must be free, not just in the weak sense that all or some of his
> acts proceed from his own character and are not externally
> compelled, but in the stronger sense that either of two or more

---

[114] Ward, 1969 p.250.

[115] Hick, 1970 (d) p.420.

[116] John Hick, 'Freedom and the Irenaean Theodicy Again' *The Journal of Theological Studies* vol.XXI (1970), referred to as Hick, 1970 (d), pp.420 -421.

[117] Holten, 1999 p.46.

[118] See Hick, 1976 p.251.

alternatives may be chosen, and the choice cannot be predicted in advance by any knowledge even of the agent's nature. For God is the Creator of natures of all men; and if men were only free in that they did what their natures caused them to do, God would be directly responsible for human acts.[119]

However Hick would argue that as God has already created us with a desire for communion with God, there will be no need to override our freedom or patronize us in order to ensure that all people eventually accept God. Rather, each person will eventually act on their desire for God. The objection is of course made that this means we are predetermined to accept God. Although our natures are God-given, they are surely not as 'pure' as Ward suggests, in the sense that our nature is not a static entity which, alone, fully determines all of our actions. Our natures are influenced by our experiences and environment, and thus can determine our actions only in a general sense and not in a totally predictable sense as Ward suggests.

Hick writes, 'I have suggested that man has been made by God so that he will in the free out-working of his own nature eventually come to love and worship his maker'.[120] Hick continues: 'Is not this simply to say, in effect, that his response to God has been predetermined by the way in which he has been created?' Hick's response is that this question is based on a wrong supposition, 'that beings have or could have chosen their own nature'.[121] Indeed Hick's description of freedom as 'limited creativity' attempts to show that our actions can loosely be determined by our natures. Geivett comments:

> The notions of a determined human nature giving rise to certain decisions and of the possibility of unpredictable twists in the moment of decision are compressed to form a richer conception of freedom.[122]

Hick believes that we do have God-given natures,[123] and that our decisions are loosely caused by our natures. However he suggests that simultaneously there can be other factors at work in our decision making. He writes, 'whilst the action proceeds from the nature of the agent, the nature from which it proceeds is that of "the actual self alive in the moment of decision"'.[124] Thus Hick attempts to show that actions which proceed from the nature of the agent still allow genuine freedom.

This account of salvation means that Hick does not have to choose, as Swinburne does, between salvation and freedom. Swinburne concludes that strong freedom is the most important gift that God gives us. Hick would claim that

---

[119] Ward, 1970 pp.222-223.
[120] Hick, 1976 p.254.
[121] Hick, 1976 p.254.
[122] Geivett, 1993 pp.160 - 161.
[123] Hick, 1976 p. 254ff.
[124] Hick, 1966 p.312, he quotes Hartshorne, 1962 p.20.

salvation is a greater gift even than this. However his account of freedom as limited creativity means that Hick can assume that God gives the gifts of freedom and salvation to every person. Thus it is possible that every person's desire for God will mean that all people will ultimately freely accept God. Hick could look at God's knowledge in order to strengthen his position. However, as we have seen, he does not discuss this in any detail. In the following chapter I will discuss the benefits of God's foreknowledge and middle knowledge for this sort of universalist position.

Good World

Hick's theodicy lays great importance on the freedom we have to choose good or bad. Hick does believe that it is a coherent suggestion that God could have created us so that we were only able to choose between different good choices and yet we would still be genuinely free. Thus Hick must account for God's decision in choosing not to do this. Hick's response is, of course, that the choice between good and bad creates the best possible world. However Mesle does not accept that our freedom to sin enhances our environment:

> I want to challenge a basic value assumption underlying Hick's theodicy. Why should we assume that the freedom to choose evil is so wonderful? I believe that meaningful freedom can exist where there are meaningful choices between goods – as when someone decides between devoting their life to art or science.[125]

Mesle continues:

> Freedom can be meaningful even when it is 'limited' to choices which are good, loving, creative and enriching ... there are freedoms which do not make our lives better or richer. There are 'freedoms' which only weaken us, limit us, enslave us, which loving and wise people confidently restrain.[126]

Hick believes, however, that it is the freedom to choose wrong and the kind of environment in which people suffer which allows us to develop.

Griffin argues that God did not need actually to make us as free beings, in order for us to believe that we are developing through our free choices. He writes:

> All that we human beings would need, in order to enjoy the feeling of being authentically virtuous would be the *belief* that we are genuinely free. Hick's God could have created us such that we were absolutely

---

[125] Mesle, 1991 p.31.
[126] Mesle, 1991 p.42.

convinced that we were free, even though we only did what God willed.[127]

Hick responds to this idea:

> I find it hard to take seriously Griffin's suggestion that God's purpose in creation might be satisfied by giving us the mere illusion rather than the reality of freedom. The kind of God he is talking about must be morally and intellectually limited as well as limited in power.[128]

Indeed it does not seem probable that a loving God, who, according to Hick, allows us to have freedom for the benefit of our own development would pretend to give us freedom. Hick does not merely emphasize the importance of humans believing that their actions are free, but claims that in order to have a genuinely valuable relationship with God our actions must be free. Thus the illusion of human freedom would not allow God the genuine relationship with creation which Hick thinks God desires.

As far as Hick is concerned, a freedom limited to only good choices, or the belief that we are free when actually we are not, would not result in a better world than the actual world. The importance of the soul-making environment in Hick's theory is clear and either of these proposed worlds would prevent the process of soul-making which he believes to be so important.

Conclusion

Hick does advocate a single predestination, however he does not believe that this deprives us of freedom. Hick advocates a compatibilist freedom which allows us to be free whilst acting according to our natures which are God-given. This means that every individual will eventually act in accordance with his/her desire for communion with God and thus accept God and so be saved. Although our natures are God-given this constitutes only a weak, or soft, determinism, as our natures develop and are influenced by our environment. Thus we are not fully determined in the sense of never being able to do other than we do, but often because of our natures, we cannot reasonably be expected to do other than we do. The epistemic distance from God at which we are created is essential to Hick's theory and he demonstrates that because of our inherent desire for God, and God's nature we would not be free if we were made fully aware of God. The compelling nature of a full encounter with God will be important to the conclusions of this book, and although Hick demonstrates this adequately, I will return to it in the following chapter. Although Hick believes that we could logically be made free but still

---

[127] David R. Griffin, 'Critique' in Davies (ed.) 1981 p.54.

[128] John Hick, 'Response to Critics' in Davies (ed.) 1981, referred to as Hick, 1981 (b), p.65.

always choose the good he rejects this idea as such a good world would be unable to fulfil God's purposes for us, namely soul-making and the resulting development into children of God. In conclusion, it is not his account of freedom which is most problematic for Hick, as he shows that the inherent desire for God is compatible with our free choices.

God's Knowledge

In order to affirm an universalist outcome Hick must assert at least that God has foreknowledge. Otherwise this result cannot be known. Also I have made the point that a discussion of God's knowledge and an appeal to middle knowledge would strengthen Hick's position significantly. With the benefit of middle knowledge, Hick could argue not only that our desire for God will ultimately lead to universal salvation, but that God *knows* that this will be the outcome because all people will eventually fulfill this desire by accepting God. Hick could contend that should any possible person have freely chosen to reject God, despite his/her inherent desire for God, then God would not have actualized such a person. However the omission of a discussion of God's knowledge leaves a chink in the armor of Hick's defence of universalism and thus creates a weakness in his theory. It would seem that a discussion of middle knowledge could save Hick's theory or at very least strengthen his case. In the final chapter I will develop an account of universalism which is dependent on middle knowledge.

Conclusion

Although there are several difficulties with Hick's universal salvation, in my judgement he responds adequately to many of the criticisms. The major criticism of Hick's universalism is that it does not allow for genuine human freedom. Hick's whole theory stands or falls on his understanding of human freedom. However he demonstrates that in line with compatibilist freedom, his account of freedom as 'limited creativity' both allows us finally to fulfill our God-given natures and also to act with genuine human freedom. Thus, if compatibilist freedom is accepted, and it seems that on the grounds of it allowing genuine human freedom it can be accepted, this major obstacle to acceptance of Hick's theory is removed. Hick shows that our inherent desire for God and God's nature mean that if we had full awareness of God we would not be able to choose freely but would submit our wills to God's.

Hick's progressive afterlives are criticised as they are far removed from any traditional Christian thought. Indeed it seems that they are not the solution that Hick hopes they will be, as they cannot affirm ultimate universal salvation. A further difficulty arises from the lack of discussion concerning God's knowledge, and it seems that for Hick's theory to work he needs to appeal to God's foreknowledge and middle knowledge. Without these, Hick cannot affirm that

God's desire for universal salvation will ultimately be efficacious, or that there will be anything more certain than a contingent universalism. However Hick's claim that universalism can be supported by the New Testament, and his responses to general criticisms of universalism, are adequate. Therefore with some discussion of God's knowledge and further discussion of epistemic distance it will be possible to remodel Hick's theory into a coherent, Christian universalism and I will do this in the following chapter.

Chapter 6

Firm Universalism

Introduction

In this chapter I will put forward an alternative to Swinburne and Hick's theories of hell and universalism. In previous chapters I have largely rejected Swinburne's account of salvation and hell. Although I am more in sympathy with Hick's thought on this subject, I have rejected some of his proposals and pointed to areas not developed by Hick which would be beneficial to his universalist position. The main area is God's knowledge which I shall discuss in this chapter. I hope to demonstrate that it is a plausible theory that although we are free to reject God, God knows that in the end no one will choose this option.

The premises for this argument are drawn from the conclusions of discussions in earlier chapters. There are three main premises: first, God's universal salvific will. As we have seen, Hick asserts this strongly and Swinburne weakly. In agreement with Hick, I will assert this strongly and assume that this would be God's overriding desire in creation; that it is more important than the freedom of individuals. God's universal salvific will can be defended both Biblically and as a consequence of divine love. By 'God's universal salvific will' I mean that God strongly desires to save every person. This includes the belief that God not only wills the salvation of all people, but further designed creation to make this a likely outcome in two specific ways. First, that God creates us with a deep longing for God, and second, that God provides every person with sufficient grace and opportunity to accept God.

The second premise is compatibilist human freedom. Having rejected Swinburne's case for libertarian freedom, and argued for the coherence of this understanding of freedom throughout this book, I will not discuss it again in this chapter, but will refer to the conclusions already drawn. These are that compatibilist human freedom (in relation to both determinism and divine foreknowledge) is both coherent, and further is the most accurate account of our human freedom. The third premise is that God has both simple foreknowledge and middle knowledge. The compatibility of divine foreknowledge and human freedom has already been discussed and again I will draw on the conclusions reached rather than return to this topic. As neither Swinburne nor Hick particularly discuss God's middle knowledge that remains to be done. Although it has been touched on in previous chapters, and I have concluded it is coherent to talk of God's middle knowledge, some further discussion of the implications of this knowledge are needed to support my position. In this chapter I will discuss what it means for God to have middle knowledge and show that with the benefit of middle knowledge, God need not create any person who would not be saved, and thus would not create any world in which all are not saved.

So God's universal salvific will, which is a consequence of divine love necessarily leads to universal salvation, because God, being able to create a 'universalist world' (one in which all people are saved), would not create any world which did not have this outcome. This position relies on both the coherence of middle knowledge and a universal opportunity to encounter God, to arrive at what I will term 'firm universalism'. In this chapter I will attempt to establish that with the benefit of middle knowledge, God is able to create a world in which God knows that all will be saved, and that an encounter with God after death would be efficacious in providing all people with the opportunity freely to choose God. However, I will begin by looking at the Biblical evidence for hell and universalism. I have looked at this previously and in chapter 5 concluded that Hick's position was adequate. However it will be helpful to return here to the question of the relevant Biblical material in order both further to establish the first premise and to consider the approaches a universalist may take to Scripture and whether the Bible can ultimately support a universalist position.

Bible

Neither Swinburne nor Hick provide a systematic account of the relevant Biblical material and thus so far the engagement with Biblical material has been sparse. Although the evidence and testimony of Scripture is, of course, essential in establishing a Christian position, the aim of this book is primarily to explore the topic of hell in relation to concepts of philosophy of religion. Although my primary concern has not been with Biblical material, I do believe that my position is compatible with the teaching of the New Testament. There is not the space here nor is it the purpose of this study to go through every single Biblical passage which may be relevant to the question of hell and salvation to show that it can be interpreted to support universalism. There has been much written on the Bible and the subject of hell and salvation which does not need repeating here. Instead, I will begin by looking at one particular approach and then looking at the key texts. Jan Bonda has attempted to show that the whole thrust of Scripture is to encourage us to work and hope for the salvation of all and so I will begin by discussing his work.

An Universalist Approach To Scripture - Jan Bonda

Bonda's book *The One Purpose of God - An Answer to the Doctrine of Eternal Punishment* looks in considerable detail at passages from Scripture which are relevant to God's salvific will and the ultimate state after death. Bonda's position is interesting because he writes as an evangelical who affirms the authority of Scripture and yet firmly believes that we should hope for the eventual salvation of all people. Bonda was a pastor in the Dutch Reformed Church and in the first chapter describes several pastoral situations which had prompted him into thinking and writing about the one purpose of God. His approach is to look at the texts in light of what Sanders refers to as 'control beliefs'.[1] Bonda proposes that we search the Bible with the question in mind 'Do the Scriptures really teach us that there is no hope for those who died in that state? [without God.] Is it true that God wants us passively to accept the fact that our fellow human beings are lost?'.[2] Bonda believes that we have learnt to read the Scriptures with the assumption that some are damned, and that there is nothing we can do about it.

> Since Augustine our tradition has taught us that God has two separate goals. He has predestined a small percentage of humankind to salvation, to eternal life. The rest of humanity has been predestined to eternal damnation. Since it is his will that many will be lost, we have no option but to acquiesce.[3]

Bonda explicitly rejects the idea of there being two separate goals. As is clear from the title of his book, Bonda wishes to affirm that God in fact has only one goal, which although the majority of the Church fails to apprehend, the New Testament writers understood. He comments: 'Apparently we have lost something in our faith tradition, something of the hope by which the New Testament believers lived. It is imperative that we know more about this hope!'.[4]

Thus Bonda's main control belief is that the salvation of all people is God's one purpose. Bonda further believes that God wishes to achieve this end in co-operation with humans, rather than by simply forcing salvation upon us.

> God wants salvation for Israel, and through Israel he wants to reach all nations with his redemption. He wants to achieve this through human beings (mortals!) who share in the same aim, and who want that so eagerly that they are willing to put their own salvation at risk! We completely miss the point Scripture is trying to make if we argue that God would have done this anyway, since it had been predetermined what he would do! No, God himself puts everything at risk. If Moses had not intervened, Israel would not have received the forgiveness required for the fulfilment of the promise to the fathers.[5]

---

[1] See Sanders, 1992 pp.31-34. He explains that 'The views that we take on such subjects [as christology, faith, the nature and means of grace, the value of general revelation, the ministry of the Holy Spirit, and epistemology] are of immense importance because they serve as "control beliefs" that guide and control the way we investigate and interpret evidence on other topics ... Control beliefs can be extremely powerful in influencing what we "see" in a text.' p.31.
[2] Bonda, 1993 p.2.
[3] Bonda, 1993 p.256.
[4] Bonda, 1993 p.3.
[5] Bonda, 1993 pp.62-63.

Thus God uses people to help bring about the salvation of all people and the responses of individuals to their calling, according to Bonda, demonstrates their suitability for assisting God with this task.

One example that Bonda discusses in some detail is Genesis 18:22 - 33, where Abraham intercedes for the people of Sodom. Bonda notes: 'In asking for the salvation not only of the righteous but of the entire city, Abraham does exactly what God intends'.[6] Indeed it is 'precisely because he [Abraham] intercedes for Sodom, [that] he demonstrates that he is the man through whom God will lead all nations to the salvation he has prepared for them'.[7] Abraham shows himself to be worthy of this task, precisely because he does not simply acquiesce to God's threat to destroy the city but instead pleads for the people. Bonda emphasises: 'Whoever is called by him is called not to accept passively the doom people have brought upon themselves. And those who do acquiesce cannot be the tools through which God realises his purposes'.[8]

Two Sets of Passages - Universalist and Separatist Texts

In his book, Bonda is particularly concerned with the teaching of the Old Testament prophets and the writings of St Paul. However he also discusses the story of the Lost Son (Luke 15: 11-32) which he believes 'perfectly expresses what God is like'.[9] Bonda uses this story, which is told in Luke's Gospel, along with the preceding parables of the Lost Sheep and the Lost Coin as a 'control' picture of God, and interprets other scriptural material in the light of these parables. It is clear that the New Testament contains two distinct sets of teaching concerning the afterlife. First are the warnings of the separation of the good and bad, and the fires of hell that will be experienced by the latter. Then there are also the sayings that refer to the eventual reconciliation of all people with God. The question then is how

---

[6] Bonda, 1993 pp. 46-47 Bonda further questions why the city can be saved only if God can find ten righteous people. He asks, 'why this bottom line? Lower than ten will not do. There must be a *people* that calls upon the name of the Lord. Ten represented the smallest unit of the people of Israel (Exodus 18:21). It is the smallest number: A people of ten! For we are concerned with the *people*'. He makes the point in a footnote that 'the Jewish concept of *Minjan* is further proof that ten is the minimum number for a people. There must be minjan - a minimum of ten Jewish adult males - for any corporate act of worship' p.47.
[7] Bonda, 1993 p.48.
[8] Bonda, 1993 p. 63. The city of Sodom is not of course saved and once Lot has left 'the Lord rained on Sodom and Gomorrah brimstone and fire from the Lord out of heaven'. Genesis 19:24. Bonda asks 'How does this conversation make sense, if this is the end of Sodom? God knows what he was about to do. He knows that he cannot find ten righteous persons. Does he simply go through the motions with Abraham, knowing that Sodom will come to nothing?'. Bonda writes that the answer to this is 'No, because Sodom will not come to nothing. The story does indeed concern the coming judgement of God. But this judgement is not discussed before it has been made clear what is in God's heart. He wants Sodom to be saved, even when he executes judgement on the city'. Bonda concludes, 'therefore the judgement will not be the end of Sodom!' p.48.
[9] Bonda, 1993 p.63.

are we to reconcile these seemingly opposing teachings? One response has been that they must be held alongside one another. Bonda does not accept that the two sets of statements should be held in tension.

> The parables of the searching shepherd and the compassionate father (Luke 14 - 15) lose their meaning if Scripture teaches both! For in these stories Jesus tells his disciples not to accept passively the perdition of the many, not even of one of them. The shepherd and the woman keep on searching until they have found what was lost - the one sheep and the one coin. How can we follow that example if, simultaneously, we are told that God has destined most people to perdition? What keeps us from giving in to despair even in apparently hopeless situations? It is the certainty that there can be no case in which he does not support us; he is the One who desires the salvation of that particular individual, and he will never stop wanting it ... There are no other statements in the Bible that attribute another attitude to the Father. 'For the Son of God, Jesus Christ, whom we proclaimed among you, ... was not "Yes and No", but in him it is always "Yes" (2 Corinthians 1:19)'.[10]

So Bonda's response is that we should read passages which teach separation and damnation in the light of the universalist passages.

Many claim that passages which speak of separation and damnation are warnings to encourage repentance and acceptance of faith, rather than accurate predictions of what will take place. For example, Bauckham and Hart write, 'In the preaching of Jesus ... judgement is always a warning to avoid the path to final condemnation, a summons to decision and repentance'.[11] Sachs comments: 'Paradoxically, it would seem that both the universality of salvation and the inescapable threat of damnation seem to have been a part of Jesus' own preaching'.[12] However he concludes:

> Eschatological descriptions concerning final judgement are best understood as ways in which the Bible speaks about human freedom and responsibility before God. Properly understood, therefore, such biblical texts offer no proof whatsoever that anyone will in fact be damned. The preaching of the gospel, on the lips of Jesus and in the ministry of the Church, is an 'open situation'.[13]

---

[10] Bonda, 1993 p.69.

[11] Richard Bauckham and Trevor Hart, *Hope Against Hope - Christian Eschatology in Contemporary Context* (1999) London: Dartmann, Longman and Todd p.144.

[12] Sachs, 1991 p.229.

[13] Sachs, 1991 p.238.

Robinson, takes the slightly different view that universalism 'can finally establish itself only if it also preserves intact two other truths upon which the Bible is equally insistent. These are the reality of human freedom and the seriousness of hell'.[14] For Robinson, the passages on hell are more than just a warning and yet he believes that universalism will be the final outcome. However in the meantime, Robinson thinks that these sets of texts must be held together. He claims that the tension arises from seeing them as literal predictions. He writes, 'they are not forecasts, but represent alike elements in the total Christian understanding of the end which must be retained together'.[15] Thus Robinson believes that these different passages can be synthesised if properly understood. One way of understanding these contrasting texts is then to suppose that they refer to different stages of the afterlife. There will be judgement and punishment as is taught but these will precede the final stage when all will be permanently reconciled with God. Sachs proposes a different understanding where the separatist texts are understood as existential warnings and not theological predictions.

Similarly Balthasar claims that the two sets of passages cannot be brought into synthesis and that the texts that speak of judgement are not referring to future actions, but apply now. He writes, 'what we have here are two series of statements that, in the end, because we are under judgement, we neither can nor may bring into synthesis'.[16] Whilst Balthasar does not want to deny the possible reality of the passages which speak of separation and damnation, neither does he want them to override the message of the universalist passages.

> I only dispute that the series of threats invalidates the cited universalist statements. And I claim nothing more than this: that these statements give us a right to have hope for all men, which simultaneously implies that I see no need to take the step from the threats to the positing of a hell occupied by our brothers and sisters, through which our hopes would come to nought.[17]

Thus Balthasar also denies that they are predictions which we must simply accept, of the fate of some people. For Balthasar and Bonda these passages have a strong element of warning, but a warning aimed at those who believe that they are already in the way of salvation. The warning is not to leave brothers and sisters who may not be in Christ to this fate, but to hope and work for the salvation of all people. Bonda concludes:

> Everything the Bible says about judgement, from Sodom onward, is said to people who were called by God not to accept passively the perdition of their fellow human beings. We may argue about the exegesis of certain texts and can point to other passages, but there

---

[14] Robinson, 1950 p.109.

[15] Robinson, 1950 p.100.

[16] Balthasar, 1988 p.22.

[17] Balthasar, 1988 pp.186 - 187.

can be no difference of opinion regarding this calling, for there simply is no other calling.[18]

Thus Bonda believes that God has called all people to salvation, and those that have accepted that calling, are further required to work for the salvation of others, so that God's one purpose may be achieved. The passages that speak of damnation and separation do not challenge this conclusion, but rather for Bonda, they reinforce it.

Reading Universalist Texts

Richard Bauckham in his article 'Universalism: A Historical Survey' discusses several different universalist approaches to the evidence of Scripture.

> Almost all universalists before this century thought it necessary to argue for a universalist interpretation of those texts of the New Testament which seem to teach eternal punishment or final condemnation, and the standard approach to such texts was to deny the everlasting or final character of the punishment.[19]

These discussions largely centred around the meaning of the word αιον. Bonda explains that 'the Greek word for eternity (αιον) is translated both '*age*' – 'this age' and the 'future age' (Matt 12:32) - and *world* [referring to] 'the end of the world' (Matt 13:40,49; 28:20)'.[20] Bonda asserts that 'in both cases a time period is intended that has an end'.[21] However, many claim that αιον refers to a time period that does not have an end, and thus is most accurately translated 'eternal'. The passage most relevant to this discussion is the parable of the sheep and the goats in Matthew 25: 31 - 46. Although Matthew 18:8 states that the fire is eternal, this is the only explicit statement that the punishment will be eternal (v46).[22] The

---

[18] Bonda, 1993 pp. 256 - 257.

[19] Bauckham, 1978 p.52.

[20] Bonda, 1993 p.70.

[21] Bonda, 1993 p.70.

[22] For other passages thought to teach eternal punishment of the wicked, see for example Mark 9:43- 50. This is the only use by Mark of the Hebrew word gehenna but is found in a similar form twice in Matthew, 5: 29-30 and 18: 6-9. D.E. Nineham says of this passage that 'certainly it affords no ground for attributing to Jesus the later fully developed doctrines of eternal punishment'. D.E. Nineham, *Saint Mark* (1963) London: SCM Press p.258. John 3:36 states 'he who does not obey the Son shall not see life, but the wrath of God rests upon him'. Bray writes: 'The only suggestion that the wrath of God might have a duration is in John 3:36, where it is said that "the wrath of God remains on them", though this is hardly a solid basis on which to build a doctrine of eternal punishment!' Bray, 1992 p.21. See also 2 Thessalonians 1:7-9: the Lord Jesus will be 'inflicting vengeance upon those who do not know God and upon those who do not obey the gospel of our Lord Jesus. They shall suffer the punishment of eternal destruction and exclusion from the presence of the Lord.' Jude 6

difficulty in claiming that αιον here is referring to a finite period of time, is that the same word is used for the fate of the sheep and the goats. Thus if the goats are sentenced to a period of punishment, the sheep are only receiving a period of life, rather then eternal life. However it may be, as Robinson suggests, that these periods of punishment and reward precede the final state of universal reconciliation. The interpretation of αιον as an age, is a valid one and an unequivocal meaning for the word cannot be found. Therefore one's understanding of the meaning of αιον is probably determined by one's control beliefs. Those who assume that the Gospels teach an eternal punishment may well understand αιον as 'eternal' and those who are denying that the Gospels teach an eternal punishment will read αιον as 'an age'.

Bauckham observes that during the twentieth century two different approaches have been developed with regard to universalist readings of Scripture:

> One is a new form of exegesis of the texts about final condemnation, which acknowledges the note of finality but sees these texts as threats rather than predictions. A threat need not be carried out ... The second approach to the exegetical problem is simply to disagree with the New Testament writers' teaching about a final division of mankind, which can be said to be merely taken over from their contemporary Jewish environment, while the texts which could be held to support universalism represent a deeper insight into the meaning of God's revelation in Christ.[23]

Sachs adopts this first approach. As we have seen he argues that passages which teach separation and damnation should be understood as warnings rather than predictions. He writes that Matthew 25:

> Does not give us information about an eternal hell after death, as if we could conclude that it has already been determined that a certain number will in fact be saved (the sheep) and a certain number be damned (the goats). Texts like this have a paraenetic function which impresses upon the hearers the critical urgency of their own situation as a situation of judgement.[24]

The second approach is obviously open to the criticism that it at best ignores the Bible, and at worst directly contradicts it. Although in response to some passages

---

refers to angels being kept in 'eternal chains' however it is clear that this will only last 'until the judgement of the great day'. And Revelation has several references to eternal; see 14:11, 19:3, 20:10. These texts fall into Sanders fifth category, and as we can see, have been interpreted by universalists in the light of the overall message of the New Testament.

[23] Bauckham, 1978 p.52.

[24] Sachs, 1991 p.238.

Hick adopts the first of these approaches,[25] he also uses the second one. His justification for this is threefold. First he claims that we cannot be sure that the passages which teach damnation and separation are authentic.[26] Second, Hick cites, as Bauckham observes, the influence of Jewish culture on Jesus' teaching. Hick claims that Jesus is simply using the language of the time.[27] The main defence of this sort of position however, is that the overall message of the New Testament is more important than specific passages, and Hick, amongst others, believes that this supports universalism.[28] Bauckham concludes that this is a common position for universalists to take with regard to the Bible. He claims that this approach is sufficiently acceptable in mainstream Christianity to have removed what for many has been a stumbling block to universalism and has encouraged the growth of universalism.

> Thus the modern universalist is no longer bound to the letter of the New Testament; he can base his doctrine on the spirit of New Testament teaching about the love of God ... This more liberal approach to Scripture has probably played quite a large part in the general spread of universalism in this century.[29]

As well as explaining the texts which seem to contradict universalism, and claiming that the overall message of the New Testament supports universalism, the universalist can appeal to specific texts which seem to teach that all will be saved.

Categories of Universalist Texts

The texts which are of particular significance to the universalist can, according to Sanders, be helpfully divided into five different categories. He defines these as being, first, texts that 'affirm God's desire to save all people' and second, 'those that proclaim the unlimited atonement of Christ'. The third set of texts are those which articulate 'the implications of the universal atoning work of Jesus', and the fourth are those which speak of the 'consummation of God's plan of salvation in which all people are finally redeemed'. The final set are the passages which refer to damnation and separation which universalists interpret 'in a way consistent with what they see as the overriding theme of the New Testament'.[30] Even in the passages which refer to the atonement made by Christ and its implications, the importance lies in the emphasis on the universality of this work. Thus for our purposes, the universalist texts can be separated into two broad categories. They are texts that refer to *all* and texts that refer to *world* or *universe*.

---

[25] See Hick, 1968 (b) pp.600-601 and Hick, 1976 p.183.

[26] Hick, 1983 pp.58-59.

[27] Hick,1966 p.346.

[28] Hick, 1966 (b) p.193.

[29] Bauckham, 1978 p.52.

[30] Sanders, 1992 pp. 83 - 85.

'All' Texts

In several passages which may be claimed to support universalism, we come across the Greek, παντας. Whether or not these passages can assist the case for universalism depends whether or not we can rightly translate παντας to mean *all* people. According to Sanders, the most important of these passages is Romans 5: 12 - 19. The verse of particular interest to us is v.18: 'Then as one man's trespass led to condemnation for all (παντας) men, so one man's act of righteousness leads to acquittal and life for all (παντας) men. This is similar to Paul's claim in 1 Corinthians 15: 22, 'For as in Adam all (παντες) die, so also in Christ shall all (παντες) be made alive'. Clearly these passages could be understood as stating that Christ brings eternal life for every person. Indeed Marshall writes, 'in Romans five the language of "many" and "all" indicates a divine provision of salvation that is as universal as the human state of condemnation because of sin'.[31]

However, many have argued that Paul's words cannot be understood to include all people. N.T. Wright writes:

> If we are to maintain, on the basis of the word 'all' in Romans 5 and 11, that Paul was a universalist, we would do so in the teeth of (eg.) Romans 2:6-16, 14:11 - 12 and such other passages as 2 Thessalonians 2: 7 - 10. Nor will it do to say that Paul had not thought through the implications of Romans 5: the epistle is far too tight-knit for that.[32]

Thus Wright suggests that these passages should be viewed in the light of the rest of Paul's writing, and that when this is done, Paul cannot be said to be a universalist and so consequently these passages cannot be proclaiming universal salvation. The writers of the ACUTE report claim that 'Romans 5 is dealing with comparisons of, rather than parallels with, the word 'all'. The most likely meaning would therefore appear to be: "How much *more* then will salvation come to many through one man's act of righteousness"'.[33] In their discussion of 1 Corinthians 15:22 they argue that 'the "all" who are "made alive" in Christ are clearly those who *already belong* to Christ'.[34] Thus, although to the universalist these passages may seem to be clearly teaching universal salvation, to the separatist there is no such message, explicit or implicit, in the text. Indeed Davies writes:

> To affirm that God is ultimately victorious over all enemies and that God's authority will one day be universally recognised is one thing

---

[31] I. Howard Marshall, 'Universal Grace and Atonement in the Pastoral Epistles' in Clark H. Pinnock (ed.), *The Grace of God, The Will of Man* Grand Rapids, Michigan: Zondervan Publishing House (1989) p.61.

[32] N.T. Wright, 'Towards a Biblical View of Universalism' *Themelios* vol.4 (1978) p.55.

[33] ACUTE, 2000 p.29.

[34] ACUTE, 2000 p.30.

and will be agreed on by all Christians. But to say that every person will eventually be reconciled to God is quite another, and can only be based on a surprisingly literalistic interpretation of such terms as 'all', 'all things', 'every knee', and 'the world' in the passages cited. It is odd that universalists, who typically protest against literalistic interpretations of the many texts that seem to teach separationism, appear themselves to adapt a kind of literalism here.[35]

Thus he claims that these passages only suggest universal salvation when they are interpreted literally and that this is incongruous with the insistence of many universalists that the separatist passages should not be taken literally.

Another 'all' passage often appealed to by universalists, is Philippians 2: 10-11: 'At the name of Jesus every (παν) knee should bow ... and every (πασα) tongue confess that Jesus Christ is Lord, to the glory of God the Father'. Bonda comments on this passage, 'when Paul says that every tongue will praise God, there is no alternative: This includes everyone ... Now if it be true that all people will praise God, how can it be denied that God's salvation includes all people? Why else would they sing his praises if they are not redeemed by him?'.[36] This question has not been left unanswered. Helm responds: 'This language implies that the impenitent will recognise the essential justice of their plight. For they too recognise Christ's Lordship, and confess him, not with love and adoration as a Saviour, but as their Lord'.[37] Similarly, the ACUTE report comments on this passage: 'While this draws a picture of all humanity coming into the presence of Christ, it cannot be taken to justify universalism, since the bowing takes place at his judgement seat'.[38]

I do not think that Paul was a universalist. However I do think that Paul believed that it was possible that all people would be saved, and rejoiced to think that one day every knee would bow and every tongue confess Christ as Lord. Or as Hick puts it: 'Sometimes as he wrote about the saving activity of God the inner logic of that about which he was writing inevitably unfolded itself into the thought of universal salvation'.[39] Paul certainly did not hold a doctrine of universalism, but his belief in the grace of God allowed him the vision of all people being restored through Christ and singing his praise. As Bonda writes: 'Paul has encountered God's love in Jesus Christ, and this encounter has awakened in him a limitless hope. If God is able to save him, a persecutor of the church, God can save all people'.[40] Thus we may class Paul as a hopeful universalist as his belief in God's saving power at times seemed to stretch to all people.[41]

---

[35] Davies, 1990 p.176.

[36] Bonda, 1993 p.221.

[37] Paul Helm, *The Last Things* (1989) Edinburgh: The Banner of Truth Trust p.116.

[38] ACUTE, 2000 pp.29-30.

[39] Hick, 1976 p.248.

[40] Bonda, 1993 p.91.

[41] Most of the passages which particularly seem to support universalism are from Paul's letters. For other 'all' passages, see Romans 11:26, 32, 14:11; 2 Corinthians 5: 14-15, 19;

'*World*' *Texts*

The other set of passages to which the universalist may appeal, is those which refer to the world. The clearest universalist passage in this group is, again, Pauline. In Romans 8:21 he writes, 'the creation (κτισις) itself will be set free from its bondage to decay and obtain the glorious liberty of the children of God'. Bonda asks: 'What is this glory of the children of God?'.[42] He claims: 'This freedom and this glory are the gifts God intended them to have: the honour and the glory of being created in his image and after his likeness. It is his ultimate goal for humanity'.[43] Bonda concludes: 'Paul's statement in Romans 8:19-21 confirms that salvation is not limited to believers. In fact, it allows for no doubt whatsoever on this point'.[44] This passage is the only one in which κτσις is used in this sort of context. In 2 Corinthians 5:19, Paul writes: 'In Christ God was reconciling the world (κοσμον) to himself'. Again Paul is expressing God's plan for creation, but here describes it as the world. The other passages of specific interest to the universalist also use κοσμον. Three of these are found in the Gospel of John, 1:29, 3:17 and 12:47 and one in the First Letter of John, 2:2. The relevance of these texts to the universalist is obvious, the use of world, implies a universal scope for the reconciliation taking place. However, as with the 'all' texts, those who reject universal salvation claim that there is no such inference in the texts. Blanchard claims:

> In none of his writings on the subject did John ever use 'world' in a statistical sense, but rather to mean people of every kind and nation … John is not saying that Jesus paid sin's penalty for every human being in history, but that in all the world's history there is no other propitiation.[45]

It is far from clear that this is a more obvious reading of the text than one which takes 'world' to refer to all people. It is only obvious in the light of Blanchard's control beliefs, one of which must be that God has ordained a final separation of the sheep and the goats.

Ephesians 1:10; Colossians 1:19 - 20; 1 Timothy 2:3-6, 4:10; Titus 2:11; For non-Pauline passages, see John 12:31-32; Hebrews 2:9 and 2 Peter 3:9.

[42] Bonda, 1993 p.117.

[43] Bonda, 1993 p.117.

[44] Bonda, 1993 p.119.

[45] John Blanchard, *Whatever Happened to Hell?* (1993) Darlington: Evangelical Press p.197.

Apokatastasis

The other passage in the Bible of particular interest to the universalist is Acts 3:21. Here we find the only occasion when αποκαταστασις is used in the Bible, although the word is familiar as the doctrine of universalism is sometimes referred to as belief in apokatastasis. Balthasar writes: 'Two translations are equally possible: "until the time of universal restoration of which God spoke", or "until everything predicted by God's prophets has come about"'.[46] The literal meaning is restoration, but Sachs comments: 'Turning to the scriptures, we find that language about final restoration is notably scarce'.[47] This is perhaps not surprising as Bauckham notes: 'The final unity of all things with God is more Platonic than biblical in inspiration'.[48] Although the specific use of αποκαταστασις is not prominent in the Bible, and it perhaps refers to an idea popular in Greek culture, the idea that there will be an ultimate reconciliation of all people with God is far from alien to the New Testament.

Conclusion

Although all of the universalist texts can be read otherwise, and interpreted to support a separatist position, the passages at which we have looked promise a glorious end for all people. Talbott claims:

> What the New Testament in general gives us, I would argue, is a glorious picture of how the end of salvation can be a matter of grace (already foreordained and not a matter of human effort at all), even though we are fully responsible for all our free choices made along the way.[49]

All of the passages speak of God having taken the initiative, and drawing all people to God. There is no emphasis in these texts on humans needing to achieve certain goals in order to gain salvation. It is plain that Biblical support can be found for many positions, and even passages which seem clearly to teach one thing, can be interpreted to the satisfaction of a reader holding a different position. Indeed this is exactly the process by which the universalist and the separatist explain the set of passages, present in the New Testament which oppose their position. Thus I do not want to rely on universalist passages, or a universalist interpretation of separatist passages as the crux of my argument.

What is more important, and I suggest gives greater strength to the universalist position, is the overall message of the Bible. I believe that three claims can be made from Scripture which strengthen the universalist's case. These are,

---

[46] Balthasar, 1988 p.225.

[47] Sachs, 1991 p.228.

[48] Bauckham, 1978 p.49.

[49] Talbott, 1990 p.244.

first, that the Bible is an account of the ongoing process of salvation and as such leads us to believe that God's purpose in creation is to reconcile all people with Godself. Further it demonstrates that this is by no means a straightforward process but one which God continues in each generation. Secondly, it is clear from the Bible, and particularly the New Testament, that God is a god of love. Indeed the author of the First Letter of John records that 'God is love' (1 John 4:16). Finally the message of the New Testament is that the advent of Jesus was good news for the world. These three points endorse the first premise of this chapter, that God has a universal salvific will and, I believe, also support the conclusion that there will be eventual universal salvation, because as I will claim in this chapter, what God desires must come about. The Bible records the outworking of God's love through interaction with God's people over the ages and sometimes the Biblical writers, especially St Paul recognise that the end of this process will come when all people are finally reconciled to God.

Thus whilst the universalist will encounter difficulties in appealing to specific passages, just as the separatist will, we may conclude that universalism is not against the spirit of the New Testament. Indeed the doctrine of hell often presumed to be contained within the New Testament is, on close examination, conspicuous by its absence and even though some passages contradict a universalist position, those which endorse it give a glorious picture of the eschaton, when all things will be reconciled to God, which matches the overall message of the New Testament.

Epistemic Distance

Hick and Swinburne both claim that there must be 'epistemic distance' in order to allow humans true freedom in relation to God. Their claim that God has not unequivocally revealed Godself to us in our present existence would seem to be confirmed by our own experience of the world. Many people do not believe that God exists at all and those who do are not agreed on what exactly God is. If there were a clear revelation of God in this world this would not be the case.[50] Hick and Swinburne both argue that epistemic distance protects our human freedom and allows us choice in relation to God. In our earlier discussion of epistemic distance, I concluded that this does seem to be a realistic account of our relationship with, or awareness of God in this life. However, many Christians have supposed that after death some sort of encounter with God takes place and thus this distance would be removed. In what follows I want to argue that every person after death will have an

---

[50] John Blanchard denies that this is the case. He claims, 'nobody can plead ignorance of God's existence, because we are all surrounded by evidence that he exists'. Blanchard, 1993 p.112. This seems to be a most naïve view, as clearly one who does not believe in God or even is unaware of the possibility of God, will not interpret their surroundings as evidence of God's existence.

encounter with God and further that this encounter will be efficacious in leading every person to accept God.

After Death Encounter

Hick postulates a series of after-lives in which all people continue existence and, he believes, eventually fit themselves for heaven. For many, Hick's theory is too close to reincarnation to be acceptable as part of a Christian theory. Indeed there are many difficulties with Hick's progressive after-lives, and I have rejected this proposal in the earlier discussion. Hick does not actually propose an encounter with God, at least not until one has already decided in favour of God. However, the grounds on which Hick is led to suggest that there may be further lives or a further life after death are sound. Many Christian theories have maintained that individual fates are not sealed until after death. This reflects the belief that what we decide or become in this life is in some way unfinished, or recognises that our opportunities on this earth are unequal and that the chance to come to know God does not seem to have been fairly distributed.

The belief that after death we will encounter Christ as judge is based on the New Testament and is still a widely held view, especially in the evangelical community. Strange writes: 'Pinnock believes that there is much theological sense in believing in a post-mortem encounter with Christ. He claims that all evangelicals believe that at the Parousia, all humanity will come before Christ and give an account of themselves'.[51] Others have suggested that at death one will meet God in order to be 'welcomed home'. Hick notes: 'In the earliest days there seems to have been so vivid a sense of the reality and love of God, and of Christ having overcome death, that those who had died were thought of as having gone forward into a greater fulfilment and joy'.[52]

The emphasis on relationship with Christ, which is popular in Christianity, is generally believed to be a relationship that, after death or the end of the world, will not end but will increase in importance. If heaven is conceived of as somehow being in the company of God, then of course some sort of encounter with God is necessary. However, the point of post-mortem encounter theories is that it is this encounter which seals ones fate. For Pinnock, amongst others the post-mortem encounter does not offer further evangelistic opportunity, but rather is a chance to confirm the decision already made in life.[53]

The Old Testament teaches that those who have seen the face of God must die. For example, after encountering God: 'Jacob called the name of the place Peniel (which means face of God) saying, "I have seen God face to face and yet my life is preserved"' (Genesis 32:30). Moses upon encountering the burning bush:

---

[51] Strange, 1999 pp.162-163. Pinnock appeals to Romans 14:7-12.

[52] Hick, 1976 p.207. Hick notes that Ulrich Simon writes that the dead were described as having 'gone to God' or being 'received or accepted by God'. Ulrich Simon, *Heaven in the Christian Tradition* (1958) London: Rockliff p.219.

[53] Pinnock, 1992 p.170.

'hid his face for he was afraid to look at God' (Exodus 3:6) and Elijah 'wrapped his face in his mantle' (1 Kings 19:13) so that he would not look upon the Lord. The experience of a face to face encounter with God was so significant that after such an experience one could not normally continue with one's earthly life. Hick claims:

> The notion of a direct and transforming awareness of the divine
> Reality had already excited the religious mind of the ancient world,
> so that the promise of such a *gnosis* latent within the Christian gospel
> soon began to be drawn out.[54]

Of course the idea of seeing God face to face was most commonly thought of as the beatific vision and thought to be the state of those in heaven. Hick writes: 'The theology of the eschatological vision of God begins with Irenaeus, in the second century'.[55] However he notes that it was Thomas Aquinas who expounded this idea. Aquinas explains:

> Since we reach the knowledge of intelligible things from sensible
> things, we also take over the names proper to sense knowledge for
> intellectual knowledge, especially the ones which apply to sight,
> which compared to the other senses, is more noble and more
> spiritual, and so more closely related to the intellect. Thus it is that
> this intellectual knowledge is called vision.[56]

Thus the vision of God was not supposed to be merely a sighting of God, but also a comprehension of the nature of God and it is this experience which, I believe, would be efficacious for all people in realising that they do in fact desire communion with God. In the last chapter I discussed Hick's account of epistemic distance and concluded that he was right that with full awareness of God we would not be free creatures. This is because an awareness of God would involve what Aquinas describes as 'intellectual knowledge' of God. We would not just be aware of God, but fully aware of God's nature and this would fill us with the desire to be in communion with God.[57]

The Christian tradition then has supposed that after death some sort of encounter with God will take place for the purposes of judgement or meeting one's

---

[54] Hick, 1976 pp.204-205.

[55] Hick, 1976 p.205. He quotes Irenaeus 'men therefore shall see God, that they might live, being made immortal by that sight and attaining even unto God'. Irenaeus, *Against Heresies* book IV, chapter 20 paragraph 6.

[56] Aquinas, *Summa Contra Gentiles* (1924) London: Burns, Oates and Wathburn book III, part 1 pp.181-182.

[57] Genesis 1:26 claims that we were made in the 'image and likeness of God'. In his commentary on this passage, Gerhard Von Rad claims 'everything about man points to God. With regard to the origin of both his nature and his destiny, man is completely referred to and understood from God'. Gerhard Von Rad, *Genesis - A Commentary* trans. John H. Marks (1961) London: SCM Press p.58.

maker. Thus there is significant support for the view that after death an encounter with God takes place. Further this sort of encounter with God would be irresistible to human natures.

Face To Face Encounter

I propose that after death every person will have an encounter with God. This encounter after death does not necessarily confirm the decision made in life, nor does it exactly offer a second chance. Rather each person will have their first chance to see God, as God really is. They will have the opportunity to see 'face to face'. In this situation, each person will experience the love and goodness of God, in all its fullness. This encounter will allow each person to see God's true nature, and not just to see God as they have believed God to be. Thus for every person, this will be their first chance truly to see God. Even for those who have been deeply committed to God in this life it will be their first realisation of the full glory of God. When they are able to see God as God really is and not as their traditions and religions have made God, all people will find that they do indeed have a deep yearning for God. Thus this experience will lead to all people choosing in favour of God. As Gooch and Mosher explain: 'God's love is so great that as a matter of fact no one will want to refuse it when he understands it in its glory'.[58]

In the First Letter to the Corinthians, Paul writes that after death we will know God more clearly than we can in our present life. He writes: 'For now we see in a mirror dimly, but then face to face. Now I know in part; then I shall understand fully, even as I have been fully understood' (13:12). In the Second Letter to the Corinthians, Paul writes: 'And we all, with unveiled face, beholding the glory of the Lord, are being changed into His likeness from one degree of glory to another; for this comes from the Lord who is the Spirit' (3:18).[59] In these passages Paul writes that when we recognise God, a transformation occurs. Indeed this message is at the heart of the Christian gospel. However, Paul writes how much more dramatic this transformation will be when we know God fully, when instead of seeing only reflections of God, we can see God 'face to face'. Bauckham and Hart write:

> The biblical image of seeing God thus combines the sense of being in the immediate presence of God and of knowing God in his true identity. This 'face to face' knowledge, knowing God as we are known by God (1 Corinthians 13:12), is not a purely intellectual matter but the involvement of the whole person in the fuller relationship with God of which humans are created capable.[60]

---

[58] Gooch and Mosher, 1972 p.425.

[59] Paul is making reference to the Jewish belief that one could not look upon the face of God and live. See Genesis 32:30. In the second passage he is also referring to the Jews not being able to look at Moses' face after he had spoken with God, Exodus 34:29 -35.

[60] Bauckham and Hart, 1999 p.170.

When we encounter God, we will not only know what God is like, in terms of God's attributes for example, but we will also know that we are called to a relationship with God, we are called to become children of God. This is the process that we can begin in this world. However these gradual changes, as we come to know God, are small compared to the changes that will take place when we are able to see God face to face.

This experience of seeing God face to face, will not be without a process of judgement. When we see ourselves as children of God, to borrow Hick's language, we will judge ourselves in the light of what we could have become, and what we have in fact become, during our earthly lives. When we recognise the potential within us fully to become children of God, we will realise that we have not lived up to our potential. In the face of our creator we will suffer shame and remorse for the way that we have lived. In his *Dream of Gerontius* Cardinal Newman has the Soul ask the Angel: 'Shall I see my dearest Master when I reach His throne?' and the Angel replies: 'Yes, - for one moment thou shalt see thy Lord. One moment, but thou knowest not, my child, what thou dost ask: that sight of the Most Fair will gladden thee, but it will pierce thee too'.[61] The angel explains that the encounter with God will be joyful, but also painful because of the judgement we will make on ourselves in the light of God's goodness. Thus we will judge ourselves, but at the same time will be taken into God's love and want to become fully, children of God. The transformation that occurs is not one whereby we gradually develop into children of God through existence in soul-making environments as Hick proposes, but rather one where we want God to take us and make us fully God's children. It is the realisation that we were made to become children of God and the desire for God to make us complete. This transformation, is a complete submission to the will of God.

This process will happen in the afterlife realm, and it is not possible to say whether this process will be instantaneous or whether it will be gradual. However I do suggest that it will happen without there being any further stages before this point of encounter with God.

Objections to the Face to Face Encounter

It may be objected that at the time of our death we have not progressed sufficiently to be ready to become children of God. This is what Hick argues and David Brown makes a similar objection.[62] The main objection of this view is that we will not be the same person if we are changed so radically at death. Brown explains:

> My claim is that such an abrupt transition to moral perfection in essentially temporal beings is not the sort of claim to which clear

---

[61] John Henry Newman, *The Dream of Gerontius* (1986) London: Mowbray.
[62] David Brown, 'No Heaven Without Purgatory' *Religious Studies* vol.21 (1985) pp.447-456.

sense can be attached, and so conceptually we have every reason to believe that, if Heaven exists, then so must purgatory.[63]

Brown raises three specific objections to the claim that we could be instantly perfected. First he objects that we do not have the sort of goodness necessary for heaven and that the sort of goodness required cannot be acquired instantly. He writes: 'Only when moral action arises spontaneously from an ingrained natural disposition or habit, in short only when a virtue is present, may that person properly be called good'.[64] However I do not believe that our entrance into heaven will in anyway rely on our goodness of character. Brown continues: 'The very notion of such a habit suggests practice, and practice implies time, time in which to practise overcoming the opposing habit, time in which to practise reinforcing the new'.[65] I am not proposing that we need to acquire a virtuous character in order for this transformation to take place. Although we will not at this stage develop virtues, which as Brown claims can only happen over a period of time, we will develop a character that is the fulfilment of our earthly character. Our goodness will not depend upon us learning more and more consistently to choose the good in a range of situations. Rather we will make one choice in favour of God and consequently become a fulfilled people, children of God. Again this will not mirror the transformation of those who choose in favour of God in this life. Now, we continually make choices and often struggle to live up to the good choices we make. There are no requirements for getting into heaven, other than a desire for communion with God. With this desire comes the desire to be transformed into a child of God and this will involve aligning our will with God's will. Thus a transformation takes place but not one which we need to work at or practise, but one where we recognise what we have the potential to be, and chose to become it. After we have been transformed, we will live in a different realm with different choices to those in this life and thus although our characters will be good, they will be suited to our new existence.

Brown's second objection is: 'Unless there is an intermediate stage between earth and Heaven, the resurrected individual could have no reasonable grounds for believing himself to be the same person as the person to whose earthly existence he allegedly corresponds'.[66] However it is not clear that this is the case for I am not proposing that an individual simply wakes up in the afterlife and finds that he/she is a transformed being. Rather the individual participates in the transformation through desire and consent. The transformation which takes place is the fulfilment of a person and not the annihilation of him/her. It is not inflicted on individuals but is desired by them once they encounter God. At this point they recognise not only God's true nature but also what their own true nature could and should be.

---

[63] Brown, 1985 p.447.
[64] Brown, 1985 p.450.
[65] Brown, 1985 p.450.
[66] Brown, 1985 p.450.

Finally Brown objects:

> It seems clear that God is under a moral obligation to see that the
> individual concerned personally endorses each aspect of the
> transformation of his character. That being so, the existence of
> Purgatory is a legitimate deduction from the goodness of God ... the
> decision to redeem those parts of the personality that are hitherto
> unredeemed will be a decision of both God and the individual.[67]

I believe that the individual will 'endorse each aspect of the transformation of his
character'; indeed this will characterise the individual's response to his/her
encounter with God. It will not be our works, or the extent to which we have
already become children of God in this world which enable us to respond
favourably to our encounter with God. It will be the experience of seeing God, face
to face in all of God's glory and the realisation that we are made for communion
with God.

Brown claims:

> There is even a strong moral argument for saying that the individual's
> first confrontation with God after death should be as he is, warts and
> all. For only then can God properly be said to have accepted the
> individual for what he is as a whole, rather than merely for what he
> can allegedly instantaneously become.[68]

This is an important point and Brown is right that God accepts the unperfected
individual and not the already perfected one. As I have said above the process of
encountering God will involve judgement and the individual will recognise both
what they are and what they have the potential to become. That God accepts us as
we are may well be a further spur to becoming a child of God, a fulfilled person. It
will be our 'warts and all' in the face of God's glory that will allow us both to judge
ourselves for what we have been and see what we could become.

It may be difficult to see how we will retain our freedom if such a process
is to take place. Submitting our will to God's, sounds as though we revoke our
freedom and to an extent this is true. There has always been a tension in the
Christian religion, between freedom and service. However a more helpful
description might be to say that we completely align our will with God's. These
words from C.S. Lewis' *The Great Divorce* are often quoted by those defending the
weak view of hell: 'There are only two kinds of people in the end: those who say to
God, "Thy will be done," and those to whom God says, in the end, "*Thy* will be
done"'.[69] I suggest that ultimately the two parties identified by Lewis will be one
and the same party. I believe that finally, this will be the same thing. Our will, will

---

[67] Brown, 1985 p.454.

[68] Brown, 1985 p.454.

[69] C.S. Lewis, *The Great Divorce* New York: Macmillan (1946) p.72.

be God's will and thus both our will and God's will will be done. After an encounter with God, we would be interested in no other way than God's way. This does not involve us sacrificing our freedom, we will remain free beings but our choices will forever be to do God's will.

It could be objected that if we are free, then however amazing a face to face encounter with God is, some might still choose to reject God. Indeed this remains a possibility. However it is my belief that God would not create a person who would not respond favourably to such an encounter, and I shall be pursuing this argument in the following section. So, although God knew that all people would ultimately accept God, and has designed the world to bring this about, our acceptance of God is still a free choice. According to both Swinburne and Hick, such a revelation would inevitably lead to an individual being compelled to love God, they would be unable to do other than respond to God. The evidence of the face to face encounter is awesome, but we accept it because of our internal desire for God, and longing to be in communion with God and not because it is externally forced upon us. Thus God creating the world so that we have a deep desire for God, and further ensuring that all people are offered grace to submit to God's will, does not conflict with our compatibilist human freedom.

Sachs writes: 'The finality which human freedom is ultimately directed toward, like the very possibility of freedom itself, is a gift from God and something which in the end, is not achieved but received'.[70] When we encounter God, we realise that the fulfilment of our existence is in God, and thus we desire to accept the gift of grace which God gives in order to enable us to be transformed into children of God. This end is not contrary to human freedom, it does not override it, but rather as Sachs writes, it is the fulfilment of it. He writes: 'It would seem to be more accurate to say that human freedom is simply and most radically the capacity for God, not the capacity for *either* God *or* something else. Human freedom is created for one end alone: God'.[71] In the encounter with God, every free person recognises this capacity for God and freely accepts this end. Every person will choose to submit his/her will to God's.

The further objection may be made that if epistemic distance can be removed after death, why is it necessary in our pre-mortem existence? If ultimately, epistemic distance does not destroy our freedom with regard to God, there must be some other reason why epistemic distance is beneficial in the pre-mortem existence. For God initially to have created us at an epistemic distance from Godself, there must be something to be gained from it. It might be that without having this distance from God initially, we would not be people who would recognise that in God was our fulfilment. It may be that the soul-making journey that takes place in this life is exactly what enables us to respond favourably to God when we see God face to face. Indeed it may be that without initially having this distance from God, we would not be able to become ourselves, let alone become children of God. If we were made, always aware of the presence of God, we would not be able to develop

---

[70] Sachs, 1991 p.249.
[71] Sachs, 1991 p.247.

characters of our own, we would not have a will to align with God's will, from the start we would have only known God's will.

G. Stanley Kane argues that according to Hick's theodicy, we endure a great deal of suffering for the purpose of soul-making, which is important to fit us for the end state. However in the eschaton there is no suffering to endure and no difficulties to overcome.

> It is hard to see how character traits can have any value apart from the actions and behaviour, or potential actions and behaviour, to which they tend to lead. In Hick's eschaton, however, there is no potential for ever showing these character traits in actions or behaviour.[72]

Thus Kane observes that it seems a strange requirement for the end state to equip ourselves with virtues which, in this realm we will not need.

> One wonders what bearing the claim that persons in the eschaton possess courage and compassion has on life then and there in the final state. Is heaven to be a place where the redeemed pride themselves on what they would and could do if only they were not in heaven?[73]

Such a heaven, he argues, is actually an unsuitable place for the sorts of persons who possess courage and compassion. Kane assumes that the response might be made that God values these attributes and therefore requires them of the redeemed. However he concludes:

> Is heaven to be a place where the redeemed are loved and respected by God primarily for what they would and could do if only they were some place else? ... Furthermore, to say the importance of these qualities is that God values them is only to say that God has chosen to require them of men, it is not to give a reason why he should have required them. If there is no sufficient reason why he should have done this, then God's choosing to value them is arbitrary, and in imposing these requirements on men he is merely tyrannising over them, exercising raw power. The suggestion, then, that the significance of these values is simply that God values them leads to abandonment of the doctrine that God is good in the sense that is required by theistic religion.[74]

---

[72] G. Stanley Kane, 'The Failure of Soul-Making Theodicy' *International Journal for the Philosophy of Religion* vol.6 (1975) p.13.

[73] Kane, 1975 p.13.

[74] Kane, 1975 p.14.

For God to require the sorts of qualities that are acquired through living in a soul-making environment and therefore enduring suffering and pain simply because God has chosen to require them does, as Kane argues, challenge the view that God is good. However this is to misunderstand the purpose of the soul-making existence. Rather than allowing individuals to acquire certain qualities which can then be ticked off on God's checklist, it enables individuals to develop both their character and potential as children of God.

Kane makes the further objection:

> There seems to be an inconsistency in maintaining that the struggle against evil is a great intrinsic value while also holding that the final perfected state of men will be one in which there is no such struggle. How can a final state be perfect if it lacks such a great value?[75]

The value of the struggle is not intrinsic but the value is in the result of the struggle. Through living in this sort of environment we develop and grow and become people with distinct wills and characters. In the final state every person will have freely chosen to align his/her will with God's will and thus value the qualities which God values such as compassion and courage. Although the eschaton might not be an environment where these qualities are needed, it will be an environment where good qualities are valued, as all people having accepted God, will recognise good. Thus epistemic distance allows us, in this life, to develop into the sort of people we have the potential to become and the final state allows us to exist as such perfected people.

The post-mortem encounter with God is, then, crucial to allow us to come freely to accept God. During our earthly existence, we will live at an epistemic distance from God and thus develop our own will.[76] After death, we will see God 'face to face' and find our true fulfilment in God. We will freely submit our wills to God's and allow God to transform us into the children of God, which we were created with the potential to be. Thus although epistemic distance is important in

---

[75] Kane, 1975 p.14. Kane notes that his objections would not apply 'if it were logically possible to develop and to manifest the traits of character that Hick values in a world that is free of evil'. p.14.

[76] Of course not all have opportunity to develop their character. The most obvious group would be those who die in infancy. It would seem that if God is good at all then there must be some good purpose to our present soul-making existence which seems much harder to define for those who die in infancy than for those who live long enough to develop their character. I do not think that the lives of those who die in infancy are any less valuable then those who live for a longer period of time. A God with middle knowledge will know that their earthly lives will be short and yet still chooses to actualize these people. This cannot be just for the soul-making value of those who die young for others: there must be some intrinsic value in their existence. Those who die in infancy have always challenged theories about the afterlife. For a discussion of this see Sanders' appendix 'Infant Salvation and Damnation', Sanders, 1992 pp.287-305.

the pre-mortem existence, it is removed after death to enable all people to see God 'face to face'.

Middle Knowledge

Although I have touched on the subject of middle knowledge in previous chapters, we have seen that Swinburne rejects it as a coherent account of God's knowledge and Hick does not discuss it. A discussion of middle knowledge would help to strengthen Hick's position and it is integral to my own. Having concluded that God does have this sort of knowledge, it will be necessary to discuss what difference middle knowledge makes to God's power and what are the consequences of this regarding hell and salvation. Amongst the proponents of middle knowledge there is disagreement over whether having this type of knowledge will enhance God's power. If God having middle knowledge makes no difference to God's providential control, then it may be that middle knowledge is irrelevant to this discussion. However I do not think that this is the case.

The Use of Middle Knowledge

Although middle knowledge means that God knows all counterfactuals of freedom, it does not mean that God controls these counterfactuals. Basinger writes: 'As most proponents of middle knowledge also grant, God does not determine which hypothetical conditionals of freedom are true'.[77] Similarly, Craig asserts: 'Middle knowledge is like natural knowledge in that such knowledge does not depend on any decision of the divine will; God does not determine which counterfactuals of creaturely freedom are true or false'.[78] Indeed a theory which claimed that the counterfactuals of freedom were directly under God's control would not be middle knowledge but some sort of determinist knowledge whereby God would know all of the different ways that God could make people behave. Hasker insists that 'it is an absolutely essential feature of the theory of middle knowledge that the counterfactuals of freedom are not under God's control'.[79] Thus middle knowledge does not allow God to determine different human choices, but simply to know what they would be.

If God has no control over the counterfactuals of freedom, it could be argued that middle knowledge does not enhance God's power over the outcome of creation. Hunt argues that middle knowledge cannot contribute to divine providential control,[80] and Basinger similarly argues:

---

[77] Basinger, 1991 p.132.

[78] Craig, 1989 p.178.

[79] Hasker,1991 p.385.

[80] David P. Hunt, 'Divine Providence and Simple Foreknowledge' *Faith and Philosophy* vol.10 (1993) p.400.

God sees all actualizable worlds in their entirety and has total control over which of these worlds, if any, he will actualize. But since God cannot control which choices will freely be made in any given context, he cannot ensure that any given possible world will be an actual creative option ... Accordingly, a God with middle knowledge could find himself *disappointed* in the sense that there may well be many possible worlds he can envision that he would like to actualize but simply cannot. God may have to settle for much less than the best.[81]

Basinger thus concludes that, 'generally speaking, the providential capacities of God with middle knowledge have been greatly overstated'.[82] Thus Basinger, amongst others, claims that the value of middle knowledge is actually minimal, and so it does not, as some have thought, give God extra providential control and consequently does not help our understanding of either God's providence or the problem of hell or the problem of evil. Indeed, it might be worse for God to have middle knowledge in this case, as it would allow God to see the sort of world God would like to create, but not allow God actually to create that sort of world. Hasker, states that middle knowledge is 'on balance ... a detriment rather than a help to an adequate understanding of providence'.[83] Thus he does not think that discussing middle knowledge assists in our attempts to think about God's control. However, middle knowledge should not be so quickly dismissed.

Many have argued that middle knowledge does in fact give God significant additional control over the world. Gordon and Sadowsky claim that if God has middle knowledge then God 'need by his decision to create, never allow the world to get into a position requiring his interference'.[84] Hasker responds that this would only be the case if the counterfactuals of freedom were 'extremely favourable for the fulfilment of his purposes'.[85] He continues: 'There is no reason to suppose that this is in fact the case - and Christians, who hold that God has massively intervened in the incarnation, would seem to have little motivation for holding such a view.'[86] Although Christians would indeed want to say that God had intervened in the world through Jesus and perhaps in many other instances, there is no reason to deny that middle knowledge gives God the position stated by Gordon and Sadowsky. It may be that God *need* never intervene, but that when creating the world, God *chose* to interfere in specific ways. With middle knowledge, God would know the consequences of intervening. It seems more than feasible that God would choose from the beginning to make these particular interventions. Although we are

---

[81] Basinger, 1991 p.133.

[82] Basinger, 1991 p.138.

[83] Hasker, 1992 p.97.

[84] David Gordon and James Sadowsky, 'Does Theism Need Middle Knowledge' *Religious Studies* vol. 25 (1989) p.81.

[85] Hasker, 1993 p.112.

[86] Hasker, 1993 p.112.

created at an epistemic distance from God, that does not preclude God having any interaction with the world. God does want to show God's love for creation and thus God builds into the pattern of the world specific interventions, or revelations. An obvious example of this would, of course, be the Incarnation. However it is understood, the life of Jesus is, for Christians, an event of immense significance through which God intervened in the world. If God could have set up the world so that God need never intervene, God could also have set up the world so that God need never intervene except on those occasions which God had planned from the beginning.

Thus with the use of middle knowledge, God can plan the world as God desires to. Consequently, the actual world, is the one which God chose to create over all others. If we adopt this view of middle knowledge, that must include the understanding that the evil which exists, is part of God's plan. Hasker claims that if we accept middle knowledge, we must also accept a view of meticulous providence. Hasker explains that meticulous providence entails:

> Every single instance of evil that occurs is such that God's permitting either that specific evil or some other equal or greater evil is necessary for some greater good that is better than anything God could have brought about without permitting the evil in question.[87]

Thus God knows and allows all the evil in the world to take place. This, of course, creates a difficulty for the theodicist, as most defences of evil rely on the free will defence and claim that the evil is not permitted by God, but bought about by sinful humans. Evil is a consequence of our free will, rather than being part of the divine plan. This is not the case with meticulous providence. Hasker writes:

> It also follows that God intends the evils which actually occur - not, to be sure, that God regards these evils as inherently desirable, but he intends them as necessary parts of that world which, among all feasible worlds, he regards as best and most worthy of being actualised.[88]

Indeed Hasker concludes: 'Molinism lends itself to an extremely strong view of divine providence; in all likelihood, the strongest view possible if Calvinism is excluded'.[89] However, this comparison to Calvinism may be misleading. We have seen that God does not control the counterfactuals of freedom, and thus this is not, unlike Calvinism, a determinist theory. Therefore meticulous providence does not involve God ordaining the instances of evil which take place. God knows, through

---

[87] Hasker, 1994 p 146. Hasker notes that meticulous providence is argued for in response to the molinist's problem of evil by Michael Peterson *Evil and the Christian God* (1982) Grand Rapids, Michigan: Baker Book House pp.79 -99.
[88] Hasker, 1993 p.116.
[89] Hasker, 1992 p.95.

his middle knowledge and foreknowledge, the specific instances of evil that will occur, and God, by actualising this world, allows them to occur. Therefore God's decision to actualise this world and not a different world, must mean that according to God, this is the best possible world. Consequently God allowing specific instances of evil is no different to God creating a soul-making environment, as Hick claims, because that is the best possible world.[90] God's culpability is not changed by creating a world in which God knows exactly what evil there will be, and creating a world in which God knows that evil will take place.

The actual world then, must be the least evil of all the feasible worlds, or one of several 'least evil' worlds. It is obviously difficult to measure evil[91] and to know on what criterion a world would be, overall, more or less evil. It may be that this world has the combination of the least evil and the most saved. It may be that a world in which just one person is finally lost is a world less desirable to God than a world with even more evil than the actual world but where all people are finally saved. Perhaps the combination of God creating free beings, but ones that will finally be reconciled to God, involves a significant degree of evil in the pre-mortem existence. If God desires to create people, all of whom will ultimately be reconciled to God, to live in communion with God, then a world in which this is the outcome will be the world which God actualises. If the consequences of creating free people is the existence of evil, then God may well prefer to actualise a world with a significant degree of evil in the pre-mortem existence, rather than one with any evil in the post-mortem existence.

So, if we are to accept that God has middle knowledge, and that this knowledge gives God greater knowledge with regard to the consequences of actualising a particular world, we must accept that the actual world, is the best world God could have actualised.

God's Providential Control

Those who adhere to the free will theory claim that God must rely on 'luck' to execute God's plan. Swinburne, amongst others would state that God cannot know, and certainly cannot determine what will happen in the world because God has chosen to create free creatures. Hasker claims a God with middle knowledge is still reliant, in part, on luck.

> Molinism is also dependent on 'luck'. Here, to be sure, the 'luck' confronts God at an earlier point, not in the actual making of a choice by the human being (that is guaranteed by God's knowledge of the counterfactuals of freedom), but rather in the counterfactuals of freedom God is confronted with in the creation situation. These counterfactuals are contingent truths, but their truth is not controlled

---

[90] Hick, 1966 p.253ff.
[91] Plantinga makes this point, Plantinga, 1974 p.190.

by God; rather they are just 'there' and God must make the best of what he finds.[92]

Although the truth of counterfactuals of freedom are not controlled by God, it is not the case that God is simply left to make the best of what he finds. It is after all, God who makes humans as they are. Hick writes: 'God has formed the free human person with a nature that can find its perfect fulfilment and happiness only in active enjoyment of the infinite goodness of the Creator'.[93] Thus if God chooses to create us so that we long for communion with God, God does not directly control our free choices. However this desire for God will surely influence the choices that we make. There is a significant difference between God making us as the sort of people we are, with the sort of desires we have and God controlling counterfactuals of freedom.

Geisler explains that God having influenced our desires in creating us, is not the same as God causing us to act.

> God-given desires, reasoning and persuasion can be conditions of a free choice. But they are not the cause. That is, they are not the sufficient causal condition of our action. If they are, then the human agent is not the efficient cause of the action, but only the instrumental cause through which God's action is exercised.[94]

Just because God made us as free beings does not mean that God is detached from the nature of these free beings. God has created beings with an inherent desire for God, yet they are still free beings who can choose how to respond to this desire. Through middle knowledge, God can know how every being will finally respond to this desire.

Apart from God's influence in creating us as beings with a longing for God, God, through middle knowledge, has a further control over the world. Although God cannot change how individuals will freely choose, God can change the circumstances in which they find themselves. Basinger gives the example of whether or not Bill will freely choose to steal an apple. He writes:

> Middle Knowledge does allow God to know beforehand exactly what Bill would do if actually faced with the decision. But if God knows that Bill would freely choose to steal the apple if faced with the

---

[92] Hasker, 1992 p.103.

[93] Hick, 1966 p.344.

[94] Norman Geisler, 'Norman Geisler's Response' in Basinger and Basinger (eds.), 1986 p.48.

decision, then God cannot actualize W^1, that possible world in which
Bill *freely* chooses not to steal the apple.[95]

It is true that God cannot actualise a world in which Bill freely refrains from
stealing the apple, in exactly the same situation. However, God could actualise a
world, where Bill encounters slightly different circumstances and freely chooses
not to steal the apple. God could actualize a world in which a starving Bill had just
visited a soup kitchen and thus chooses not to steal the apple. God could create a
world in which there are no apples and so Bill will never choose to steal one.
Although God cannot change the free choices that one would make in any given
situation, through middle knowledge God is able to change the situations in which
one will make those choices. Thus if God can actualise the appropriate
circumstances, God could, with the benefit of middle knowledge, bring about
universal salvation. Thus if God knew that every person would accept God after a
face to face encounter, God could create a world in which each individual at some
point had such an encounter. Unless such a world was not feasible for God, and we
have no reason to suppose that to be the case, God could actualise these
circumstances and thus create a universalist world.

Craig, writes: 'If He has middle knowledge, then God can so plan the world
that His ends will be achieved through the free decisions of creatures'.[96] That is to
say, that God could ensure that all people would be in a situation where they freely
made the choices that God desired them to make. Talbott believes that if God has
middle knowledge, God can bring it about that each person freely chooses God. He
gives the example:

> iv) If God were to subject Smith to experiences A, B and C, then
> Smith would freely repent of all wrong doing.
> v) If God were to subject Smith to experiences A and B but not C,
> then Smith would freely refuse to repent of all wrong doing.[97]

Talbott continues: 'if God knows iv) and v) are both true, he is in a position to
bring it about (weakly) that Smith freely repents of all wrong doing and to bring it
about (weakly) that Smith freely refuses to repent of all wrong doing'.[98] Talbott
concludes that God would surely choose to bring it about that Smith freely chooses
to repent. The only reasons why God would not do this would be if the world in
which Smith freely repents is not a world actualizable by God, or if Smith's free
repentance can only be achieved in a world in which a greater number of people

---

[95] Basinger, 1991 p.132. In this article W represents the world in which Bill freely chooses
to steal the apple and W^1 represents the world in which Bill freely chooses not to steal the
apple.
[96] Craig, 1991 p.244.
[97] Talbott, 1990 p.234.
[98] Talbott, 1990 p.234.

would not freely repent. Talbott argues that if the first were true, God would have avoided creating Smith at all, knowing that he could not be redeemed.[99]

The objection may be made that God manipulates our freedom by placing us in some situations and not others. But it is clear that this is the kind of free existence that we do have. We do not always have control over which situations we find ourselves in. To adopt Talbott's distinction, God by choosing the circumstances in which we will be actualised, brings it about weakly that we respond in a particular way. Therefore, with the benefit of middle knowledge, God could ensure that all people will freely choose to accept God and so be saved. Thus middle knowledge does increase God's providential control because it allows God to ensure that the world which is actualised is one in which all people will find themselves in certain circumstances. For this purpose, all people will find themselves in the situation where they choose freely to accept salvation. So God could be said to bring it about weakly that all people will accept salvation. However this does not infringe on our compatibilist freedom.

Sanders writes: 'The concept of middle knowledge is used in a couple of ways then, - both to allow for the salvation of the unevangelized and to rule it out'.[100] Having discussed how middle knowledge could allow God to bring about universal salvation, I will now look at the use of middle knowledge, to preclude universal salvation.

Transworld Damnation

The objection may be made that there is no possible world in which Bill would freely choose not to steal the apple. No matter what circumstances he had encountered previous to the opportunity to steal the apple, Bill will always freely choose to steal the apple. Craig has formulated such an argument by claiming that there is transworld damnation. He believes that some people's creaturely essence[101] is such that they would be lost in any possible world that God could have created. Craig further suggests the possibility that God could only create a world which contained a mixture of the saved and lost.

> Suppose that the only worlds feasible for God in which all persons receive Christ and are saved are worlds containing only a handful of persons. Is it not at least possible that such a world is less preferable to God than a world in which great multitudes come to experience His salvation and a few are damned because they freely reject Christ?[102]

---

[99] Talbott, 1990 p.235.

[100] Sanders, 1992 p.170.

[101] This is Plantinga's clarification. Craig does not actually use this description. I have included it here as I think it will be helpful to the discussion. Plantinga, 1974 p.188.

[102] Craig, 1989 p.182.

In claiming that God would actualise the world with the ultimate balance of saved and lost, Craig is asserting that salvation is indeed of prime importance. Indeed he suggests that it is so desirable to God, that God would rather actualise a world where a large number are saved, but an even larger number lost than a world in which only a few are saved but none lost. Therefore not only is it important that some are saved, but the larger the number of the saved the better. Thus Craig values salvation even though it will cost some being lost. However, he justifies this by asserting that God will create the best balance of saved and lost that it is possible to create.

> It is possible that in order to create the actual number of persons who will be saved, God had to create the actual number of people who will be lost. It is possible that the terrible price of filling heaven is also filling hell and that in any other possible world which was feasible for God the balance between saved and lost was worse.[103]

However, it turns out that this balance was not very favourable to the saved. Craig does not suppose the number who are damned to be 'a few'.

> Such persons who are not sufficiently well-informed about Christ's person and work will be judged on the basis of their response to general revelation and the light that they do have. Perhaps some will be saved through such a response; but on the basis of Scripture we must say that such 'anonymous Christians' are relatively rare.[104]

Thus only Christians and a relatively rare number of anonymous Christians are saved. Although it is unclear what sort of number of non-Christians Craig is thinking of, this probably leaves the majority of humanity damned. If this world has, as Craig claims, the optimum ratio of saved compared to lost, it would seem that God could not create a world in which more people would be saved than lost. This surely raises the question of whether God knowing this, would have proceeded with creation at all. Craig preempts this objection and suggests: 'Given his will to create a world of free creatures, God must accept that some will be lost'.[105]

Craig further argues:

> It is simply irrelevant whether it seems intuitively possible that God could in some possible world or other win a free affirmative response to His grace on the part of any person. For it is possible that in every world realizable by God in which persons are free with respect to salvation, some people irrevocably reject God.[106]

---

[103] Craig, 1989 p.183.
[104] Craig, 1989 p.186.
[105] Craig, 1989 p.185.
[106] Craig, 1991 (b) p.299.

Although that may well be possible, we have so far been provided with no reason to think that it is so. There only needs to be one potential world in which the combination of people and circumstances will be such that all will freely choose God. If there is one such actualizable world, then that is the world which God would actualise. If there is no such actualizable world, then would God have actualised a world at all? Gray raises an important point and one that lies at the heart of this debate.

> A question of immense theological proportions is the 'why' of God's creation. Although neither party ever draws this out in the debate, Craig assumes that God's purposes in creation are sufficient, even given the fact that God knew some would be damned in this creation. Talbott replies that if this were so, then the price of creation was too high. Why would God create if he knew some were to be damned?[107]

Craig pre-empts this sort of objection and claims:

> The tragic fact that every world feasible for God is one involving persons who are lost would not force Him to refrain from creation or to annul creaturely freedom lest the blessedness of the saved be undermined, for it is possible that the reality of lost persons is a fact the pain of which He alone shall endure for eternity.[108]

Talbott does not accept that under these conditions God would have proceeded with creation. He notes two criticisms of what he terms the Rejection Hypothesis:

> i) If God could have populated a universe with free agents none of whom are irredeemable in the sense that they freely reject him forever, then he would most certainly have done so.
> ii) If God could not have so populated a universe, and knew that he could not, then he would have faced a catastrophe of such

---

[107] Gray, 1996 p.348.

[108] Craig, 1991 (b) p.308. Craig explains, 'In shielding His redeemed people from the painful knowledge of the estate of the damned and bearing it Himself alone, God extends the suffering of the cross into eternity. The terrible secret of the condition of the lost is buried for eternity deep within the breast of God, a burden whose gravity only He can fully feel and yet which He willingly takes upon Himself in order that He might bring free creatures into the supreme and unalloyed joy of fellowship with Himself' p.307. There is not room here properly to consider this defence; however it seems to create more difficulties than it has solved. God is not the only one aware of the state of the damned. Presumably they are also aware of their condition and are suffering for eternity. Further God is deceiving those in heaven about the state of their lost brothers and sisters. Craig's description of God bearing this secret sounds almost like God is ashamed of the secret of the damned, it seems strange to propose that God would create such a situation even if this were the only feasible world.

proportions that he would have had no choice but to prevent it, either by not creating any persons at all or by interfering with human freedom as the lesser evil.[109]

According to Talbott, there would have been no need for God to have been saddled with Craig's rather dismal world. If the only world actualizable was a world in which many freely rejected God, God could have overridden their freedom to bring them salvation. Although I do not think it will be necessary to resort to this conclusion, I think that Talbott is right that this response of God would have been preferable to the outcome Craig envisions.

So Craig claims that the only worlds that God can create are ones where a large number of people will be lost. He further justifies God's action in actualizing a world with this number of lost, by claiming that they would be lost in any possible world. That is to say that they suffer from transworld damnation. Thus some people whom God has created are irredeemable in any possible situation. These are very controversial claims of Craig's and ones which he does not seem to justify. Talbott objects: 'The very concept of an irredeemable person is deeply incoherent'.[110] Similarly, Sachs asks:

> Is it really possible to imagine a human being utterly devoid of good, so completely evil that there is absolutely nothing for God to heal and fulfil in the resurrection? One could not even speak of a truly human person unless there had been at least some minimal, mutual experience of love.[111]

It is certainly difficult to imagine such a person, and even more difficult to imagine why God would create such a person. Craig of course, claims that without such people to account for the lost, there would not be any saved. He argues that the only worlds it is possible for God to create are worlds with such a balance of saved and lost. Hunt suggests: 'It appears that Craig has no better reason for defining transworld damnation in terms of worlds feasible for God than the fact that these are the worlds in terms of which Plantinga defined transworld depravity'.[112] It is clear that Craig relies heavily on Plantinga for this argument.

Plantinga claims that it is at least possible that in all of the worlds which were feasible for God to create, people would suffer from transworld depravity. This is because Plantinga concludes that every free person it would be possible to actualise would choose to do wrong in at least one act. Plantinga explains:

---

[109] Talbott, 1990 p.228.
[110] Talbott, 1990 p.236.
[111] Sachs, 1991 p.237.
[112] David P. Hunt, 'Middle Knowledge and the Soteriological Problem of Evil' *Religious Studies* vol.27 (1991) p.15.

> It is possible that every creaturely essence suffers from transworld depravity. But suppose this is true ... if every such essence suffers from transworld depravity, then no matter which essences God instantiated, the resulting persons, if free with respect to morally significant actions, would always perform at least some wrong actions.[113]

Therefore whatever different world God made, the transworldly depraved people in it, would mean that that world was not free of moral evil. Whilst Plantinga shows that this is at least possible, he cannot of course, prove that it is the case. However Plantinga's suggestion has one considerable strength, and that is that it explains the nature of the actual world. It is clear to us that God has not made beings who always freely choose to do good and thus Plantinga's account succeeds in offering an explanation of why the actual world is the best possible world God could make, even with the amount of evil it contains.

Craig however cannot appeal to our experience of the world. He assumes that in this world some are damned and therefore develops an explanation which shows this to be the best possible world God could actualise. But how does Craig know that some are damned? Neither he nor anyone else (except, of course, God) can know this. Thus Craig's argument for transworld damnation, does not have the advantage that Plantinga's argument for transworld depravity has, in that he is not seeking to explain a state of affairs of which we have direct experience. Plantinga must only demonstrate that transworld depravity is possible, for us to have reason to believe that it is actual. But for Craig to show that transworld damnation is at least possible will not suffice, unless one starts with the strong belief, as he does, that all are not saved.

Another difficulty for Craig is Plantinga's claim that every creaturely essence is transworldly depraved. If they were not, then God would have created only those creatures who did not suffer from transworld depravity.[114] Craig does not, of course, claim that every creaturely essence is transworldly damned, this would be a most difficult claim to reconcile with Christian thought. However, if not all creaturely essences are transworldly damned why did God not only actualise the essences that were free from transworld damnation? Craig would presumably resort to the response that God had to actualise a certain number of the transworldly damned in order for there to be any saved. But why should this be the case? In what way can there being a number of saved rely on there also being a number of lost? Plantinga claims that God actualises the transworldly depraved, because these are the only free people who can be actualised. However Craig can make no comparative claim. The transworldly damned are not the only people that God can actualise and thus it seems there is no convincing reason for thinking that God would actualise any transworldly damned essences, let alone a majority of

---

[113] Plantinga, 1974 pp. 188-189.
[114] Plantinga, 1974 p.189.

transworldly damned. William Hasker points out a further difficulty with the idea of the transwordly damned. In a footnote he writes:

> For one thing, we may be perplexed by the apparent geographical and racial bias in the incidence of transworld damnation. On Craig's account, transworld damnation must have affected very nearly the entire human race, aside from Jews, at the time of Christ; since then its incidence has gradually decreased as the Gospel has been spread throughout the world. It would be interesting, to say the least, to know Craig's explanation for this phenomenon.[115]

This is a serious difficulty for Craig's account and as it stands it seems that we must reject of transworld damnation on the grounds that it is inadequately defended by Craig.

The Best Possible World[116]

So far I have assumed that Plantinga's account of transworld depravity is coherent. Even if we were to reject transworld depravity and suppose that God could arrange circumstances in which people would always freely choose to do good, we might conclude that God would have reason not to create such a world. It may be that the combination of good and evil, is the best environment for us and indeed this is what I have concluded in previous chapters. However, because God may consider a world in which we can freely choose to do wrong the best world to actualise, does not mean that God would also chose to create a world in which anyone would decisively choose to reject God. If, on the other hand, transworld depravity is true, it does not mean that transworld damnation is also true. It is possible that every creaturely essence would do moral evil with regard to a certain act, but it does not follow that every creaturely essence would also reject God. Thus Craig relies too heavily on Plantinga's established argument in order to support his own which differs significantly.

Is Plantinga right that every creaturely essence suffers from transworld depravity? It is quite clear that God has not designed the world so that nobody will ever steal an apple, to return to Basinger's example. God has not created free beings who will always choose the good. Does this mean then that even with the benefit of middle knowledge God could not do this? Hick argues that although God could do this, our free choices are infinitely more valuable when they are a result of our competing desires, than if they were made without any effort on our part. Swinburne more strongly claims that only free choices made from a range of good and bad options are truly valuable. Swinburne would claim that God could not

---

[115] Hasker, 1991 p.387 fn.8.

[116] It has of course been argued that the idea of a 'best possible world' is incoherent. However I will argue that this world is the 'best possible' which combines human freedom and an universalist outcome.

bring it about that our freedom to choose is always between good options, as he would assume that in this situation we would not be significantly free. However, I have already rejected Swinburne's understanding of human freedom. Hick claims that God could give us only good choices should God choose to, and it seems that this would be a feasible world for God. I do not think it can be objected that in such a world we would not have genuine freedom. In this good world, we would be able to freely decide what to do in all situations we found ourselves in. Our choices would not be compelled externally, and would perhaps be more difficult to make than choices in this world thus they would still be the result of our own desires and decisions. Indeed it seems to me that we would have the same freedom that we have in the actual world, although the range of choices would be differently limited. If this world would have been feasible for God, there must be some reason why the actual world is better than this good world.

Hick, of course, states that this is the best of all possible worlds because of the soul-making environment it offers. Each good decision made out of a choice of good and bad, is infinitely more valuable, according to Hick, than each good decision made out of a choice of different goods. Thus this world is vastly preferable to God because individuals, through their own choices, eventually become children of God, rather than being created as perfected beings in the first place.[117] So even if Plantinga is right, and every actualizable person suffers from transworld depravity, this did not mean that God could not go ahead with creation. In fact this means that they were actualised in the best possible world.

Basinger writes:

> As an all-loving being, God is committed to creating the 'best' possible world. And, even though God does not find the torment faced by those in hell to be intrinsically desirable, this world, even with such torment is, on balance, a better world than any other God could have actualised, including any other world in which no one spends eternity in hell.[118]

This again raises the question, how can Basinger, or anybody else, be certain that in the actual world some face the torment of hell? It seems uncontroversial that God should want to create the 'best' possible world, and therefore that the actual world is the best possible world. However we do not know whether in the actual world, there is a hell in which some people are suffering eternally. Given that we believe the actual world is the best possible world, it would seem more appropriate to conclude that it does not contain a hell, rather than that it does.

---

[117] Hick, of course, is prepared to state that all people will eventually undergo this process. One obvious objection would be that through our free choices we become self-centred and bad, the opposite of the result Hick envisages.

[118] Basinger, 1992 p.2.

Conclusion

Throughout this argument, I have had two main premises which are:

Premise 1: God will actualise the best world it is possible to actualise.
Premise 2: God's overriding purpose for humans is that they freely come to love God and choose to be reconciled to eternal communion with God.

Given these premises, the conclusion must be that if it is possible to actualise a world in which all people are saved, that is the world which God will actualise. That God will actualise the best world that can possibly be actualised is an uncontroversial Christian claim. That the best possible world would be a universalist world, I hope to have shown in this chapter. We do not know whether or not the actual world is a universalist world but if we believe that this would be the best possible world, then we must conclude that the actual world is a universalist world.

I have rejected Craig's argument that it is not possible for God to actualise a universalist world on the grounds that he can offer no convincing reason as to why God must create a certain number of damned in order to ensure a certain number of saved. I have further claimed that with middle knowledge God would be able to ensure that all people that are actualised will experience the circumstances necessary for them freely to accept God. In the previous section I suggested that this circumstance would be a face to face encounter with God after death. Thus God's middle knowledge means that God already knows that all people will freely respond favourably to this encounter and so God is able to create the actual world knowing that there is no risk of losing any eternally, and indeed knowing that it is the best of all possible worlds. Therefore, hell does not exist because God knows that it will not be required by our human freedom as even though any could choose to reject God, in the end none will.

Firm Universalism

The three premises with which we began this chapter were God's salvific will, compatibilist human freedom and God's foreknowledge and middle knowledge. I hope to have demonstrated that these are all coherent premises and that they lead to us being able to assert ultimate universal salvation. Which of the definitions of universalism laid out in chapter one will most accurately describe the universalist position at which I have arrived? In chapter one I wrote that I hoped to establish the difference between necessary and hard universalism. Necessary universalism entails that there is no possible world in which all will not be saved. As Kvanvig writes, the 'free will position can be false and yet still undermine necessary universalism. All that is required is that the free will position is *possibly* true, for necessary universalism claims that in no possible world could any person end up in hell'.[119] Hard universalism claims that ultimately God will allow no other outcome. Talbott, suggests that if all people did not reach a decision in favour of God, God would override their freedom in order to ensure that salvation.[120] If God could not have created free beings who would all eventually be joined with God, it does not seem unreasonable given God's salvific will, to suppose that God would ultimately sacrifice their freedom, or even refrain from actualising creation altogether, rather than risk the loss of some of God's creation.

However, I do not believe that this is a choice that it was necessary for God to make. If we accept that human freedom is not of the strong libertarian kind, but of the compatibilist kind and that God has middle knowledge and foreknowledge, these factors can work together to ensure that the eventual destiny of all free peoples will be the company of heaven. Thus hard universalism must be rejected on the grounds that God, having created limitedly free beings does not withdraw this freedom in order to achieve universal salvation. Necessary Universalism must also be rejected on the grounds that I am not claiming that in no possible world would anyone go to hell. Because we are free, there are many possible worlds in which people could go to hell. Thus although the eventual reconciliation of all people with God is the result of free choice, God who has middle knowledge and foreknowledge, knows for certain that this will in fact be the outcome. Thus although in one sense this is a contingent universalism as it follows from the free actions of humans, it cannot really said to be contingent because God ensures that this will be the result before actualising creation. Thus neither contingent, hard or necessary universalism accurately describe this position and so I will term this theory of universal salvation 'firm universalism'.

Although it may be philosophically coherent, 'firm universalism' to fulfil the purpose of this book also needs to be a viable option for a Christian. This study has been conducted within the broad parameters of a Christian framework, and I hope has resulted in a Christian position. In chapter four I defined a broad Christian framework as belief in a God of love as revealed in Jesus Christ. Firm universalism falls within this definition. The face to face encounter after death I take to be with a God of love, and the life of heaven I understand to be continued existence in the company of the God of love. Indeed I believe the free offer of heaven to be at the heart of the Christian gospel. Sachs writes:

> It seems to me that the real 'point' of Christian doctrine and hope concerning the end is precisely the eternity of salvation: that the blessed really do, finally and irrevocably reach life and fulfilment in God, beyond every power of sin and death.[121]

---

[119] Kvanvig, 1993 p.78.

[120] See Talbott, 1990 (b) particularly pp. 37-39. Talbott thinks that universal salvation will be achieved without God having to override human freedom, but that if this was the only way to bring about universal salvation God would in fact override human freedom.

[121] Sachs, 1991 p.249.

I agree that this is the point of Christian doctrine, but further, it seems to me that the blessed must include all people whom God has created in God's own image and likeness (Genesis 1:26).

In conclusion I believe that firm universalism is a coherent, Christian position which does not require us to sacrifice human freedom. God created us with the benefit of foreknowledge and middle knowledge and thus could be sure what the outcome of creation would be. This universal salvation was God's primary purpose in creation, and an end which it is best for us to arrive at freely. Thus although we are free to reject God, God knows that in the end none will.

Conclusion

Although the debate about hell has been resumed recently, I believe that there is still much to be looked at in this area and particularly with regard to the universalist position. The contrast between Swinburne and Hick's positions highlights the relevant areas of this topic and allows for direct comparisons of their different understandings of hell and freedom. Swinburne may not be best known for his position on hell, in the way that Hick is perhaps famed for his universalism, and his defence of hell has not previously received detailed study. Swinburne's position is interesting because he often attempts to defend orthodox doctrines, by unorthodox explanations. This is the case with his understanding of hell. In order to offer a defence of hell Swinburne produces an account of hell very different to the traditional strong view. The weak view of hell is the most popular and the most convincing defence of hell today. However Swinburne, and other defenders of this view, are reliant on their account of libertarian freedom which I believe is not only an inaccurate account of the human situation but also requires one to choose strong freedom over salvation as the most important gift of God. Indeed all versions of the free will defence fail if this valuation is rejected. In order to show that we are free to reject God Swinburne makes salvation secondary to freedom.

Hick's account of universal salvation goes a lot further towards holding freedom and salvation in balance. However Hick does not adequately support his claims and thus leaves us with the feeling that he does eventually sacrifice freedom to his universal salvation, not because his account of freedom is untenable but because he is reliant on the continuing lives finally to bring all to God. Were he to discuss God's middle knowledge his case would be strengthened.

Taking many of Hick's premises, I have developed an alternative account of universal salvation which instead of requiring all people to undergo transformation into children of God through their own efforts, requires only that all people realise their desire for God, which those who have not already done will do in the face to face encounter after death. My account of universalism is clearly dependent on the after-death encounter. Although I believe this to be a common expectation of Christians, certainly in this country, it is difficult to find any writings about the hope of meeting God after death. The reader may feel that this idea is in need of further development and this question could be returned to as the subject of further study. Given God's foreknowledge and middle knowledge the outcome is assured that all will finally be saved. God knew from the outset of creation that all would be saved and would not have created any world which did not have a universalist outcome. So although we make our own free choices, God has ensured that all will ultimately choose to accept God.

Bibliography

Afterlife

Badham, Paul (1976) *Christian Beliefs About Life After Death* London: Macmillan
Badham, Paul and Badham, Linda (1982) *Immortality or Extinction?* London: Macmillan
Brown, David (1985) 'No Heaven Without Purgatory' *Religious Studies* vol.21 pp.447-456
Helm, Paul (1989) *The Last Things* Edinburgh: The Banner of Truth Trust
Jantzen, Grace (1984) 'Do We Need Immortality?' *Modern Theology* vol.1 pp.33-44
Küng, Hans (1984) *Eternal Life?* London: Collins
Simon, Ulrich (1958) *Heaven in the Christian Tradition* London: Rockliff
Stevenson, Leslie (2001) 'A Two-Stage Life After Death?' *Theology* vol.CIV pp.345-351

Biblical Studies

Brown, R. E. (1971) *The Gospel According to John I - XII* London: Geoffrey Chapman
Hill, David (1972) *The Gospel of Matthew* London: Marshall, Morgan & Scott
Marshall, I. Howard (1989) 'Universal Grace and Atonement in the Pastoral Epistles' in Clarke H. Pinnock (ed.) (1989) *The Grace of God, The Will of Man* Grand Rapids, Michigan: Zondervan Publishing House
McNeile, A. H. (1938) *The Gospel According To Matthew* London: Macmillan
Nineham, D. E. (1963) *Saint Mark* London: SCM Press
Rad, Gerhard Von (1961) *Genesis - A Commentary* trans. John H. Marks London: SCM Press
Reicke, Bo (1964) *The Epistles of James, Peter and Jude* New York: Doubleday
Robinson, John A.T. (1962) *Twelve New Testament Studies* London: SCM Press
Strawson, William (1959) *Jesus and the Future Life* London: Epworth Press
Weiss, Johannes (1971) *Jesus' Proclamation of the Kingdom of God* London: SCM Press

Christianity and other Religions

D'Costa, Gavin (1986) *Theology and Religious Pluralism* Oxford: Blackwell
Dupius, J (1997) *Toward a Christian Theology of Religious Pluralism* Maryknoll, New York: Orbis Books
Marshall, Molly Truman (1993) No Salvation Outside the Church? A Critical Inquiry Lewiston New York: Edwin Mellen Press
Mullan, David George (ed.) (1998) *Selected Readings: Religious Pluralism in the West* Oxford: Blackwell
Pinnock, Clarke H. (1992) *A Wideness in God's Mercy: The Finality of Jesus Christ in a World of Religions* Grand Rapids, Michigan: Zondervan Publishing House
Plantinga, Richard J. (ed.) (1999) *Christianity and Plurality - Classic and Contemporary Readings* Oxford: Blackwell
Race, Alan (1983) *Christians and Religious Pluralism* London: SCM Press

Sanders, John (1992) *No Other Name: An Investigation Into The Destiny of the Unevangelized* Grand Rapids, Michigan: Eerdmans

Strange, Daniel (1999) *The Possibility of Salvation Among the Unevangelised: An Analysis of Inclusivism in Recent Evangelical Theology* Ph.D. Thesis: University of Bristol

Sullivan, Francis A. (1992) *Salvation Outside the Church? Tracing the History of Catholic Response* London: Geoffrey Chapman

Troeltsch, Ernst (1901) *The Absolute Validity of Christianity* London: Hart

Troeltsch, Ernst (1972) *The Absoluteness of Christianity* London: SCM Press

Evangelical Writings on Hell

ACUTE, (2000) *The Nature of Hell* A report by the Evangelical Alliance's Committee on Unity and Truth among Evangelicals, Carlisle: Paternoster Publishing

Benton, John (1985) *How Can a God of Love Send People to Hell?* Welwyn: Evangelical Press

Blamires, Harry (1988) *Knowing the Truth About Heaven and Hell* Michigan: Servant Books

Blanchard, John (1993) *Whatever Happened To Hell?* Darlington: Evangelical Press

Blocher, Henri (1994) 'Everlasting Punishment and the Problem of Evil' in Nigel de M. S. Cameron (ed.) (1992) *Universalism and the Doctrine of Hell* Carlisle: Paternoster Press; Grand Rapids: Baker Book House

Cameron, Nigel de M. S. (ed.) (1992) *Universalism and the Doctrine of Hell* Carlisle: Paternoster Press; Grand Rapids: Baker Book House

Crockett, William (ed.) (1992) *Four Views on Hell* Grand Rapids, Michigan: Zondervan Publishing House

Davies, Eryl (1991) *An Angry God? The Biblical Doctrine of Wrath, Final Judgement and Hell* Bridgend: Evangelical Press of Wales

Dixon, Larry (1992) *The Other Side of the Good News: Confronting The Contemporary Challenges to Jesus' Teaching on Hell* Wheaton, Illinois: Victor Books

Dowsett. Dick (1982) *God That's Not Fair* Kent: OMF Books

Elson, G. (1982) *Hell and a God of Love* Bromley, Kent: Hayes Press

Fernando, Ajith (1991) *Crucial Questions About Hell* Eastbourne: Kingsway Publications

Fudge, Edward (1982) *The Fire That Consumes* Housten: Providential Press

Moore, David G. (1995) *The Battle For Hell* Lahan: University Press of America

Pawson, David (1992) *The Road to Hell: Everlasting Torment or Annihilation?* London: Hodder & Stoughton

Peterson, R.A. (1995) *Hell On Trial: The Case for Eternal Punishment* Phillipsburg: P + R Publishing

Powys, David (1997) *Hell: A Hard Look At a Hard Question* Carlisle: Paternoster Press

Wright, Nigel (1996) *The Radical Evangelical: Seeking a Place to Stand* London: SPCK

Foreknowledge

Alston, William P. (1985) 'Divine Foreknowledge and Alternative Conceptions of Human Freedom' *International Journal for Philosophy of Religion* vol.18 pp.19-32

Basinger, David (1992) 'Divine Omniscience and the Soteriological Problem of Evil: Is the Type of Knowledge God Possesses Relevant?' *Religious Studies* vol.28 pp.1-18

Basinger, David (1993) 'Simple Foreknowledge and Providential Control: A Response to Hunt' *Faith and Philosophy* vol.10 pp.421-428

Fischer, John Martin (1983) 'Freedom and Foreknowledge' *Philosophical Review* vol.92 pp.67-79

Hasker, William (1985) 'Foreknowledge and Necessity' *Faith and Philosophy* vol.2 pp.121-157

Hasker, William (1989) *God, Time and Knowledge* Ithaca: Cornell University Press

Hunt, David P. (1993) 'Divine Providence and Simple Foreknowledge' *Faith and Philosophy* vol.10 pp.394-414

Kvanvig, Jonathan L. (1986) *The Possibility of an All-Knowing God* Houndmills, UK: Macmillan

Linville, Mark D. (1993) 'Divine Foreknowledge and the Libertarian Conception of Human Freedom' *International Journal for Philosophy of Religion* vol.33 pp.165-186

Pinnock, Clarke H. (ed.) (1994) *The Openness of God: A Biblical Challenge to the Traditional Understanding of God* Carlisle: Paternoster Press

Plantinga, Alvin (1967) *God and Other Minds* London: George Allen & Unwin

Rice, Richard (1980) *God's Foreknowledge and Man's Free Will* Minneapolis: Bethany House Publishers

Robinson, Michael (2000) 'Why Divine Foreknowledge?' *Religious Studies* vol.36 pp.251-275

Freedom

Ackermann, Robert (1982) 'An Alternative Free Will Defence' *Religious Studies* vol.18 pp.365-372

Basinger, David and Basinger, Randall (eds.) (1986) *Predestination and Free Will* Downers Grove, Illinois: Intervarsity Press

Bauckham, Richard (1991) *Freedom To Choose* Grove Spirituality Series no. 39

Boër, Steven E. (1978) 'The Irrelevance of the Free Will Defence' *Analysis* vol.XXXVIII pp.110-112

Coughlan, Michael J. (1986) 'The Free Will Defence and Natural *Evil*' *International Journal for Philosophy of Religion* vol.20 pp.93-108

Davies, Stephen T. (1979) 'Divine Omniscience and Human Freedom' *Religious Studies* vol.15 pp.303-316

Dennett, Daniel (1984) *Elbow Room* Oxford: Clarendon Press

Dilley, Frank B. (1982) 'Is the Free Will Defence Irrelevant?' *Religious Studies* vol.18 pp.355-364

Double, Richard (1991) *The Non-Reality of Free Will* Oxford: Oxford University Press

Feinberg, John S. (1986) 'God Ordains All Things' in David Basinger and Randall Basinger (eds.) (1986) *Predestination and Free Will* Downers Grove, Illinois: Intervarsity Press

Flew, Anthony (1991) 'Freedom and Human Nature' *Philosophy* vol.66 pp.53-63

Geisler, Norman (1986) 'Norman Geisler's Response' in David Basinger and Randall Basinger (eds.) (1986) *Predestination and Free Will* Downers Grove, Illinois: Intervarsity Press

Geisler, Norman (1986b) 'God Knows All Things' in David Basinger and Randall Basinger (eds.) (1986) *Predestination and Free Will* Downers Grove, Illinois: Intervarsity Press

Honderich, Ted (1993) *How Free Are You? The Determinism Problem* Oxford: Oxford University Press

Lehrer, Keith (ed.) (1966) *Freedom and Determinism* New York: Random House

Lucas, J. R. (1970) *The Freedom of the Will* Oxford: Oxford University Press

Pinnock, Clarke H. (ed.) (1989) *The Grace of God, The Will of Man* Grand Rapids, Michigan: Zondervan Publishing House

Plantinga, Alvin (1974) *God, Freedom and Evil* London: George Allen & Unwin

Plantinga, Alvin (1974b) *The Nature of Necessity* Oxford: Clarendon Press

Schoenig, Richard (1999) 'The Free Will Theodicy' *Religious Studies* vol.34 pp.457-470

Sennett, James F. (1991) 'The Free Will Defense and Determinism' *Faith and Philosophy* vol.8 pp.340-353

Talbott, Thomas (1979) 'Indeterminism and Chance Occurrences' *Personalist* vol.60 pp.253-261

Talbott, Thomas (1988) 'On the Divine Nature and the Nature of Divine Freedom' *Faith and Philosophy* vol.5 pp.3-24

Talbott, Thomas (1990) 'Providence, Freedom and Human Destiny' *Religious Studies* vol.26 pp.227-245

Talbott, Thomas (1993) 'Theological Fatalism and Modal Confusion' *International Journal for Philosophy of Religion* vol.33 pp.65-88

Hell and Universalism

Adams, Marilyn McCord (1971) 'Universal Salvation: A Reply to Mr Bettis' *Religious Studies* vol.7 pp.45-249

Adams, Marilyn McCord (1975) 'Hell and the God of Justice' *Religious Studies* vol.11 pp.433-447

Balthasar, Hans Urs Von (1988) *Dare We Hope 'That All Men be Saved?'* San Francisco: Ignatius Press

Bettis, Joseph Dabney (1970) 'A Critique of the Doctrine of Universal Salvation' *Religious Studies* vol.6 pp.329-344

Bonda, Jan (1993) *The One Purpose of God: An Answer to the Doctrine of Eternal Punishment* Grand Rapids, Michigan: William B. Eerdmans

Bauckham, Richard J. (1978) 'Universalism: A Historical Survey' *Themelios* vol.4 pp.48-54

Bauckham, Richard J. (ed.) (1999) *God Will Be All in All - The Eschatology of Jürgen Moltmann* (1999) Edinburgh: T & T Clark

Bauckham, Richard and Hart, Trevor (1999) *Hope Against Hope - Christian Eschatology in Contemporary Context* London: Dartman, Longman and Todd

Bray, Gerald (1992) 'Eternal Punishment or Total Annihilation' *Evangel* pp.19-24

Clark, Kelly James (2001) 'God is Great, God is Good: Medieval Conceptions of Divine Goodness and the Problem of Hell' *Religious Studies* vol.37 pp.15-31

Colwell, John (1992) 'The Contemporaneity of the Divine Decision: Reflections on Barth's Denial of "Universalism"' in Nigel de M. S. Cameron (ed.) (1992) *Universalism and the Doctrine of Hell* Carlisle: Paternoster Press; Grand Rapids: Baker Book House

Craig, William Lane (1991b) 'Talbott's Universalism' *Religious Studies* vol.27 pp.297-308

Craig, William Lane (1993) 'Talbott's Universalism Once More' *Religious Studies* vol.29 pp.497-518

Davies, Stephen T. (1990) 'Universalism, Hell and the Fate of the Ignorant' *Modern Theology* vol.6 pp.173-186

Graham, Gordon (1988) 'The Goodness of God and the Conception of Hell' *New Blackfriars* vol. 69 pp.477-487

Gray, Tony (1996) *Hell: An Analysis of Some Major Twentieth Century Attempts to Defend the Doctrine of Hell* D. Phil. Thesis: University of Oxford

Harmon, Kendall S. (1993) *Finally Excluded From God? Some Twentieth Century Theological Explanations of the Problem of Hell and Universalism with Reference to the Historical Development of these Doctrines.* D. Phil. Thesis: University of Oxford

Hart, Trevor (1992) 'Universalism: Two Distinct Types' in Nigel de M. S. Cameron (ed.) (1992) *Universalism and the Doctrine of Hell* Carlisle: Paternoster Press; Grand Rapids: Baker Book House

Himma, Kenneth Einar (2003) 'Eternally Incorrigible: The Continuing-Sin Response to the Proportionality Problem of Hell' *Religious Studies* vol.36 pp.61-78

Holten, Wilko Van (1999) 'Hell and the Goodness of God' *Religious Studies* vol.35 pp.37-55

Jensen, Paul T. (1993) 'Intolerable but Moral? Thinking about Hell' *Faith and Philosophy* vol.10 pp.394-414

Knight, Gordon (1997) 'Universalism and the Greater Good: A Response to Talbott' *Faith and Philosophy* vol.14 pp.100-103

Kvanvig, Jonathan L. (1993) *The Problem of Hell* Oxford: Oxford University Press

Lewis, C. S. (1946) *The Great Divorce* London: Macmillan

Moltmann, Jürgen (1999) 'The Logic of Hell' in Richard Bauckham (ed.) (1999) *God Will Be All in All - The Eschatology of Jürgen Moltmann* (1999) Edinburgh: T & T Clark

Norris, Frederick W. (1992) 'Universal Salvation in Origen and Maximus' in Nigel de M. S. Cameron (ed.) (1992) *Universalism and the Doctrine of Hell* Carlisle: Paternoster Press; Grand Rapids: Baker Book House

Parry, Robin and Partridge, Chris (eds.) (2003) *Universal Salvation? The Current Debate* Carlisle: Paternoster Press

Potts, Michael (1998) 'Aquinas, Hell, and the Resurrection of the Damned' *Faith and Philosophy* vol.15 pp.341-351

Reitan, Eric (2001) 'Universalism and Autonomy: Towards a Comparative Defence of Universalism' *Faith and Philosophy* vol.18 pp.222-239

Robinson, John A. T. (1950) *In the End God* London: James Clark and Co.

Sachs, John R. (1991) 'Current Eschatology: Universal Salvation and the Problem of Hell' *Theological Studies* vol.52 pp.227-254

Seymour, Charles (1997) 'On Choosing Hell' *Religious Studies* vol.33 pp.249-266

Seymour, Charles (1998) 'Hell, Justice and Freedom' *International Journal for Philosophy of Religion* vol.43 pp.69-86

Seymour, Charles (2000) 'A Craigian Theodicy of Hell' *Faith and Philosophy* vol.17 pp.103-115

Talbott, Thomas (1990b) 'The Doctrine of Everlasting Punishment' *Faith and Philosophy* vol.7 pp.19-42

Talbott, Thomas (1992) 'Craig on the Possibility of Eternal Damnation' *Religious Studies* vol.28 pp.495-510

Talbott, Thomas (1995) 'Three Pictures of God in Western Theology' *Faith and Philosophy* vol.12 pp.79-94

Talbott, Thomas (1999) *The Inescapable Love of God* Parkland, USA: Universal Publishers

Talbott, Thomas (1999b) 'Universalism and the Greater Good: Reply to Gordon Knight' *Faith and Philosophy* vol.16 pp.102-105

Talbott, Thomas (2001) 'Universalism and the Supposed Oddity of Our Earthly Life: Reply to Michael Murray' *Faith and Philosophy* vol.18 pp.102-109

VanArragon, Raymond J. (2001) 'Transworld Damnation and Craig's Contentious Suggestion' *Faith and Philosophy* vol.18 pp.241-260

Walls, Jerry L. (1985) 'Can God Save Anyone He Will?' *Scottish Journal of Theology* vol.38 pp.155-172

Walls, Jerry L. (1992) *Hell: The Logic of Damnation* Notre Dame: University of Notre Dame Press

Wright N. T. (1978) 'Towards a Biblical View of Universalism' *Themelios* vol.4 pp.54-61

Yandell, Keith E. (1992) 'The Doctrine of Hell and Moral Philosophy' *Religious Studies* vol.28 pp.75-90

Zeis, John (1986) 'To Hell With Freedom' *Sophia* vol.25 pp.41-48

John Hick

Hick, John (1957) *Faith and Knowledge* Ithaca: Cornell University Press

Hick, John (1958) 'The Christology of D.M. Baille' *Scottish Journal of Theology* vol.11 pp.1-12

Hick, John (1963) *Philosophy Of Religion* Englewood Cliffs, New Jersey: Prentice -Hall, Inc

Hick, John (1964b) *Faith And The Philosophers* London: Macmillan & Co; New York: St Martin's Press

Hick, John (1964c) *The Existence Of God* New York: The Macmillan Company.

Hick, John (1965) 'The Purpose of Evil' *The Listener* August 12 pp.231-232

Hick, John (1966) *Evil And The God Of Love* London: Macmillan & Co; New York: Harper & Row

Hick, John (1966b) *Faith And Knowledge* Second Edition Ithaca, N.Y.: Cornell University Press; London: Macmillan & co

Hick, John (1966c) 'Faith and Coercion' *Philosophy* vol.XLII pp.272-273

Hick, John (1968) *Christianity at the Centre* London: Macmillan & Co; London: SCM Press, Ltd; New York: Herder & Herder

Hick, John (1968b) 'The Problem of Evil in the First and Last Things' *Journal of Theological Studies* vol.XIX pp.591-602

Hick, John (1968c) 'The Justification of Religious Belief' *Theology* vol.LXXI pp.100-107

Hick, John (1970b) 'The Reconstruction of Christian Belief for Today and Tomorrow: I' *Theology* vol.LXXIII pp.339-345

Hick, John (1970c) 'The Reconstruction of Christian Belief for Today and Tomorrow: II' *Theology* vol.LXXIII pp.399-405

Hick, John (1970d) 'Freedom and the Irenaean Theodicy *Again*' *The Journal of Theological Studies* vol.XXI pp.419-422

Hick, John (1971b) 'Faith, Evidence, Coercion Again' *Australasian Journal of Philosophy* vol.49 pp.78-81

Hick, John (1973) *God And The Universe Of Faiths* London: Macmillan

Hick, John (1973a) 'Coherence and the God of Love Again' *Journal of Theological Studies* vol.XXIV pp.522-528

Hick, John (1974) 'Christ's Uniqueness' *Reform* October pp.18-19

Hick, John (1976) *Death And Eternal Life* London: Collins; New York: Harper & Row

Hick, John (1977b) *The Centre of Christianity* London: SCM Press

Hick, John (ed.) (1977c) *The Myth Of God Incarnate* London: SCM Press Philadelphia: Westminster Press

Hick, John (1977d) 'Present and Future Life' *Harvard Theological Review* vol.71 pp.1-15 Reprinted in Hick (1985), chapter 8

Hick, John (1977e) 'Remarks on the Problem of Evil' in Brown, S.C. (ed.) (1977) *Reason and Religion* New York: Ithaca

Hick, John (1978) 'Living in a Multi-cultural Society: Practical Reflections of a Theologian' *Expository Times* vol.89 pp.100-104

Hick, John (1980) *God Has Many Names* London: Macmillan

Hick, John (1981) 'An Irenaean Theodicy' in Stephen T. Davies (ed.) (1981) *Encountering Evil* Edinburgh: T & T Clarke

Hick, John (1981b) 'Response to Critics' in Stephen T. Davies (ed.) (1981) *Encountering Evil* Edinburgh: T & T Clarke

Hick, John (1981c) 'On Grading Religions' *Religious Studies* vol.17 pp.451-467

Hick, John (1983) *The Second Christianity* London: SCM Press

Hick, John (1985) *Problems Of Religious Pluralism* London: Macmillan; New York: St Martin's Press

Hick, John (1989) *An Interpretation Of Religion: Human Responses To The Transcendent* Basingstoke: Macmillan

Hick, John (1990) 'Straightening the Record: Some Responses to Critics' *Modern Theology* vol.62 pp.187-195

Hick, John (1991) 'Reply' in Hewitt, Harold (ed.) (1991) *Problems in the Philosophy of Religion: Critical Studies of the Work of John Hick* Basingstoke: Macmillan

Hick, John (1991b) 'A Response To Mesle' in C. Robert Mesle (1991) *John Hick's Theodicy: A Process Humanist Critique* London: Macmillan

Hick, John (1993) *The Metaphor Of God Incarnate* London: SCM Press

Hick, John (1993b) 'Afterword' in Rupert D. Geivett (1993) *Evil and the Evidence for God* Philadelphia: Temple University Press

Hick, John (1994) 'Is The Doctrine of Atonement a Mistake?' in Alan A. Padgett (ed.) (1994) *Reason and the Christian Religion: Essays in Honour of Richard Swinburne* Oxford: Clarendon Press; New York: Oxford University Press

Hick, John (1995) *The Rainbow of Faiths* London: SCM Press

Hick, John (1999) *The Fifth Dimension - An Exploration into the Spiritual Realm* Oxford: Oneworld Publications

Hick, John (2000) *'Providence and the Problem of Evil*, Richard Swinburne' *International Journal for Philosophy of Religion* vol.47 pp.57-64

Hick, John & Goulder, Michael (1983) *Why Believe In God?* London: SCM Press

On Hick

Badham, Paul (1993) *A John Hick Reader* Basingstoke: Macmillan

Betty, L.S. (1991) 'The Glitch in *An Interpretation of Religion*' in Harold Hewitt (ed.) (1991) *Problems in the Philosophy of Religion: Critical Studies of the Work of John Hick* Basingstoke: Macmillan

Byrne, Peter (1982) 'John Hick's Philosophy of World Religions' *Scottish Journal of Theology* vol.35 pp.289-301

Carliss, R. L. (1986) 'Redemption and the divine Realities: A study of Hick and an Alternative' *Religious Studies* vol.22 pp.235-248

D'Costa, Gavin (1987) *John Hick's Theology of Religions* Lanham: University Press of America

D'Costa, Gavin (1991) 'John Hick and Religious Pluralism' in Harold Hewitt (ed.) (1991) *Problems in the Philosophy of Religion: Critical Studies of the Work of John Hick* Basingstoke: Macmillan

Dilley, Frank B. (1991) 'John Hick on the Self and Resurrection' in Harold Hewitt (ed.) (1991) *Problems in the Philosophy of Religion: Critical Studies of the Work of John Hick* Basingstoke: Macmillan

Duff-Forbes, D. R. (1969) 'Faith, Evidence and Coercion' *Australasian Journal of Philosophy* vol.47 pp.209-215

Duff-Forbes, D. R. (1972) 'Comment on Hick, Necessary Being, and the Cosmological Argument' *Canadian Journal of Philosophy* vol. 1 pp.473-483

Forrester, Duncan B. (1976) 'Professor Hick and the Universe of Faiths' *Scottish Journal of Theology* vol.29 pp.65-72

Gillis, Chester (1987) *A Question of Final Belief: John Hick's Pluralistic Theory of Salvation* Basingstoke: Macmillan

Griffiths, Paul and Lewis, Darma (1983) 'On Grading Religions, Seeking Truth and Being Nice to People' *Religious Studies* vol.19 pp.75-80

Hartshorne, Charles (1977) 'John Hick on Logical and Ontological Necessity' *Religious Studies* vol.13 pp.155-165

Henze, D. F. (1965) 'Faith, Evidence and Coercion' *Philosophy* vol.XLII pp.78-85

Hewitt, Harold (ed.) (1991) *Problems in the Philosophy of Religion: Critical Studies of the Work of John Hick* Basingstoke: Macmillan

Kane, G. Stanley (1975) 'The Failure of Soul-Making Theodicy' *International Journal for the Philosophy of Religion* vol.6 pp.1-21

Kavka, George S. (1976) 'Eschatological Falsification' *Religious Studies* vol.12 pp.201-205

Lipner, Julius (1975) 'Christians and the Uniqueness of Christ' *Scottish Journal of Theology* vol.28 pp.359-368

Lipner, Julius (1976) 'Truth-Claims and Inter-religious Dialogue' *Religious Studies* vol.12 pp.217-230

Lipner, Juilius (1977) 'Does Copernicus Help?' *Religious Studies* vol.13 pp.243-258

Mathis, T. R. (1985) *Against John Hick* Lanham: University Press of America

Meacock, Heather (1997) *An Anthropological Approach to Theology: A Study of John Hick's Theology of Religious Pluralism, Towards Ethical Criteria for a Global Theology of Religions* Ph.D. Thesis: University of Bristol

Mesle, C. Robert (1991) *John Hick's Theodicy: A Process Humanist Critique* London: Macmillan

Miller, Barry (1972) 'The No-Evidence Defence' *International Journal for Philosophy of Religion* vol.3 pp.44-50

Mosher, David L. and Gooch, Paul (1972) 'Divine love and the Limits of Language' *Journal of Theological Studies* vol.23 pp.420-429

Moule, C. (1979) 'A Comment on Professor Hick's Critique of Atonement Doctrine' in Michael Goulder (ed.) (1979) *Incarnation and Myth - The Debate Continued* London: SCM Press

Netland, H. A. (1986) 'Professor Hick on Religious Pluralism' *Religious Studies* vol.22 pp.249-261

Puccetti, Roland (1967) 'The Loving God - Some Observations on John Hick's *Evil and the God of Love*' *Religious Studies* vol.2 pp.255-268

Reichenbach, B. R. (1979) 'Price, Hick and Disembodied Experience' *Religious Studies* vol.15 pp.317-325

Reist, J. M. (1972) 'Coherence and the God of Love' *The Journal of Theological Studies* vol.XXIII pp.95-105

Rowe, William (1991) 'Paradox and Promise - Hick's Solution to the Problem of Evil' in Harold Hewitt (ed.) (1991) *Problems in the Philosophy of Religion: Critical Studies of the Work of John Hick* Basingstoke: Macmillan

Schmitt, Karl (1985) *Death and After-Life in the Theologies of Karl Barth and John Hick: A Comparative Study* Amsterdam: Rodopi

Sharma, Avinda (ed.) (1993) *God, Truth and Reality: Essays in Honour of John Hick* Basingstoke: Macmillan ; New York: St Martin's Press

Sinkinson, Chris (1995) *John Hick: An Introduction to his Theology* Leicester: RTSF

Sinkinson, Chris (1997) *The Nature of Christian Apologetics in Response to Religious Pluralism: An Analysis of the Contribution of John Hick* Ph.D. Thesis: University of Bristol

Tomm, Winnie (1980) *A Christian Approach to the World Religions: A Critical Study of Aspects of John Hick's Theology* MA Thesis: University of Birmingham

Tooley, M. (1976) 'John Hick and the Concept of Eschatological Verification' *Religious Studies* vol.12 pp.177-199

Trethowan, I. (1967) 'Dr. Hick and the Problem of Evil' *The Journal of Theological Studies* vol.XVII pp.407-416

Ward, Keith (1969) 'Freedom and the Irenaean Theodicy' *The Journal of Theological Studies* vol.XX pp.249-254

Ward, Keith (1970) *Ethics and Christianity* London: George Allen & Unwin

Wyman, Walter E. (1994) 'Rethinking the Christian Doctrine of Sin: Friedrich Schleiermacher and Hick's "Irenaean Type"' *The Journal of Religion* vol.74 pp.199-217

History of Hell

Bernstein, Alan (1993) *The Formation of Hell* Ithaca: Cornell University Press

Denzinger (1955) *The Church Teaches: Documents of the Church in English Translation* London and St Louis: B. Herder Book Company

Powys, David (1992) 'The Nineteenth and Twentieth Century Debates about Hell and Universalism' in Nigel de M. S. Cameron (ed.) (1992) *Universalism and the Doctrine of Hell* Carlisle: Paternoster Press; Grand Rapids: Baker Book House

Rowell, Geoffrey (1974) *Hell and the Victorians - A Study of Nineteenth Century Theological Controversies Concerning Eternal Punishments and the Future Life* Oxford: Clarendon Press

Walker, D. P. (1964) *The Decline of Hell: Seventeenth Century Discussions of Eternal Torment* London: Routledge and Kegan Paul

Wheeler, Michael (1994) *Heaven, Hell and the Victorians* Cambridge: Cambridge University Press.

Middle Knowledge

Adams, Robert M. (1977) 'Middle Knowledge and the Problem of Evil' *American Philosophical Quarterly* pp.109-117

Adams, Robert M.(1987) 'Middle Knowledge and the Problem of Evil' in *The Virtue of Faith* New York: Oxford University Press

Basinger, David (1984) 'Divine Omniscience and Human Freedom: A 'Middle Knowledge Perspective' *Faith and Philosophy* vol.1 pp.291-302

Basinger, David (1986)'Middle Knowledge and Classical Christian Thought' *Religious Studies* vol.22 p.420-431

Basinger, David (1991) 'Middle Knowledge and Divine Control: Some Clarifications' *International Journal for Philosophy of Religion* vol.30 pp.129-139

Bertolet, Rod (1993) 'Hasker on Middle Knowledge' *Faith and Philosophy* vol.10 pp.3-17

Craig, William Lane (1987) *The Only Wise God* Grand Rapids: Baker Book House

Craig, William Lane(1989) '"No Other Name": A Middle Knowledge Perspective on the Exclusivity of Salvation Through Christ' *Faith and Philosophy* vol.6 pp.172-188

Craig, William Lane (1991) *Divine Foreknowledge and Human Freedom* Leiden: Brill

Freddoso, Alfred J. (1988) 'Introduction' in Luis De Molina (1988) *On Divine Foreknowledge* trans. Alfred J. Freddoso, Ithaca, New York: Cornell University Press

Gordon, David and Sadowsky, James (1989) 'Does Theism Need Middle Knowledge?' *Religious Studies* vol.25 pp.75-87

Hasker, William (1986) 'A Refutation of Middle Knowledge' *Nous* pp.545-557

Hasker, William (1991) 'Middle Knowledge and the Damnation of the Heathen: A Response to William Craig' *Faith and Philosophy* vol.8 pp.380-389

Hasker, William (1993) 'How Good/Bad is Middle Knowledge? A Reply to Basinger' *International Journal for Philosophy of Religion* vol.33 pp.111-118

Hasker, William (1995) 'Middle Knowledge: A Refutation Revisited' *Faith and Philosophy* vol.12 pp.223-236

Hunt, David P. (1991) 'Middle Knowledge and the Soteriological Problem of Evil' *Religious Studies* vol.27 pp.3-26

Molina, Luis De (1988) *On Divine Foreknowledge* trans. Alfred J. Freddoso, Ithaca, New York: Cornell University Press

Otte, Richard (1987) 'A Defense of Middle Knowledge' *International Journal for Philosophy of Religion* vol.XXII pp.161-169

Sadowsky, James and Gordon, David (1989) 'Does Theism Need Middle Knowledge?' *Religious Studies* vol.25 pp.75-87

Moment of Decision

Boros, Ladislaus (1962) *The Moment of Truth: Mysterium Mortis* London: Burns & Oates

Boros, Ladislaus (1965) *The Mystery of Death* trans. Gregory Bainbridge, New York: Herder & Herder

Problem of Evil

Barry, Michael (1963) *The Meaning of Evil* London: Geoffrey Chapman

Davies, Stephen T. (ed.) (1981) *Encountering Evil* Edinburgh: T & T Clarke

Geach, Peter (1977) *Providence and Evil: The Stanton Lectures 1971-2* Cambridge: Cambridge University Press

Geivett, Rupert D. (1993) *Evil and the Evidence for God* Philadelphia: Temple University Press

Hasker, William (1992) 'Providence and Evil: Three Theories' *Religious Studies* vol.28 pp.91-103

Idinopulos, Thomas A. (1969) 'Radical Theology, Evil and Freedom' *Scottish Journal of Theology* vol.22 pp.163-174

Journet, Charles (1961) *Le Mal* Paris: Desclee de Brouwer

Moser, Paul K. (1984) 'Natural Evil and the Free Will Defence' *International Journal for Philosophy of Religion* vol.15 pp.49-56

Peterson, Michael (1982) *Evil and the Christian God* Grand Rapids, Michigan: Baker Book House
Surin, Kenneth (1986) *Theology and the Problem of Evil* Oxford: Blackwell
Wenham, John (1994) *The Enigma of Evil: Can We Believe in the Goodness of God?* Guildford, Surrey: Eagle

Richard Swinburne

Swinburne, Richard (1961) 'Three Types of Thesis about Fact and Value' *Philosophical Quarterly* vol.11 pp.301-307
Swinburne, Richard (1962) 'The Presence-and-Absence Theory' *Annals Of Science* vol.18 pp.131-145
Swinburne, Richard (1963) 'Privacy' *Analysis* vol.24 pp.127-136
Swinburne, Richard (1964) 'Falsifiability of Scientific Theories' *Mind* vol.73 pp.434-436
Swinburne, Richard (1968) *Space and Time* London: Macmillan and Co.
Swinburne, Richard (1969) 'The Christian Wager' *Religious Studies* vol.4 pp.217-228
Swinburne, Richard (1973) *An Introduction to Confirmation Theory* London: Methuen
Swinburne, Richard (1977) *The Coherence of Theism* Oxford: Clarendon Press
Swinburne, Richard (1977b) 'The Problem of Evil' in S.C. Brown (ed.) (1977) *Reason and Religion* New York: Ithaca
Swinburne, Richard (1979) *The Existence of God* Oxford: Clarendon Press
Swinburne, Richard (1981) *Faith and Reason* Oxford: Clarendon Press
Swinburne, Richard (1983) 'A Theodicy of Heaven and Hell' Alfred J. Freddoso (ed.) (1983) *The Existence and Nature of God* London and Notre Dame: University of Notre Dame Press
Swinburne, Richard (1986) *The Evolution of the Soul* Oxford: Clarendon Press
Swinburne, Richard (1989) *Responsibility and Atonement* Oxford: Clarendon Press
Swinburne, Richard (1991) Revelation Oxford: Clarendon Press
Swinburne, Richard (1994) *The Christian God* Oxford: Clarendon Press
Swinburne, Richard (1994b) 'Intellectual Autobiography' in Alan A. Padgett (ed.) (1994) *Reason and the Christian Religion: Essays in Honour of Richard Swinburne* Oxford: Clarendon Press; New York: Oxford University Press
Swinburne, Richard (1995) 'Theodicy, our well-being, and God's Rights' *International Journal for the Philosophy of Religion* vol.38 pp.77-93
Swinburne, Richard (1996) *Is There a God?* Oxford: Clarendon Press
Swinburne, Richard (1998) *Providence and the Problem of Evil* Oxford: Clarendon Press

On Swinburne

Alston, William P. (1997) 'Swinburne and Christian Theology' *International Journal for Philosophy of Religion* vol.41 pp.35-57
Aspenson, Stephen. S (1996) 'Swinburne on Atonement' *Religious Studies* vol.32 pp187-204
Bringsjord, Selmer (1986) 'Swinburne's Argument from Consciousness' *International Journal for Philosophy of Religion* vol.19 pp.127-143
Cosculluela, Victor (1997) 'Death and God: The Case of Richard Swinburne' *Religious Studies* vol.33 pp.293-302

Fouts, Avery (1993) 'Divine Self - Limitations in Swinburne's Doctrine of Omniscience' *Religious Studies* vol.29 pp.21-26

Gale, Richard M. (1994) 'Swinburne's Argument from Religious Experience' in Alan A. Padgett (ed.) (1994) *Reason and the Christian Religion: Essays in Honour of Richard Swinburne* Oxford: Clarendon Press; New York: Oxford University Press

Hasker, William (1998) 'Swinburne's Modal Argument for Dualism: Epistemically Circular' *Faith and Philosophy* vol.15 pp.366-372

Lamont, John (1996) 'Stump And Swinburne on Revelation' *Religious Studies* vol.32 pp.395-412

Levine, Michael (1993) 'Swinburne's Heaven: One Hell of a Place' *Religious Studies* vol.29 pp.519-531

O'Connor, David (1983) 'Swinburne on Natural Evil' *Religious Studies* vol.19 pp.65-73

Padgett, Alan A. (ed.) (1994) *Reason and the Christian Religion: Essays in Honour of Richard Swinburne* Oxford: Clarendon Press; New York: Oxford University Press

Quinn, Philip L. (1994) 'Swinburne on Guilt, Atonement and Christian Redemption' in Alan A. Padgett (ed.) (1994) *Reason and the Christian Religion: Essays in Honour of Richard Swinburne* Oxford: Clarendon Press; New York: Oxford University Press

Smith, Quentin (1998) 'Swinburne's Explanation of the Universe' *Religious Studies* vol.34 pp.91-102

Stump, Eleanor (1994) '*Responsibility and Atonement,* Richard Swinburne' *Faith and Philosophy* vol.11 pp.321-328

Wynn, Mark (1993) 'Some Reflections on Richard Swinburne's Argument from Design' *Religious Studies* vol.29 pp.325-335

Index